100 BULLETS: SIX FEET UNDER THE GUN

Brian Azzarello Writer **Eduardo Risso** Artist
Patricia Mulvihill Colorist **Clem Robins** Letter
Dave Johnson Original Series Covers
100 BULLETS created by Brian Azzarello and Eduardo Risso

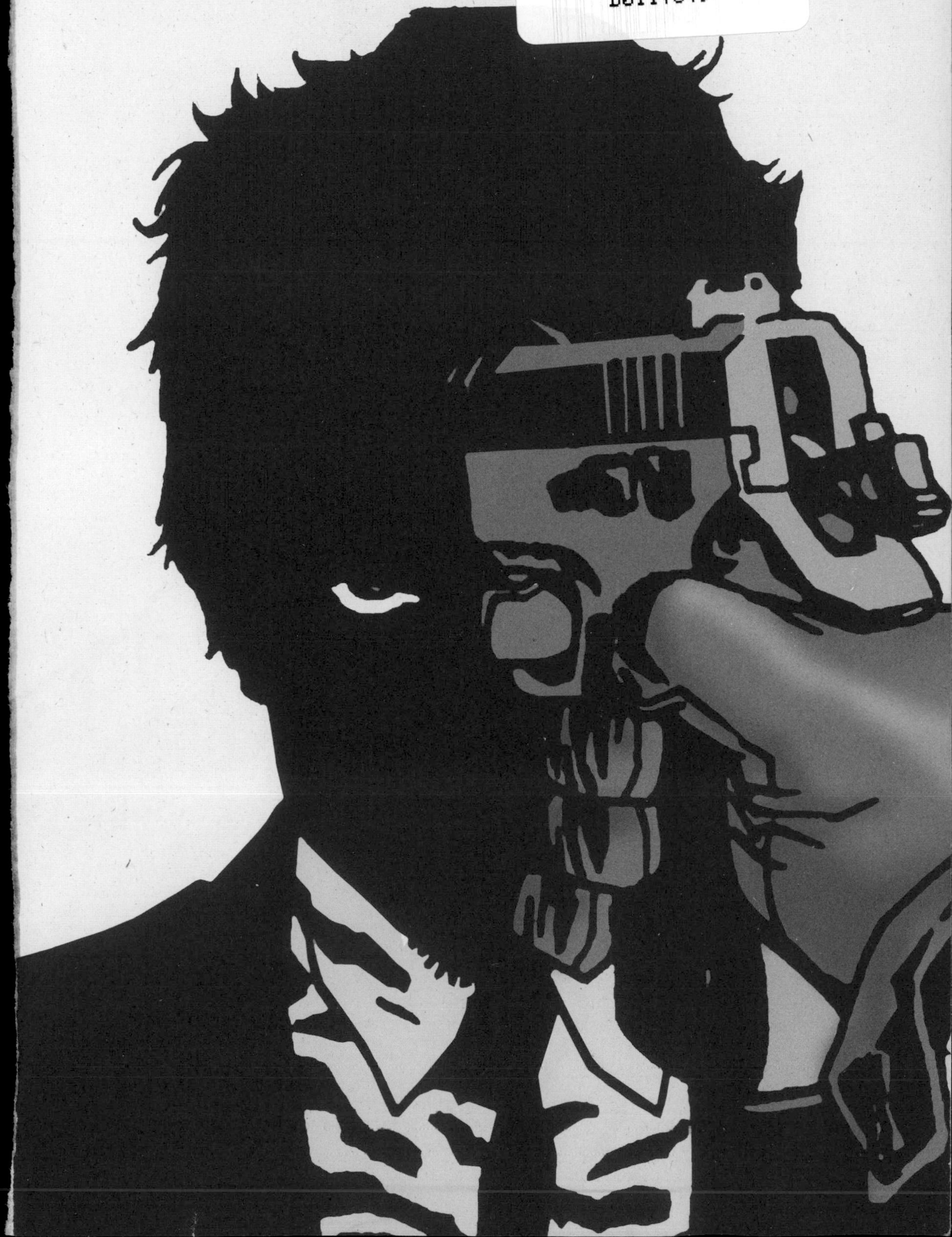

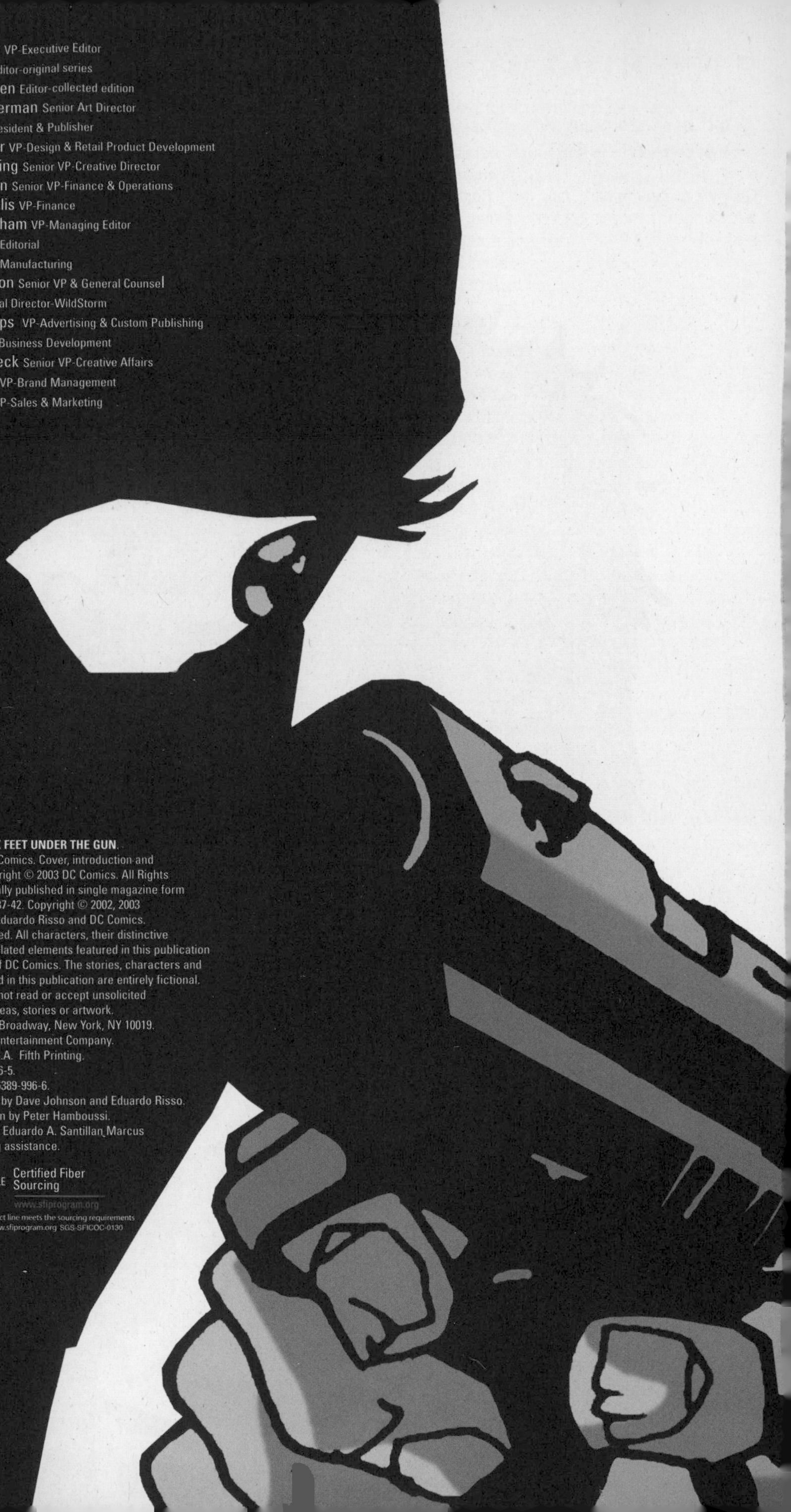

100 BULLETS: SIX FEET UNDER THE GUN.
Published by DC Comics. Cover, introduction and
compilation Copyright © 2003 DC Comics. All Rights
Reserved. Originally published in single magazine form
as 100 BULLETS 37-42. Copyright © 2002, 2003
Brian Azzarello, Eduardo Risso and DC Comics.
All Rights Reserved. All characters, their distinctive
likenesses and related elements featured in this publication
are trademarks of DC Comics. The stories, characters and
incidents featured in this publication are entirely fictional.
DC Comics does not read or accept unsolicited
submissions of ideas, stories or artwork.
DC Comics, 1700 Broadway, New York, NY 10019.
A Warner Bros. Entertainment Company.
Printed in the U.S.A. Fifth Printing.
ISBN: 1-56389-996-5.
ISBN 13: 978-1-56389-996-6.
Cover illustration by Dave Johnson and Eduardo Risso.
Publication design by Peter Hamboussi.
Special thanks to Eduardo A. Santillan Marcus
for his translating assistance.

Introduction

Fiction is as much defined by form as by genre, and comics criticism has talked genre into the grave and beyond, so enough of that already. Aside from the fact that 100 BULLETS defies genre-naming (it's Crime! No, wait, Suspense! No, no, Post-Modern Noir-Revisionism...), avoids the self-loathing of genre-busting (oooh, look, it's a comic book, but it *doesn't* have super-heroes! It *must* be good...), and comes out of the much-vaunted and oft-misunderstood Vertigo line (Vertigo? Wait, on what page will the fate of our eternal souls hang in the balance?), it is, dare I say it, literature.

Yes, you read it right, there's no qualifier. No "comics literature," no "graphic novel" double-speak. It's lit, and suck it up, that makes it Capital-"A" Art. You can pigeon-hole it later if it'll make you feel better.

This volume in the novel that is 100 BULLETS is Brian Azzarello's change-up. He's been throwing heat and a wicked slider for almost a third of the story now, laying out his threads, teasing out the mystery, the plot, the themes, the characters... in short, writing. He's posed the questions, or, more precisely, made the reader pose the questions (unlike a majority of writers working today, Brian Azzarello is in rarefied company — he actually *knows* where his story is going; getting him to tell you, that's another matter entirely). For those Hollywood types who feel the need to break all dramatic form into easy-to-digest screenplay-speak, we're out of the First Act now, and moving well into the Second, where complications will abound.

Yes, come the Third Act, you can expect a body count far higher than the last act of *Hamlet*.

And so the change-up. In the middle of the novel, a set of short stories, and hence the above-mentioned issue of form. The six issues contained herein are short stories, 22-page pieces that stand alone as character studies while, at the same time, meshing perfectly within the confines of the larger novel. That last is a nifty trick, because character work is deceptively hard to do; when it's done poorly, it's self-indulgent effluvia from the writer's brain; when it's done well, it adds dimension to a story in ways to give Stephen Hawking a migraine.

This is exceptionally well-done work, make no mistake. More than just studies in character — Dizzy Cordova's realization, with elegant finality, that she can *never* go home again; Benito Medici's entry via violence into "the game" — these are stories that forward the

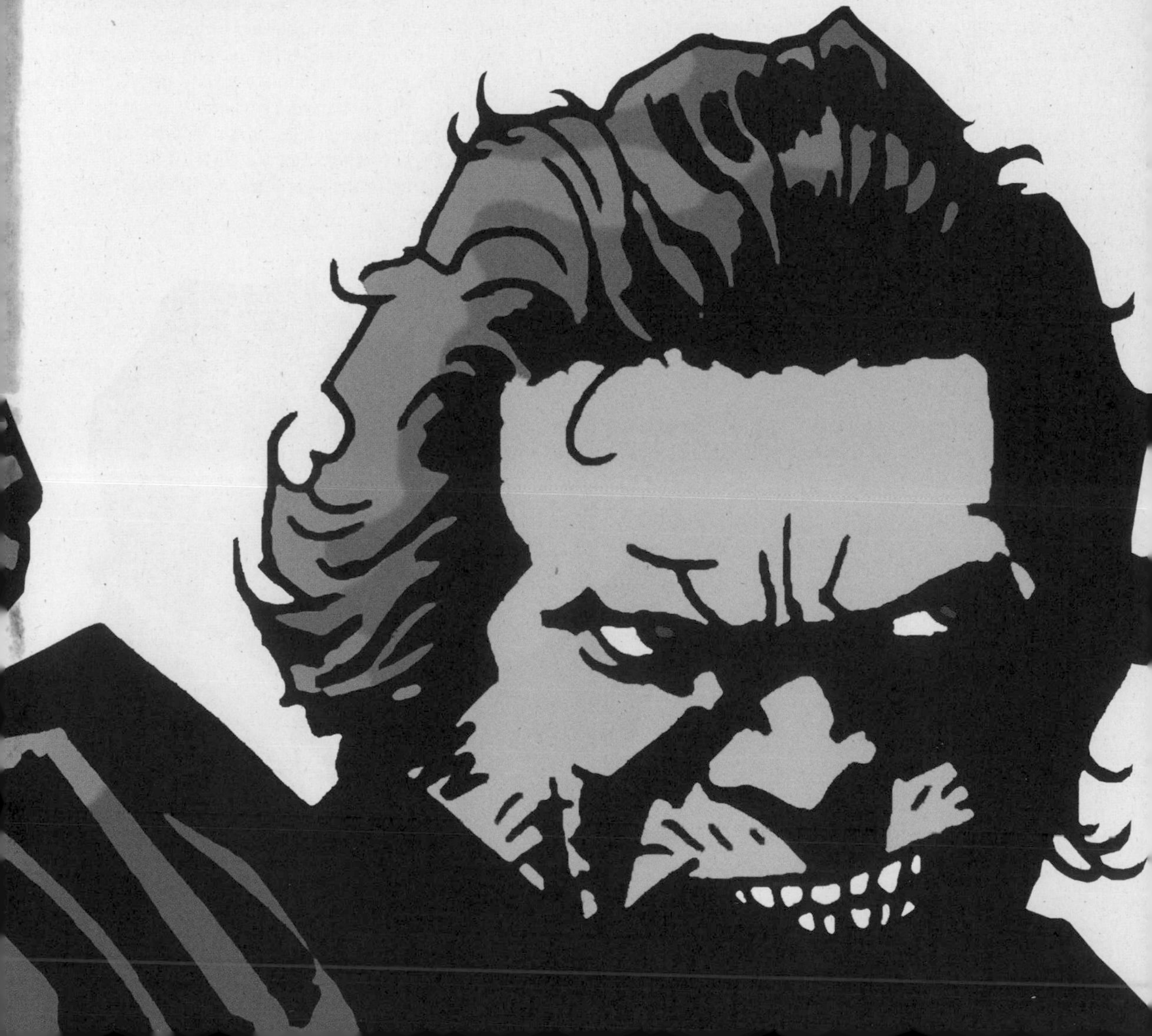

overall movement of 100 BULLETS. And while each chapter herein is topically about the title character (I refer here to the brilliant Dave Johnson covers, rather than to Azzarello's continued tongue-in-cheek wordplay in his choice of chapter names), the stories themselves thread the lives of many characters, new and old. With each story, another clue dropped, another plot forwarded, another theme reinforced. And more questions are posed, of course, as any good narrative would demand — questions both obvious (who is betraying who?) and far more sublime (regardless of whether or not she *could* go back to her life, why would Dizzy *want* to?).

Writing.

The short story, it can be argued, is the hardest damn thing in the world for a fiction writer to master. To craft a narrative of 3000 words — or 22 pages — into a cohesive, coherent narrative, one with a beginning, middle, and end, one with emotional heart and resonance, is as rare a form of alchemy as literature allows. There's a reason short story collections are so few and far between, and it's not because people aren't trying. It's because they're failing far more than they're succeeding.

These succeed, without doubt, and while it's Azzarello who's put it all into motion, it's Eduardo Risso who brings it home. There are only a handful of artists working today with Risso's gift for composition and visual narrative; of that handful, far fewer who can deliver consistently, month after month, without falter and without fail.

The Azzarello-Risso collaboration is never stronger than in these stories, and it's not by accident. Both are masters of economy, the engine of the short story, and both have mastered the oh-so-often-said and far-less-often-heeded cry of Less Is More. Every page is an exercise in restraint, to such an extent that the restraint has entered the narrative itself, tangible on the page as characters pace and plot, each looking for their moment to strike. It is no accident that Graves' chapter follows Lono's, and the contrast is telling. Lono wouldn't know restraint if it bit him on the ass; Graves' is nothing *but* restraint.

Writing.

Having said it twice, there's another truth of 100 BULLETS that must be said, which is this: Brian Azzarello *doesn't* write this alone.

He may be scripting, but Eduardo Risso is writing as well. Speaking from first-hand experience, Eduardo is an unparalleled collaborator, and the beauty of the Azzarello-Risso partnership is that the collaboration here is so seamless. Disregarding the obvious divisions of labor — I have no idea if, for instance, Brian Azzarello could draw, even if you put a gun to his head (for what little that threat might be worth, I hasten to add) — it is impossible to tell where the one ends and the other begins.

To say they complement one another is to miss the point entirely. They *don't* complement each other — they *improve* each other.

Damn.

Good.

Writing.

One hundred bullets, one hundred issues, and here are six of the best so far.

— Greg Rucka
Portland, Oregon
May, 2003

Greg Rucka is the Shamus Award-nominated author of the Atticus Kodiak series of novels (Keeper, Finder, Smoker, Shooting at Midnight, *and* Critical Space), *and the Eisner Award-winning creator and writer of the comics* Queen & Country, Whiteout, *and* Felon. *He has also won acclaim for his work on such favorite DC and Marvel characters as Batman, Wonder Woman, Wolverine, Daredevil, and Elektra. He lives with his wife and two children in a climate ideally suited to staying indoors and typing.*

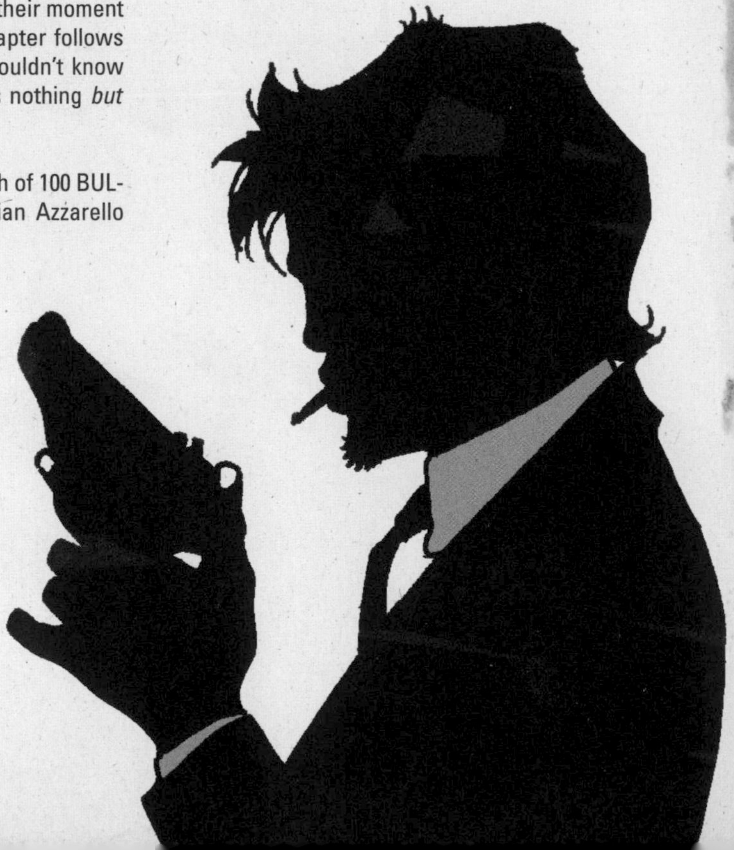

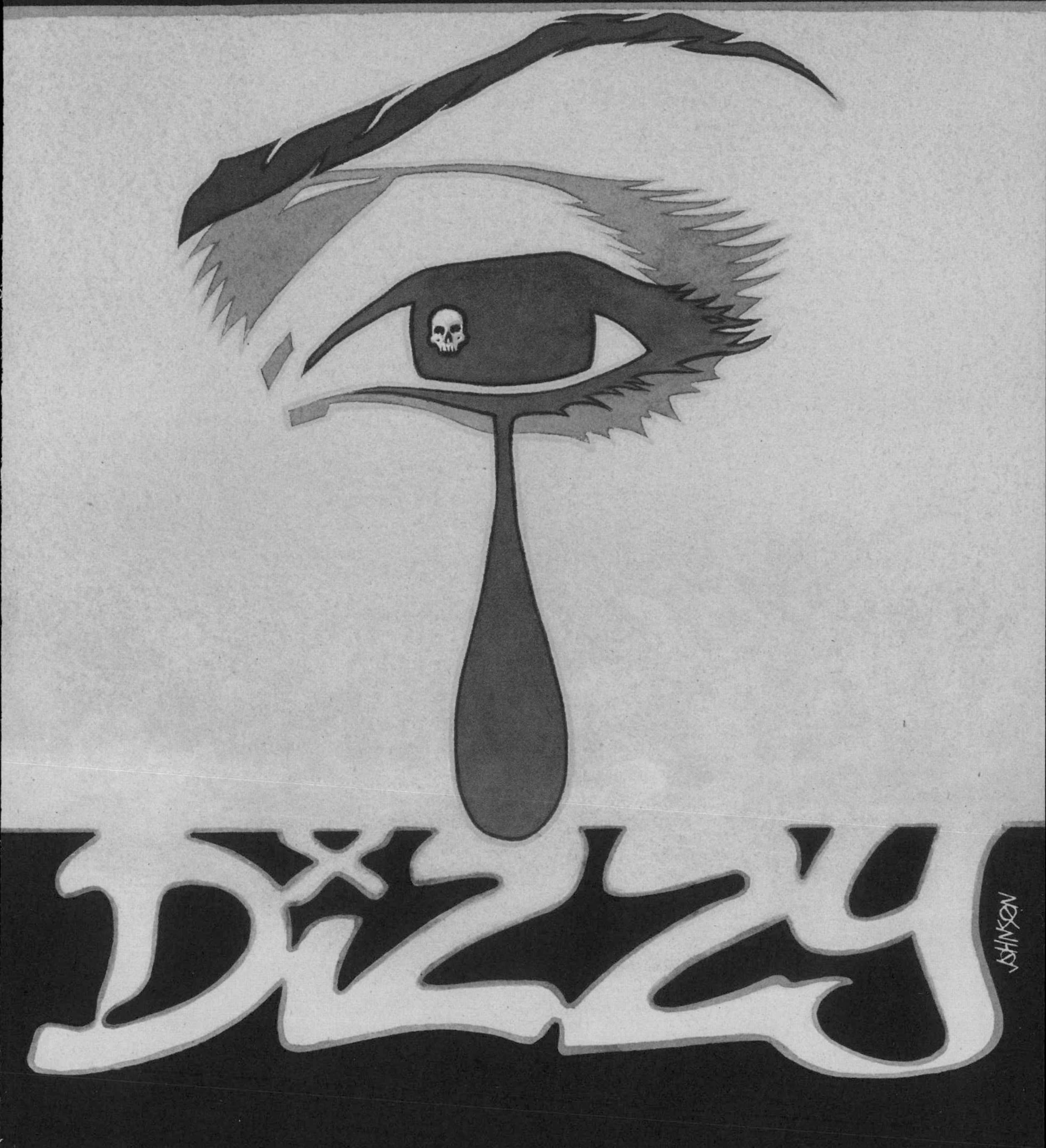
DIZZY
JOHNSON

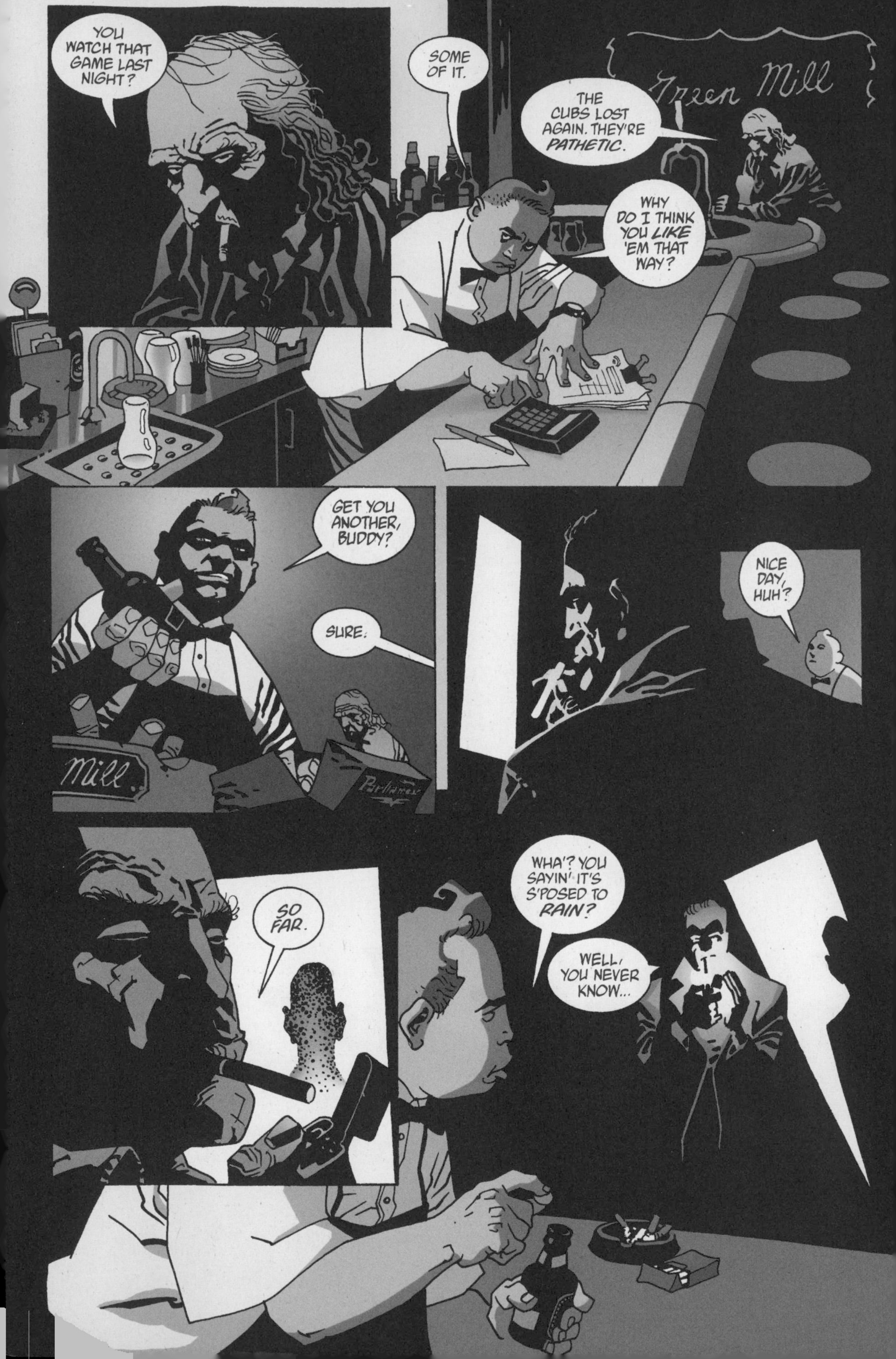
YOU WATCH THAT GAME LAST NIGHT?
SOME OF IT.
Green Mill
THE CUBS LOST AGAIN. THEY'RE PATHETIC.
WHY DO I THINK YOU LIKE 'EM THAT WAY?
GET YOU ANOTHER, BUDDY?
SURE.
Mill
NICE DAY, HUH?
SO FAR.
WHA'? YOU SAYIN' IT'S S'POSED TO RAIN?
WELL, YOU NEVER KNOW...

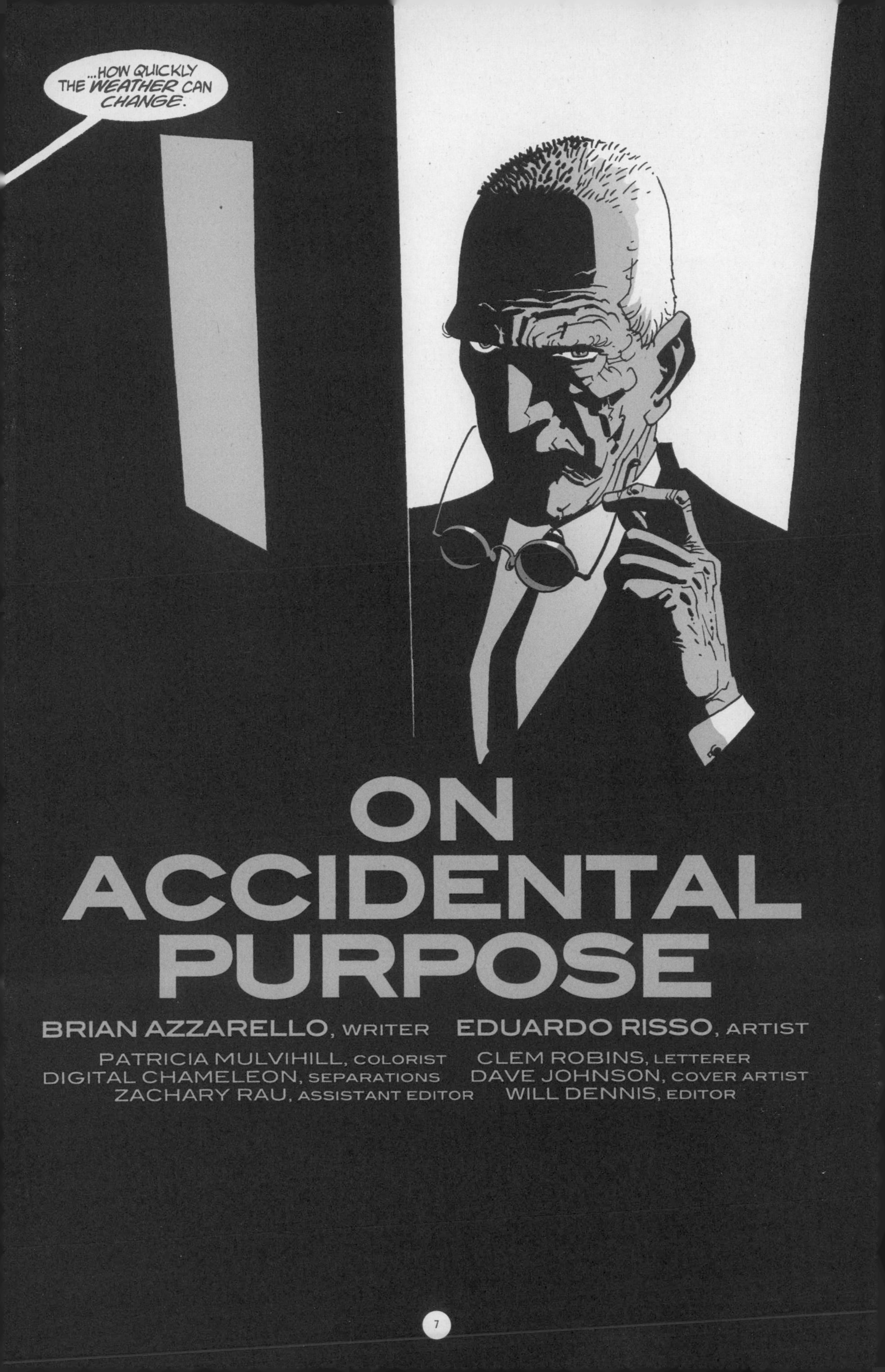
...HOW QUICKLY THE WEATHER CAN CHANGE.

ON ACCIDENTAL PURPOSE

BRIAN AZZARELLO, WRITER EDUARDO RISSO, ARTIST

PATRICIA MULVIHILL, COLORIST CLEM ROBINS, LETTERER
DIGITAL CHAMELEON, SEPARATIONS DAVE JOHNSON, COVER ARTIST
ZACHARY RAU, ASSISTANT EDITOR WILL DENNIS, EDITOR

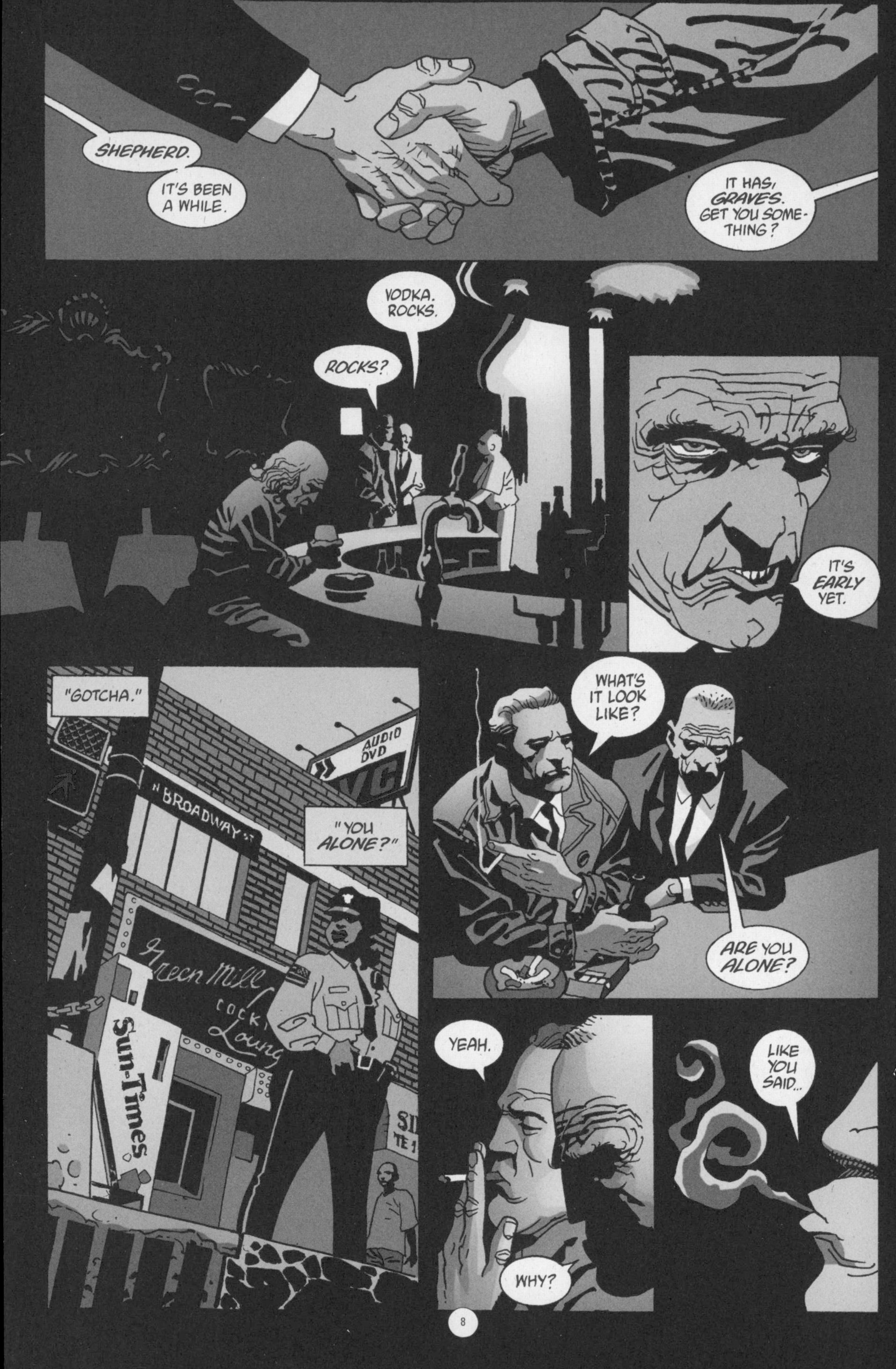
SHEPHERD.
IT'S BEEN A WHILE.
IT HAS, GRAVES. GET YOU SOME-THING?
VODKA. ROCKS.
ROCKS?
IT'S EARLY YET.
"GOTCHA."
AUDIO DVD
N BROADWAY ST
"YOU ALONE?"
Green Mill
COCK
Loung
Sun-Times
WHAT'S IT LOOK LIKE?
ARE YOU ALONE?
YEAH.
LIKE YOU SAID...
WHY?

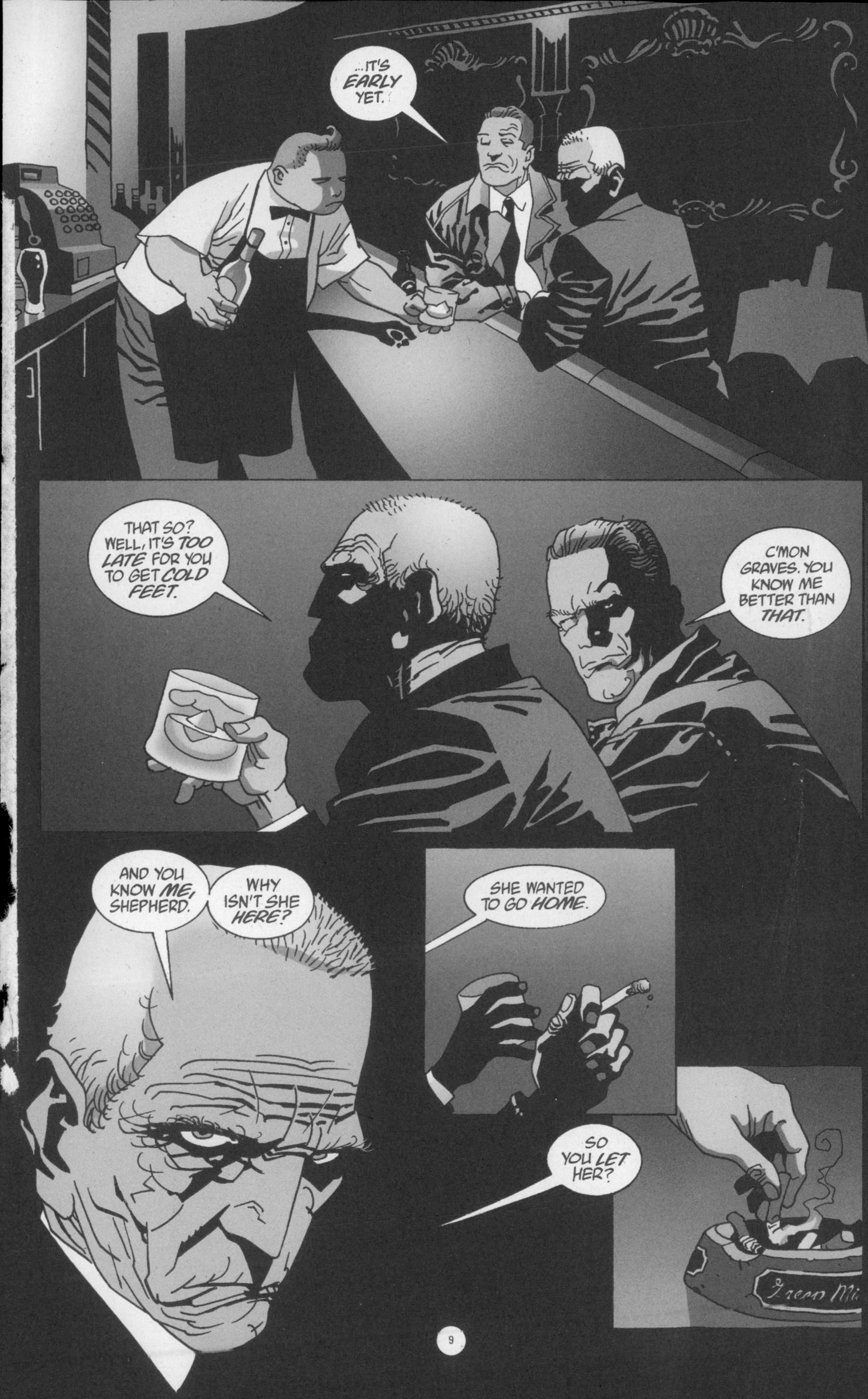
...IT'S EARLY YET.
THAT SO? WELL, IT'S TOO LATE FOR YOU TO GET COLD FEET.
C'MON GRAVES. YOU KNOW ME BETTER THAN THAT.
AND YOU KNOW ME, SHEPHERD.
WHY ISN'T SHE HERE?
SHE WANTED TO GO HOME.
SO YOU LET HER?

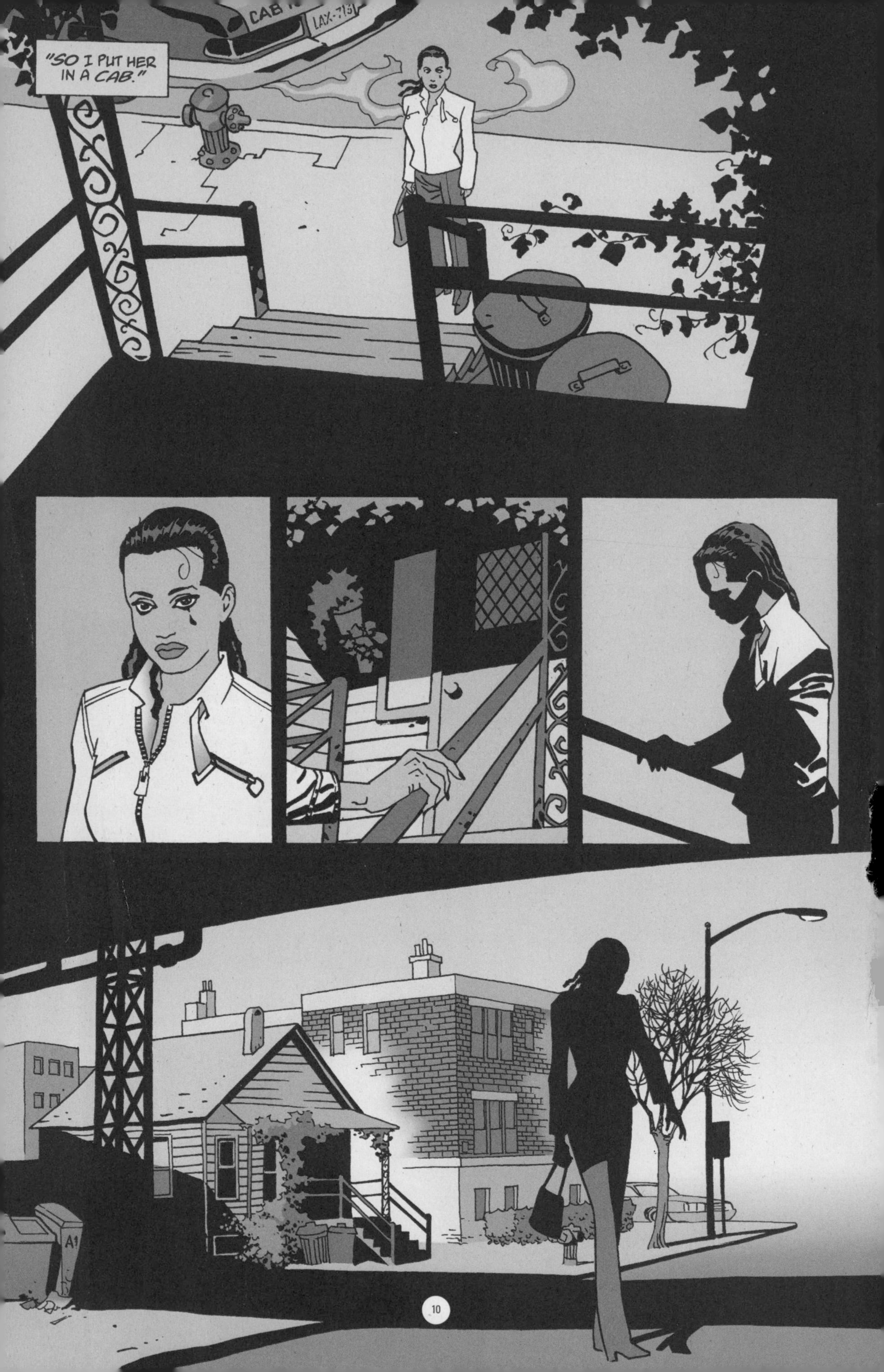
"SO I PUT HER IN A CAB."
CAB
LAX-713
A1

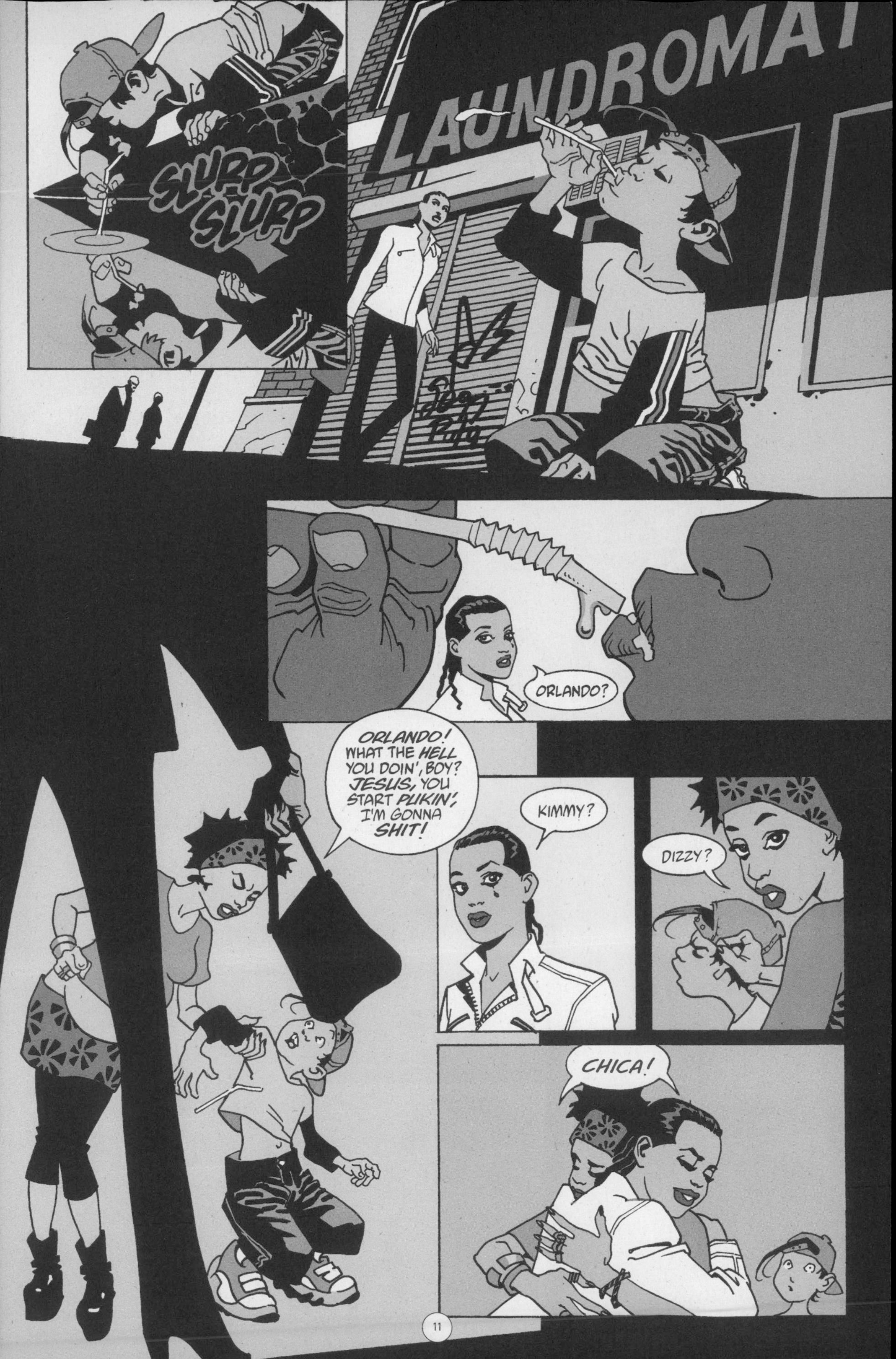
LAUNDROMAT
SLURP SLURP
ORLANDO?
ORLANDO! WHAT THE HELL YOU DOIN', BOY? JESUS, YOU START PUKIN', I'M GONNA SHIT!
KIMMY?
DIZZY?
CHICA!

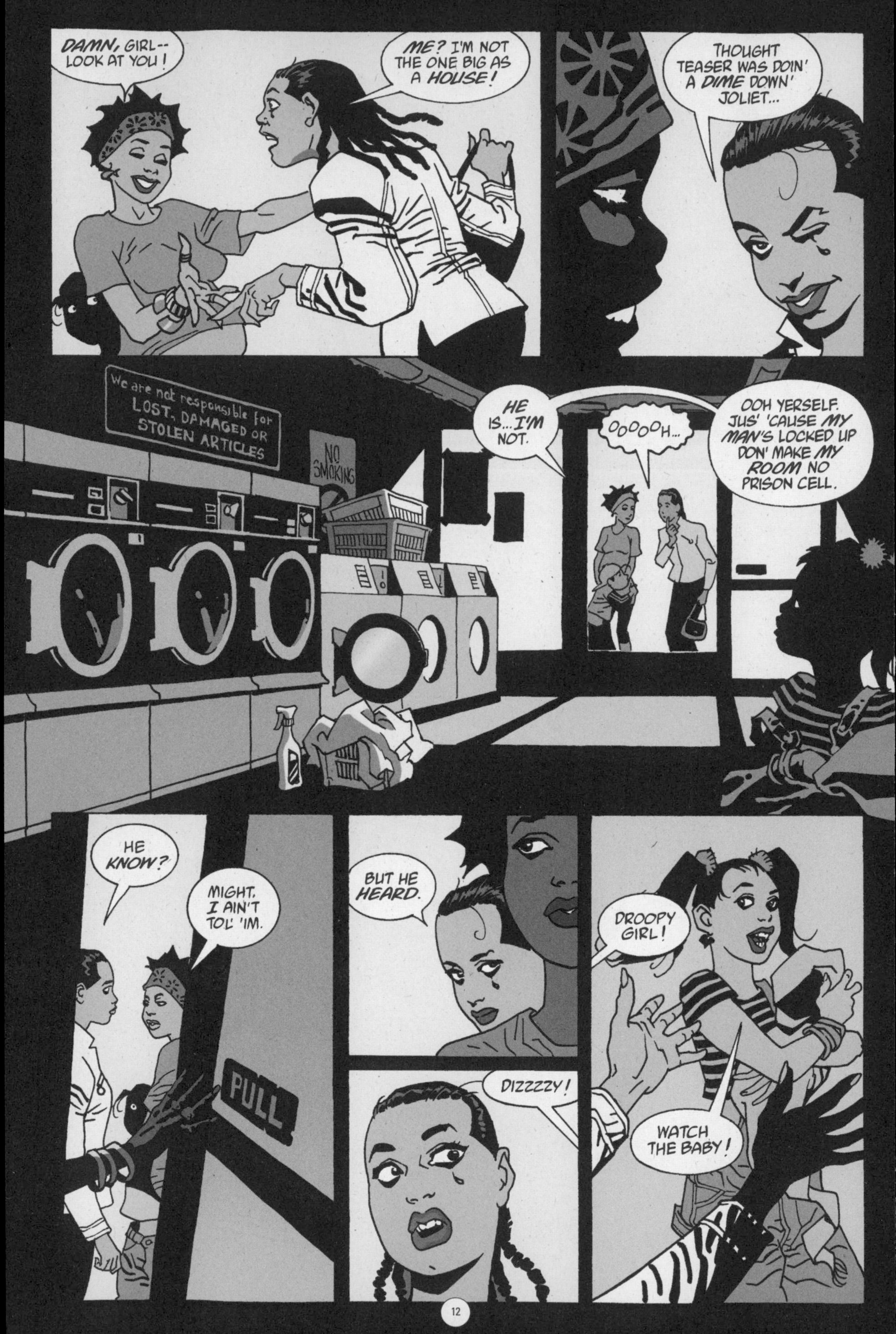
DAMN, GIRL-- LOOK AT YOU!
ME? I'M NOT THE ONE BIG AS A HOUSE!
THOUGHT TEASER WAS DOIN' A DIME DOWN' JOLIET...
We are not responsible for LOST, DAMAGED OR STOLEN ARTICLES
NO SMOKING
HE IS...I'M NOT.
OOOOOH...
OOH YERSELF. JUS' 'CAUSE MY MAN'S LOCKED UP DON' MAKE MY ROOM NO PRISON CELL.
HE KNOW?
MIGHT. I AIN'T TOL' 'IM.
PULL
BUT HE HEARD.
DROOPY GIRL!
DIZZZZY!
WATCH THE BABY!

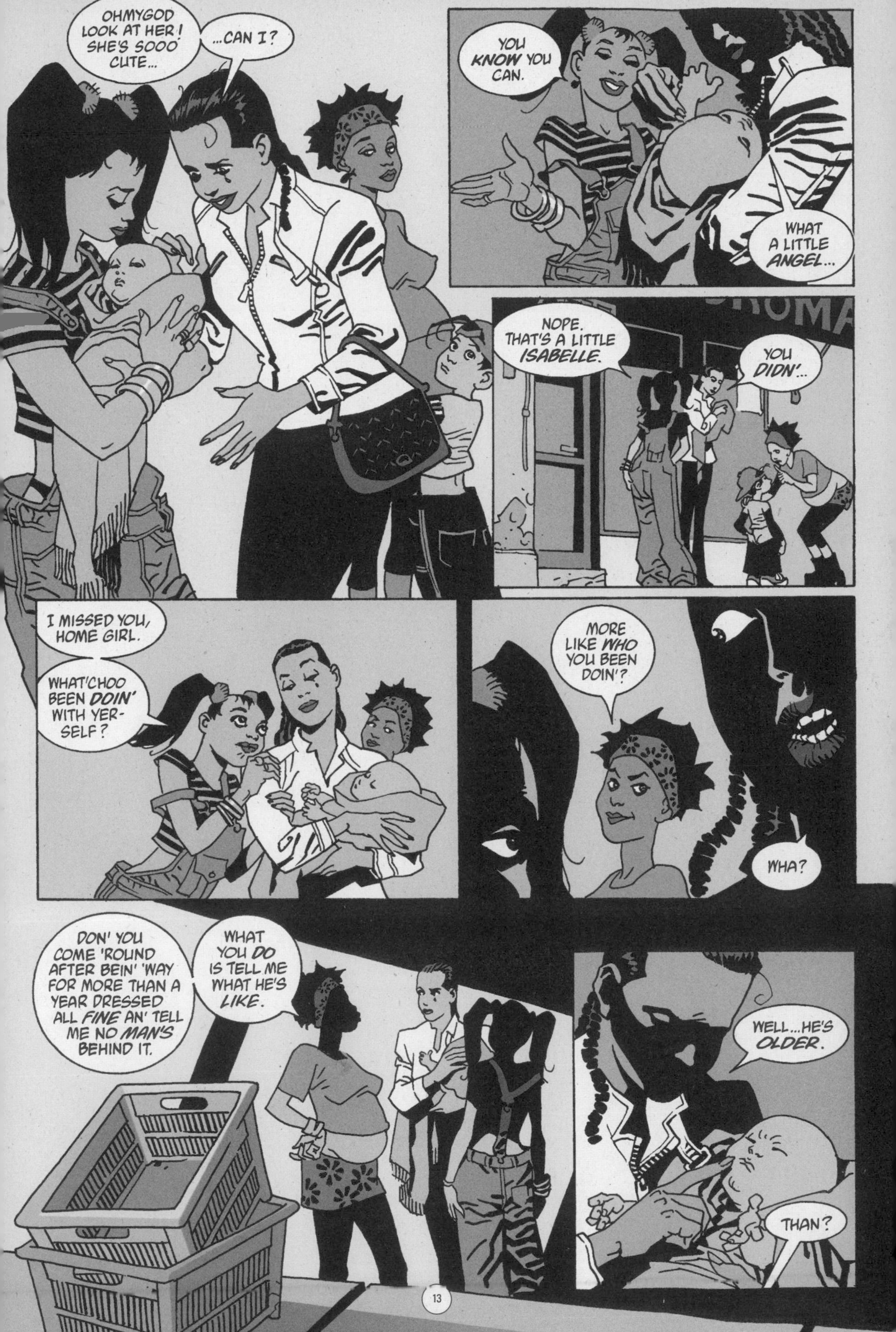
OHMYGOD LOOK AT HER! SHE'S SOOO CUTE...
...CAN I?
YOU KNOW YOU CAN.
WHAT A LITTLE ANGEL...
NOPE. THAT'S A LITTLE ISABELLE.
YOU DIDN'...
I MISSED YOU, HOME GIRL.
WHAT'CHOO BEEN DOIN' WITH YER-SELF?
MORE LIKE WHO YOU BEEN DOIN'?
WHA?
DON' YOU COME 'ROUND AFTER BEIN' 'WAY FOR MORE THAN A YEAR DRESSED ALL FINE AN' TELL ME NO MAN'S BEHIND IT.
WHAT YOU DO IS TELL ME WHAT HE'S LIKE.
WELL...HE'S OLDER.
THAN?

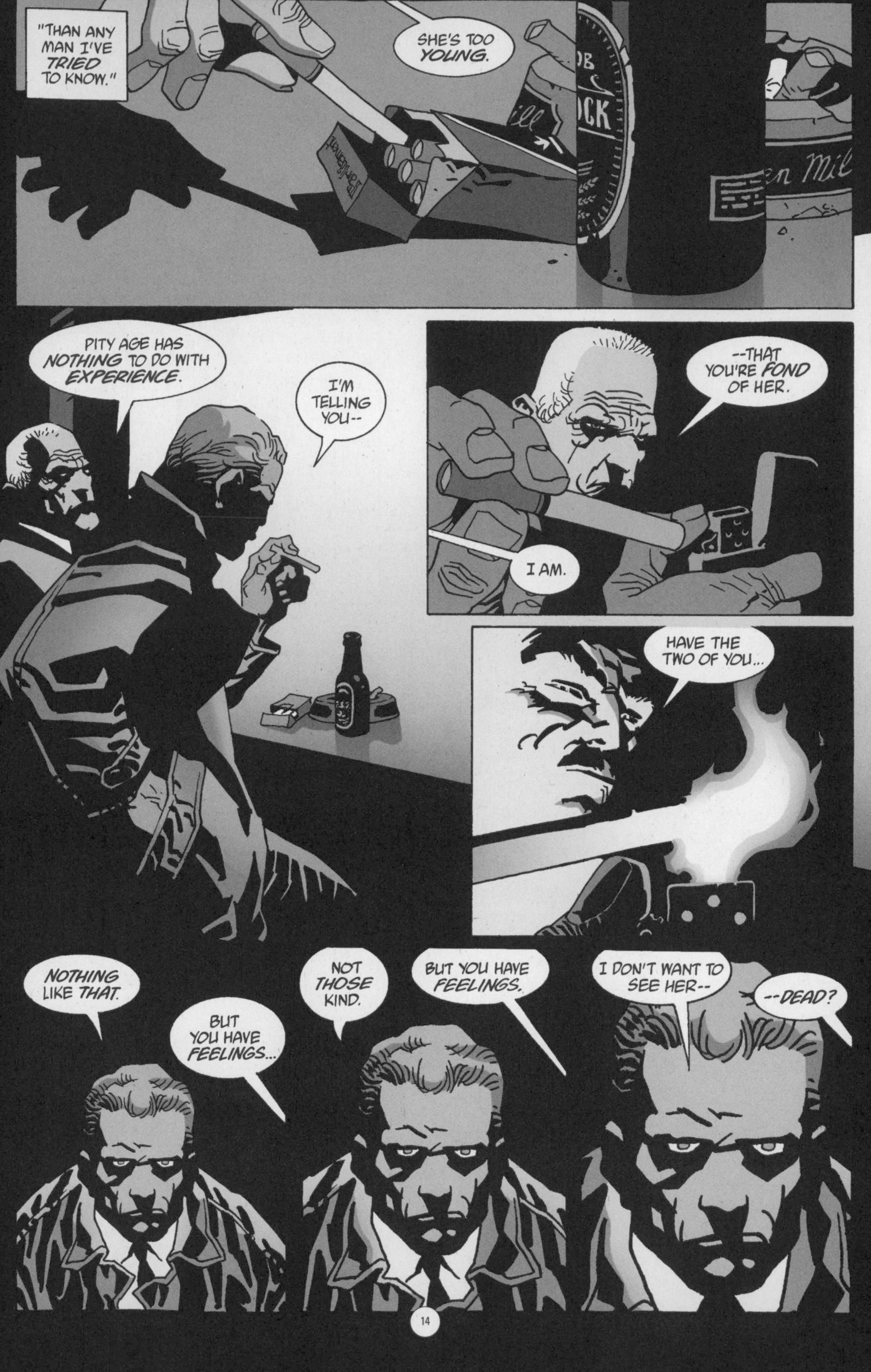
"THAN ANY MAN I'VE TRIED TO KNOW."
SHE'S TOO YOUNG.
PITY AGE HAS NOTHING TO DO WITH EXPERIENCE.
I'M TELLING YOU--
--THAT YOU'RE FOND OF HER.
I AM.
HAVE THE TWO OF YOU...
NOTHING LIKE THAT.
BUT YOU HAVE FEELINGS...
NOT THOSE KIND.
BUT YOU HAVE FEELINGS.
I DON'T WANT TO SEE HER--
--DEAD?

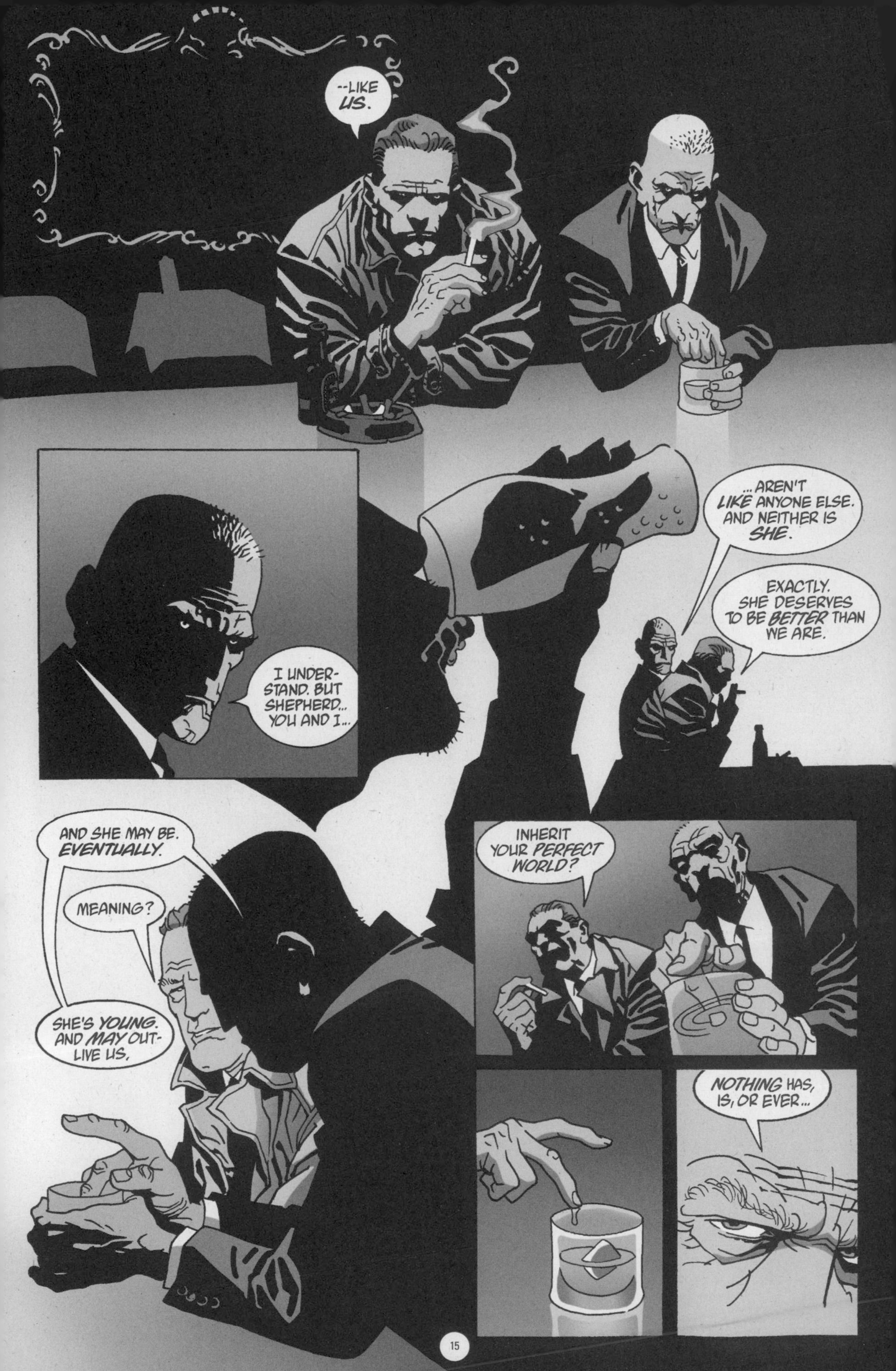
--LIKE US.
I UNDERSTAND. BUT SHEPHERD... YOU AND I...
...AREN'T LIKE ANYONE ELSE. AND NEITHER IS SHE.
EXACTLY. SHE DESERVES TO BE BETTER THAN WE ARE.
AND SHE MAY BE. EVENTUALLY.
MEANING?
SHE'S YOUNG. AND MAY OUTLIVE US.
INHERIT YOUR PERFECT WORLD?
NOTHING HAS, IS, OR EVER...

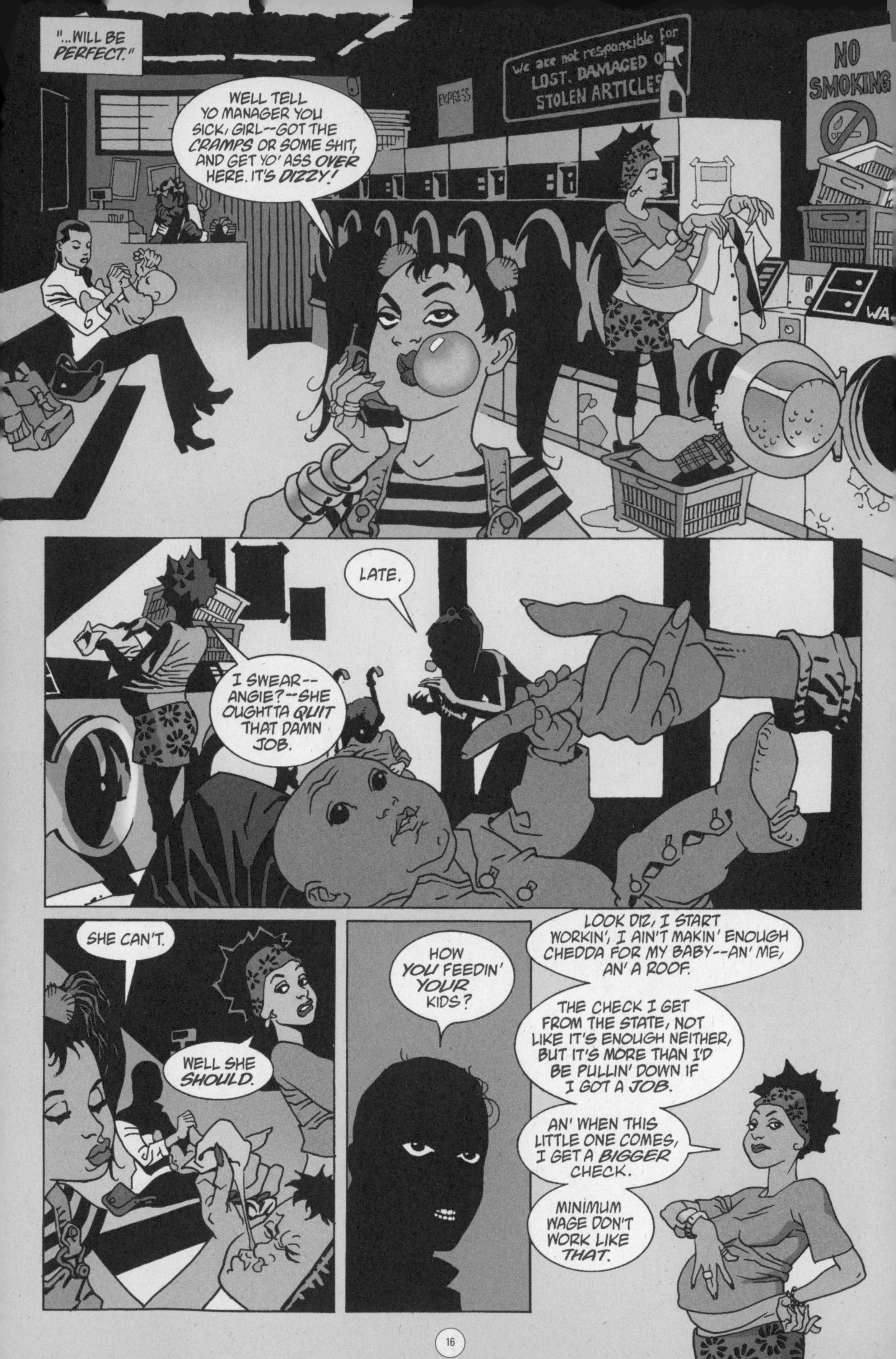
"...WILL BE PERFECT."
WELL TELL YO MANAGER YOU SICK, GIRL--GOT THE CRAMPS OR SOME SHIT, AND GET YO' ASS OVER HERE. IT'S DIZZY!
We are not responsible for LOST, DAMAGED OR STOLEN ARTICLES
EXPRESS
NO SMOKING
LATE.
I SWEAR-- ANGIE?--SHE OUGHTTA QUIT THAT DAMN JOB.
SHE CAN'T.
WELL SHE SHOULD.
HOW YOU FEEDIN' YOUR KIDS?
LOOK DIZ, I START WORKIN', I AIN'T MAKIN' ENOUGH CHEDDA FOR MY BABY--AN' ME, AN' A ROOF.
THE CHECK I GET FROM THE STATE, NOT LIKE IT'S ENOUGH NEITHER, BUT IT'S MORE THAN I'D BE PULLIN' DOWN IF I GOT A JOB.
AN' WHEN THIS LITTLE ONE COMES, I GET A BIGGER CHECK.
MINIMUM WAGE DON'T WORK LIKE THAT.

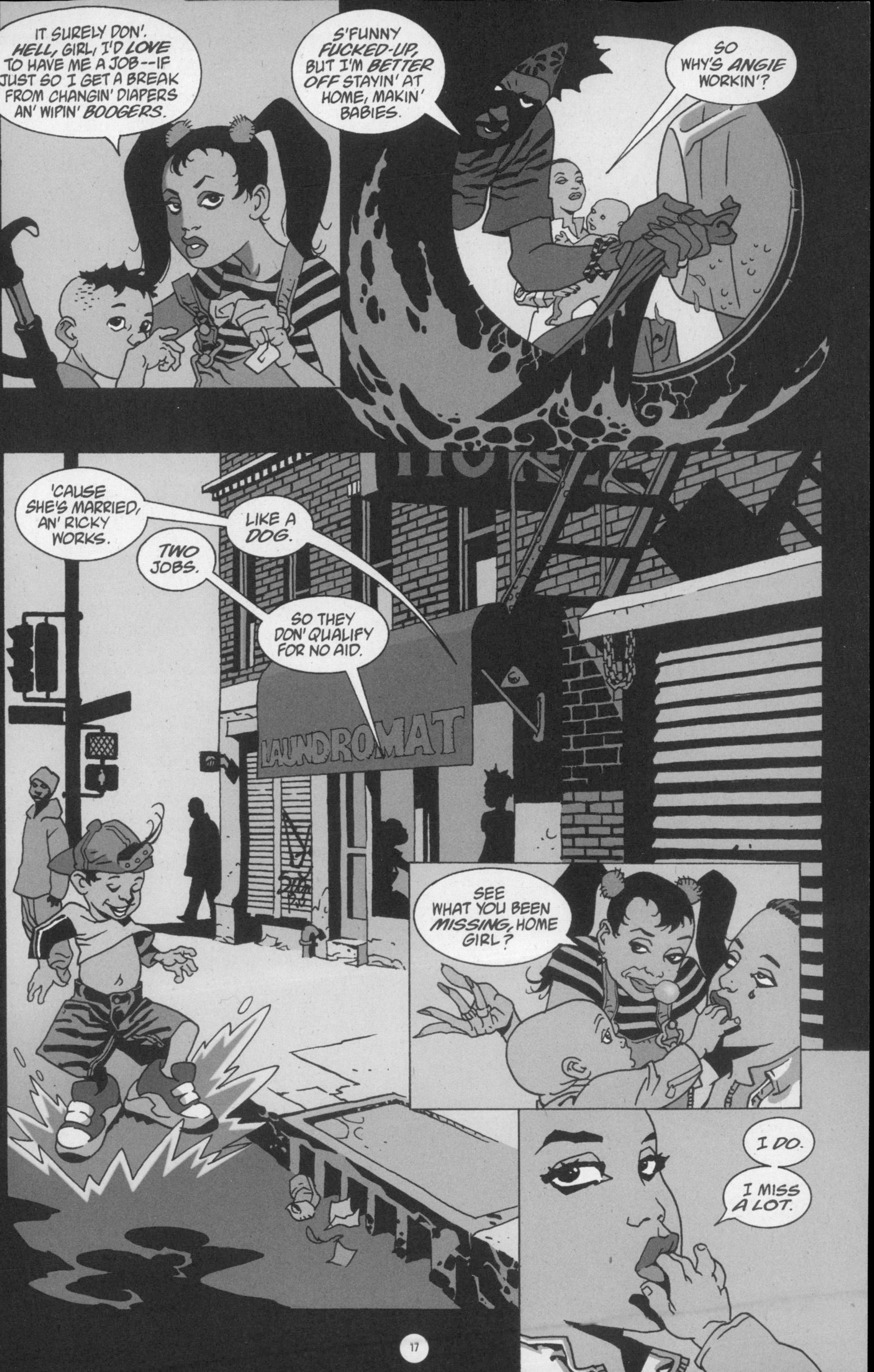
IT SURELY DON'. HELL, GIRL, I'D LOVE TO HAVE ME A JOB--IF JUST SO I GET A BREAK FROM CHANGIN' DIAPERS AN' WIPIN' BOOGERS.
S'FUNNY FUCKED-UP, BUT I'M BETTER OFF STAYIN' AT HOME, MAKIN' BABIES.
SO WHY'S ANGIE WORKIN'?
'CAUSE SHE'S MARRIED, AN' RICKY WORKS.
LIKE A DOG.
TWO JOBS.
SO THEY DON' QUALIFY FOR NO AID.
LAUNDROMAT
SEE WHAT YOU BEEN MISSING, HOME GIRL?
I DO.
I MISS A LOT.

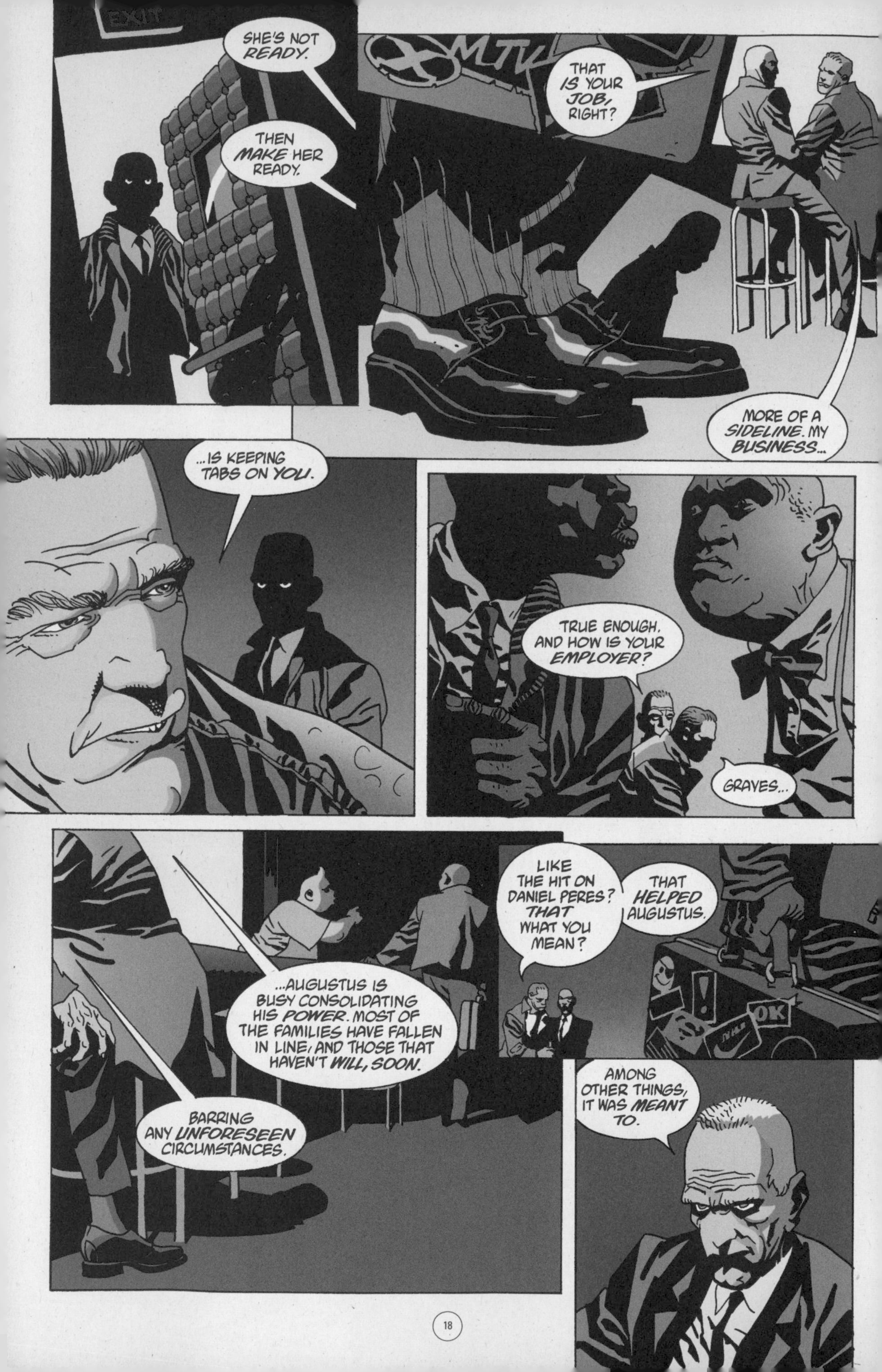
EXIT
SHE'S NOT READY.
THEN MAKE HER READY.
MTV
THAT IS YOUR JOB, RIGHT?
MORE OF A SIDELINE. MY BUSINESS...
...IS KEEPING TABS ON YOU.
TRUE ENOUGH. AND HOW IS YOUR EMPLOYER?
GRAVES...
...AUGUSTUS IS BUSY CONSOLIDATING HIS POWER. MOST OF THE FAMILIES HAVE FALLEN IN LINE; AND THOSE THAT HAVEN'T WILL, SOON.
BARRING ANY UNFORESEEN CIRCUMSTANCES.
LIKE THE HIT ON DANIEL PERES? THAT WHAT YOU MEAN?
THAT HELPED AUGUSTUS.
OK
AMONG OTHER THINGS, IT WAS MEANT TO.

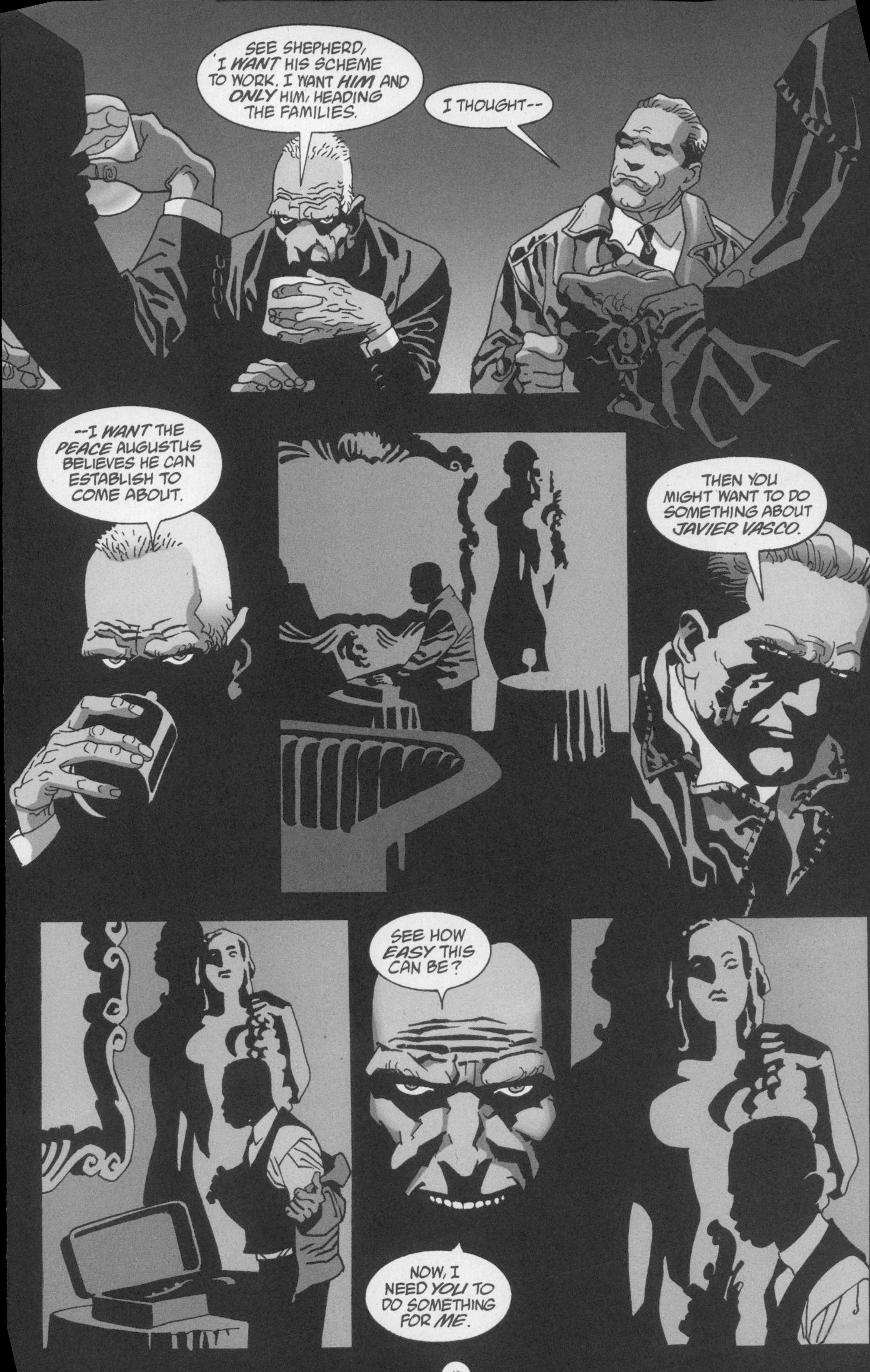

SEE SHEPHERD, I WANT HIS SCHEME TO WORK. I WANT HIM AND ONLY HIM, HEADING THE FAMILIES.
I THOUGHT--
--I WANT THE PEACE AUGUSTUS BELIEVES HE CAN ESTABLISH TO COME ABOUT.
THEN YOU MIGHT WANT TO DO SOMETHING ABOUT JAVIER VASCO.
SEE HOW EASY THIS CAN BE?
NOW, I NEED YOU TO DO SOMETHING FOR ME.

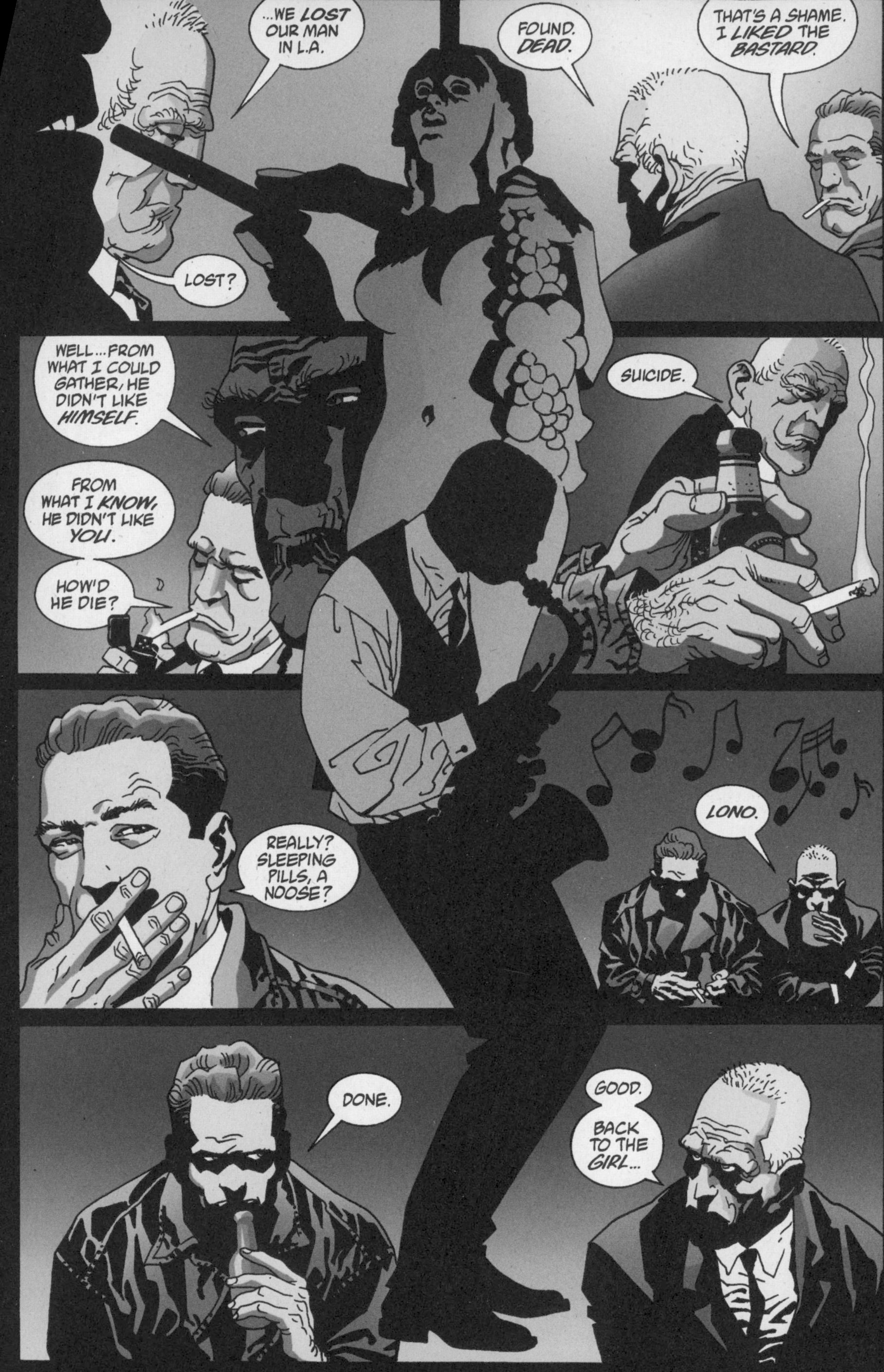
...WE LOST OUR MAN IN L.A.
LOST?
FOUND. DEAD.
THAT'S A SHAME. I LIKED THE BASTARD.
WELL...FROM WHAT I COULD GATHER, HE DIDN'T LIKE HIMSELF.
FROM WHAT I KNOW, HE DIDN'T LIKE YOU.
HOW'D HE DIE?
SUICIDE.
REALLY? SLEEPING PILLS, A NOOSE?
LONO.
DONE.
GOOD.
BACK TO THE GIRL...

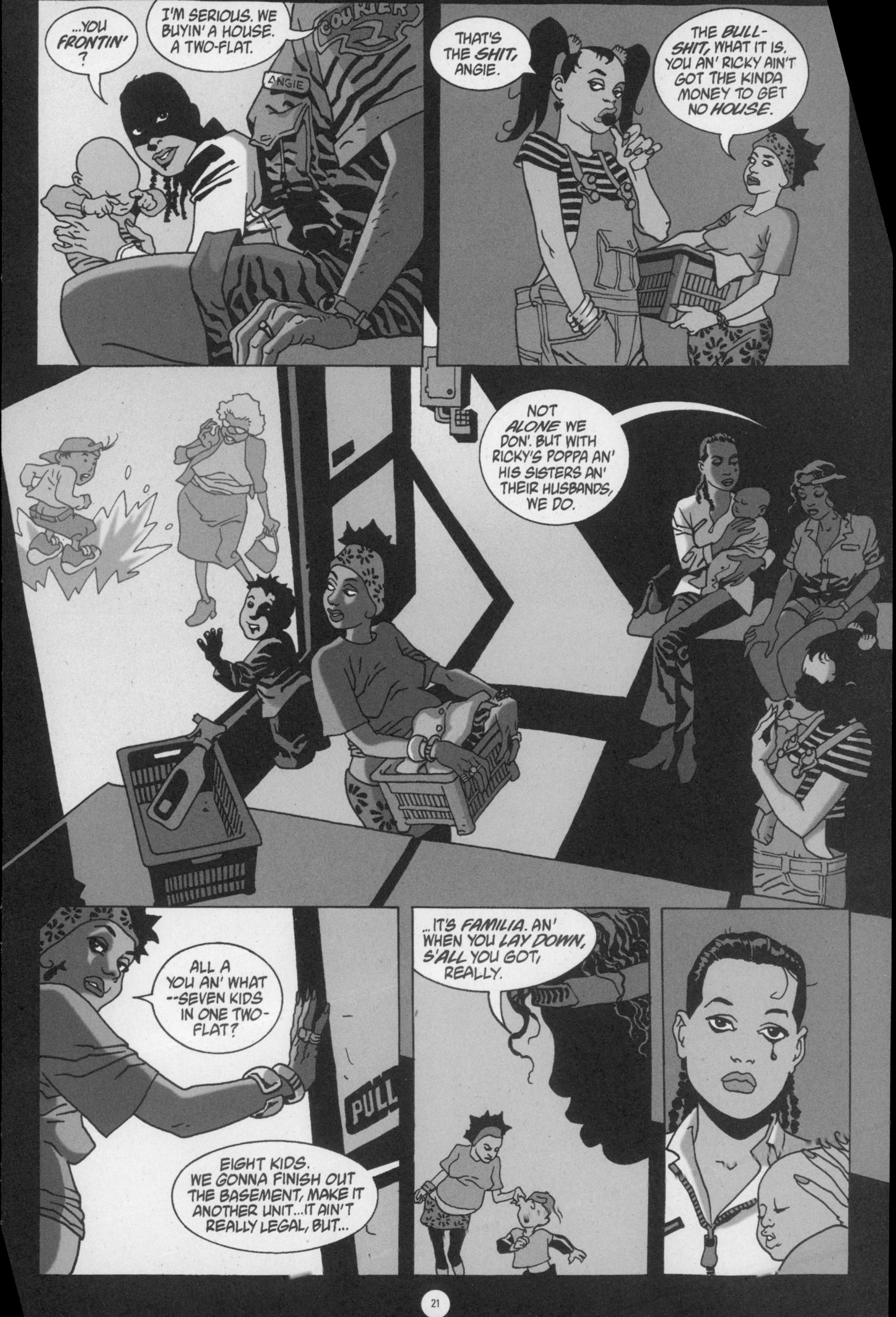

...YOU FRONTIN'?
I'M SERIOUS. WE BUYIN' A HOUSE. A TWO-FLAT.
COURIER
ANGIE
THAT'S THE SHIT, ANGIE.
THE BULL-SHIT, WHAT IT IS. YOU AN' RICKY AIN'T GOT THE KINDA MONEY TO GET NO HOUSE.
NOT ALONE WE DON'. BUT WITH RICKY'S POPPA AN' HIS SISTERS AN' THEIR HUSBANDS, WE DO.
ALL A YOU AN' WHAT --SEVEN KIDS IN ONE TWO-FLAT?
EIGHT KIDS. WE GONNA FINISH OUT THE BASEMENT, MAKE IT ANOTHER UNIT...IT AIN'T REALLY LEGAL, BUT...
...IT'S FAMILIA. AN' WHEN YOU LAY DOWN, S'ALL YOU GOT, REALLY.

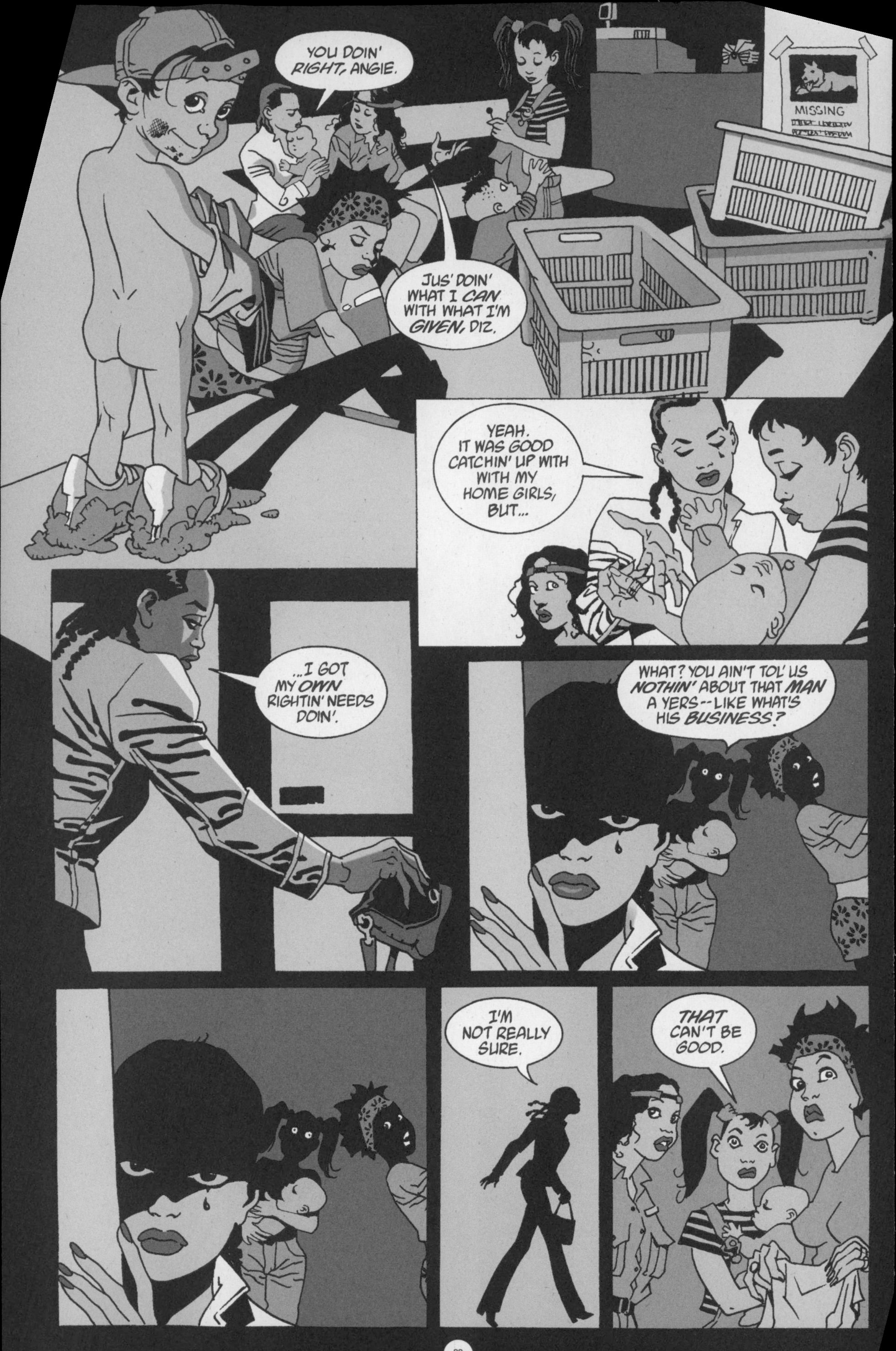

YOU DOIN' RIGHT, ANGIE.
JUS' DOIN' WHAT I CAN WITH WHAT I'M GIVEN, DIZ.
MISSING
YEAH. IT WAS GOOD CATCHIN' UP WITH WITH MY HOME GIRLS, BUT...
...I GOT MY OWN RIGHTIN' NEEDS DOIN'.
WHAT? YOU AIN'T TOL' US NOTHIN' ABOUT THAT MAN A YERS--LIKE WHAT'S HIS BUSINESS?
I'M NOT REALLY SURE.
THAT CAN'T BE GOOD.

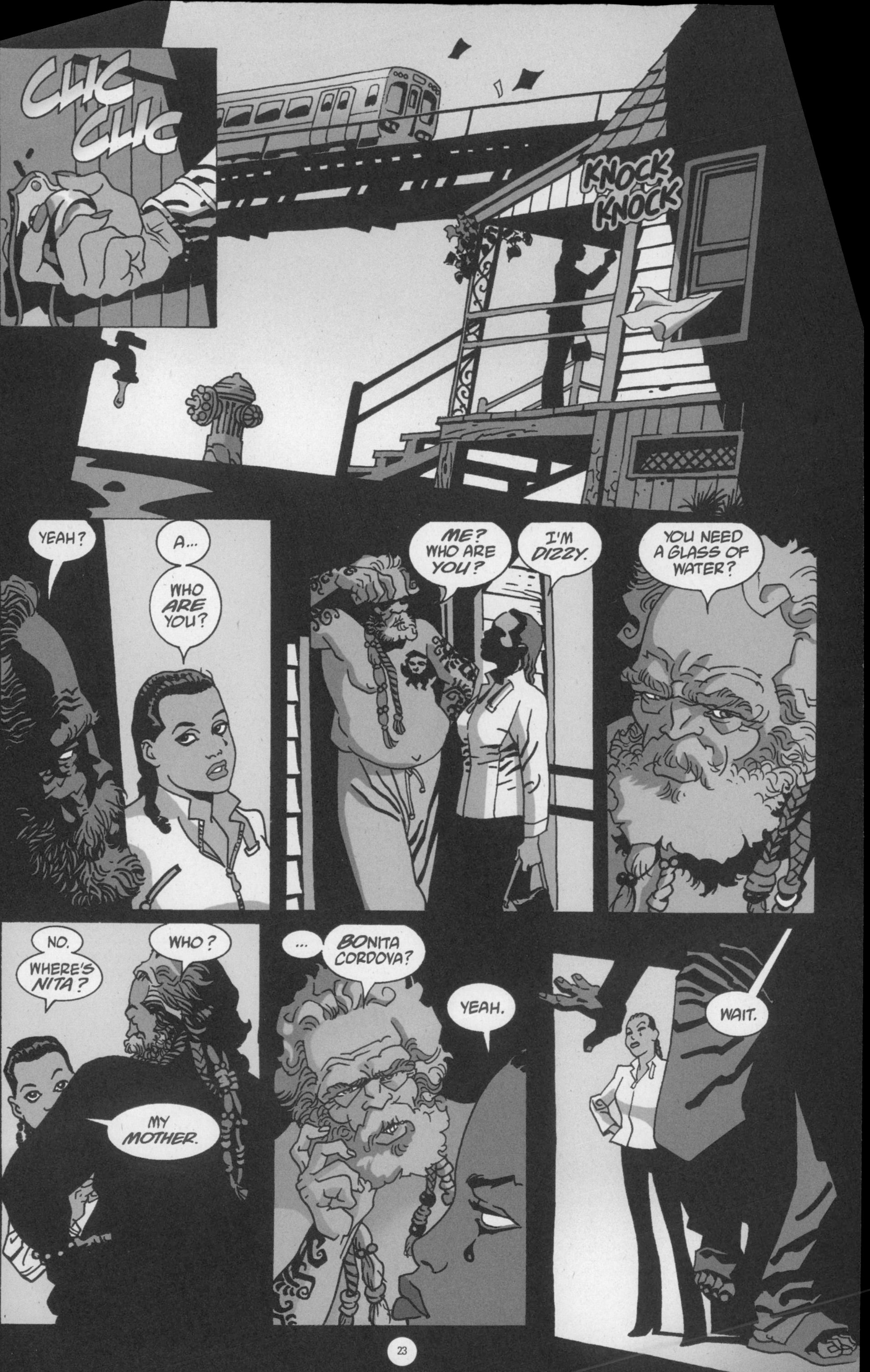
CLIC CLIC
KNOCK KNOCK
YEAH?
A...
WHO ARE YOU?
ME? WHO ARE YOU?
I'M DIZZY.
YOU NEED A GLASS OF WATER?
NO. WHERE'S NITA?
WHO?
MY MOTHER.
... BONITA CORDOVA?
YEAH.
WAIT.

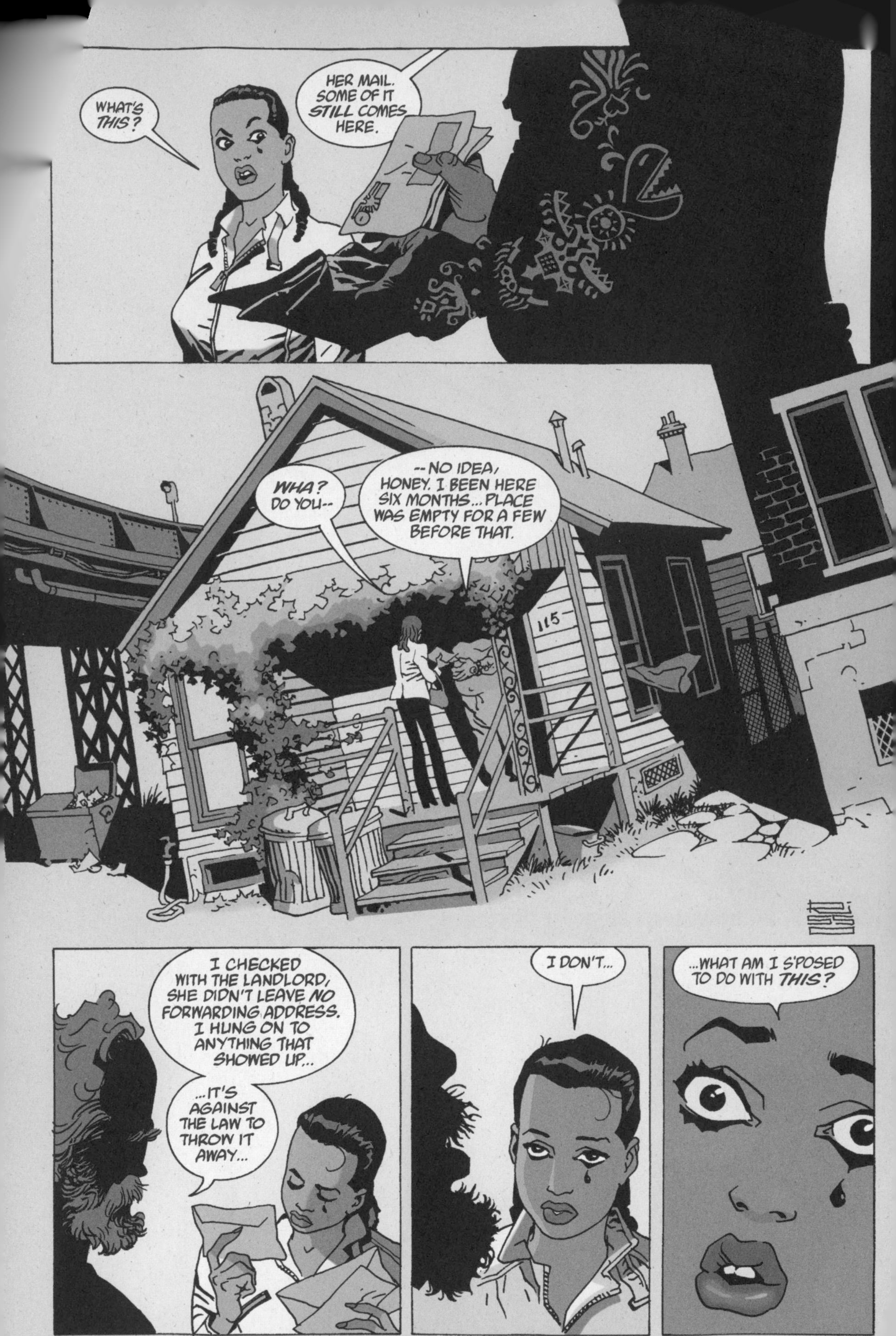
WHAT'S THIS?
HER MAIL. SOME OF IT STILL COMES HERE.
WHA? DO YOU--
--NO IDEA, HONEY. I BEEN HERE SIX MONTHS... PLACE WAS EMPTY FOR A FEW BEFORE THAT.
115
I CHECKED WITH THE LANDLORD, SHE DIDN'T LEAVE NO FORWARDING ADDRESS. I HUNG ON TO ANYTHING THAT SHOWED UP...
...IT'S AGAINST THE LAW TO THROW IT AWAY...
I DON'T...
...WHAT AM I S'POSED TO DO WITH THIS?

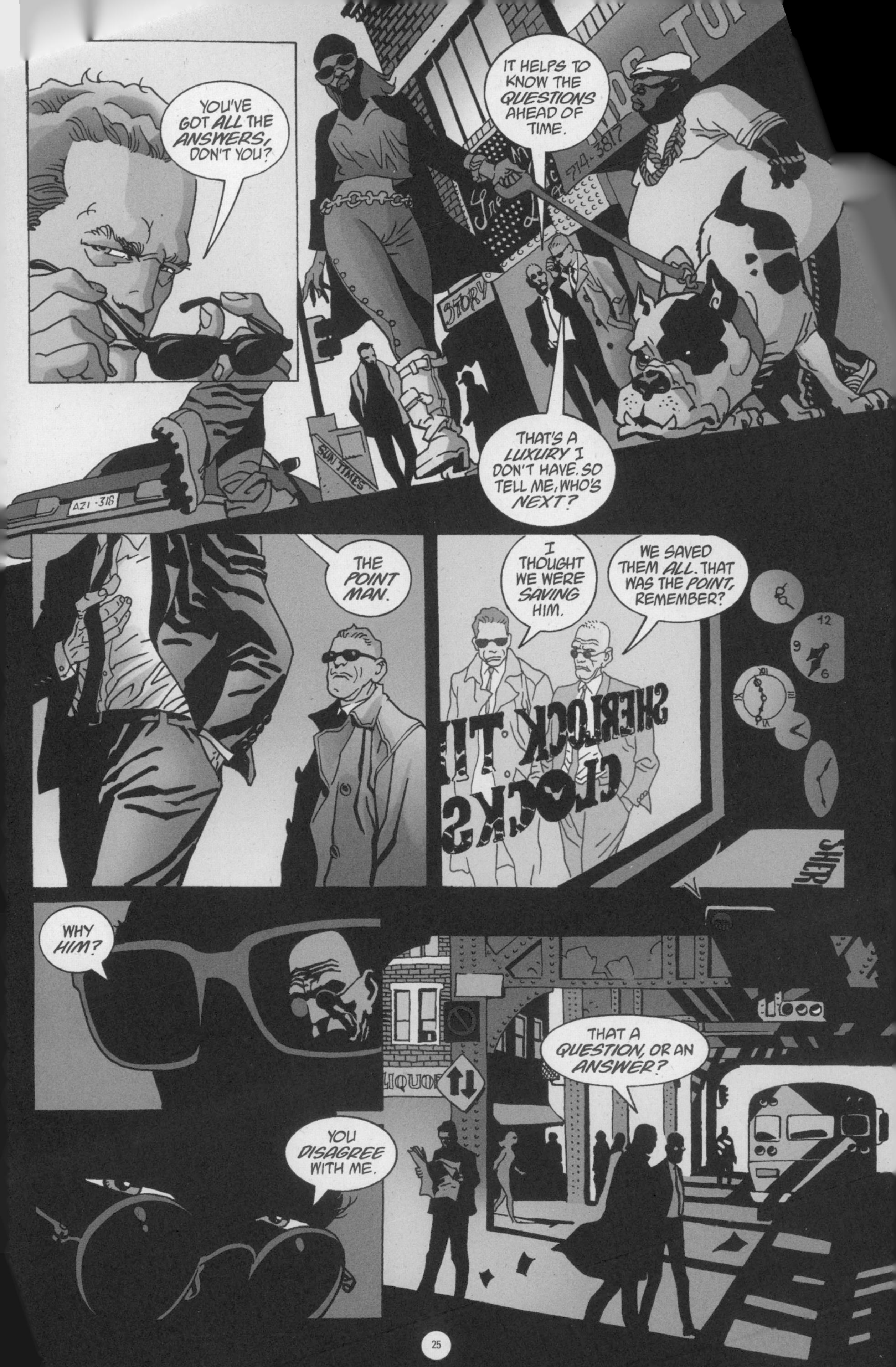
YOU'VE GOT ALL THE ANSWERS, DON'T YOU?
IT HELPS TO KNOW THE QUESTIONS AHEAD OF TIME.
714-3817
STORY
SUN TIMES
AZ1-318
THAT'S A LUXURY I DON'T HAVE. SO TELL ME, WHO'S NEXT?
THE POINT MAN.
I THOUGHT WE WERE SAVING HIM.
WE SAVED THEM ALL. THAT WAS THE POINT, REMEMBER?
SHERLOCK TI
CLOCKS
WHY HIM?
THAT A QUESTION, OR AN ANSWER?
LIQUOR
YOU DISAGREE WITH ME.

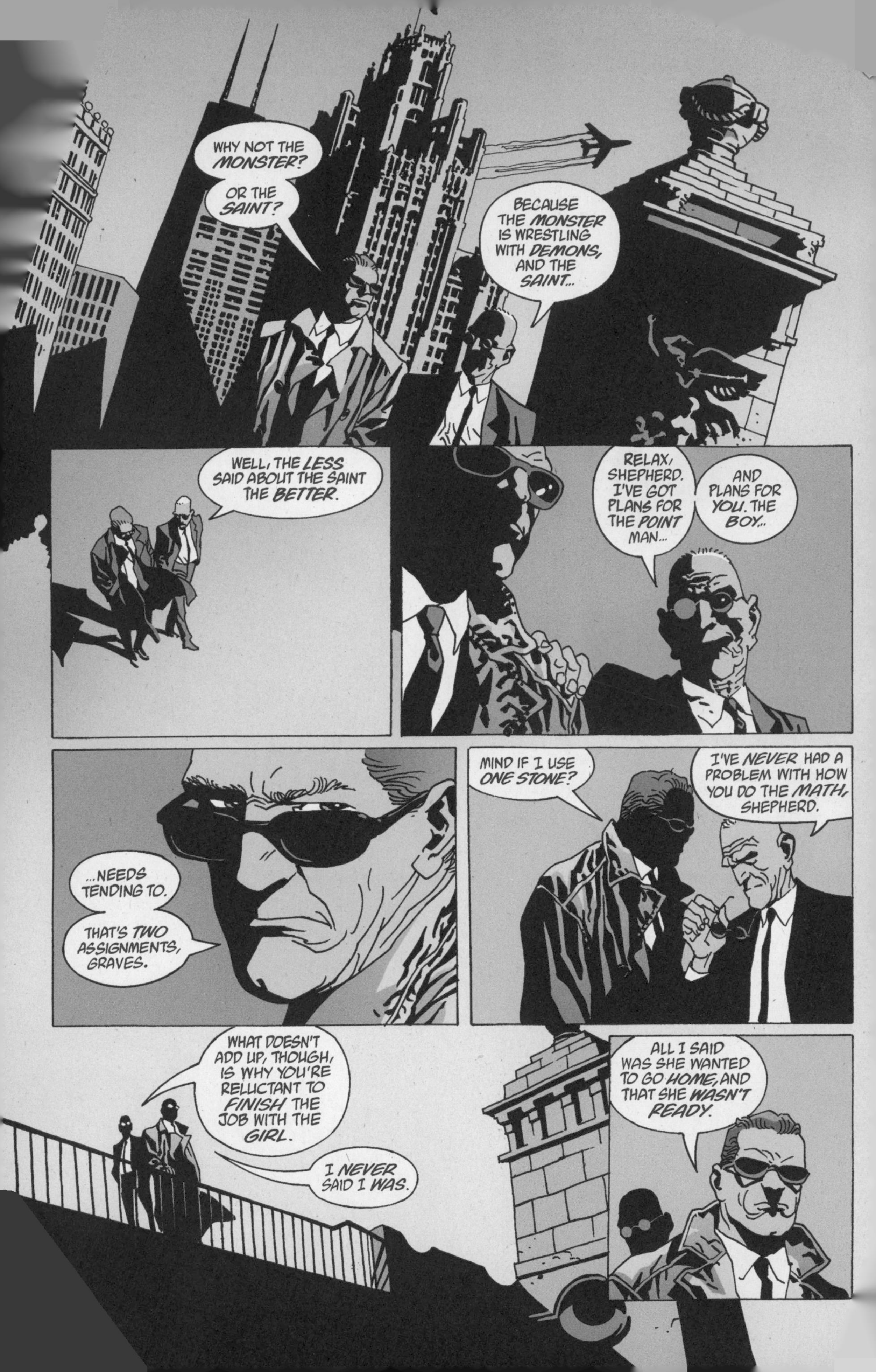
WHY NOT THE MONSTER?
OR THE SAINT?
BECAUSE THE MONSTER IS WRESTLING WITH DEMONS, AND THE SAINT...
WELL, THE LESS SAID ABOUT THE SAINT THE BETTER.
RELAX, SHEPHERD. I'VE GOT PLANS FOR THE POINT MAN...
AND PLANS FOR YOU. THE BOY...
...NEEDS TENDING TO.
THAT'S TWO ASSIGNMENTS, GRAVES.
MIND IF I USE ONE STONE?
I'VE NEVER HAD A PROBLEM WITH HOW YOU DO THE MATH, SHEPHERD.
WHAT DOESN'T ADD UP, THOUGH, IS WHY YOU'RE RELUCTANT TO FINISH THE JOB WITH THE GIRL.
I NEVER SAID I WAS.
ALL I SAID WAS SHE WANTED TO GO HOME, AND THAT SHE WASN'T READY.

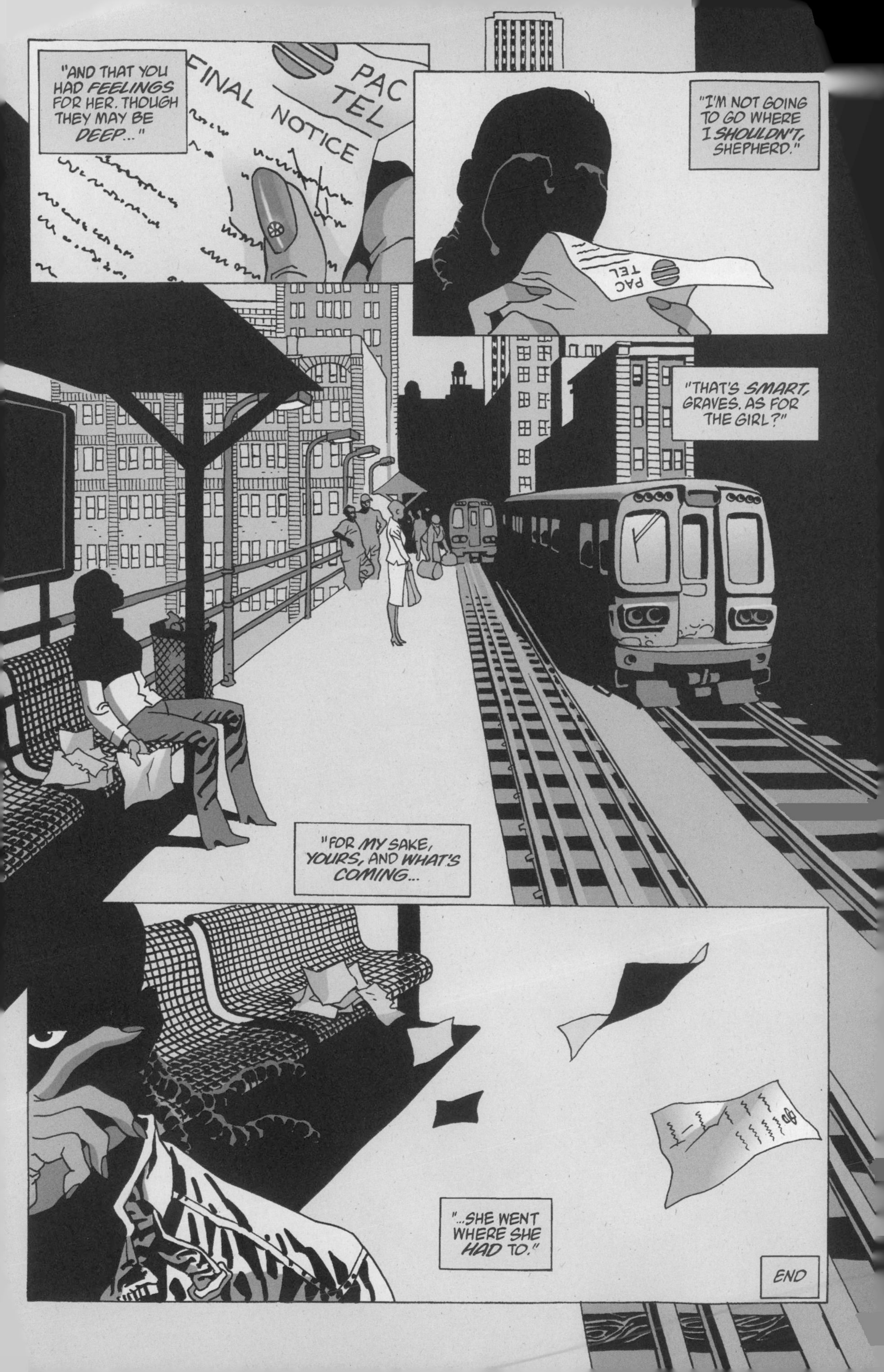
"AND THAT YOU HAD FEELINGS FOR HER. THOUGH THEY MAY BE DEEP..."
PAC TEL
FINAL NOTICE
"I'M NOT GOING TO GO WHERE I SHOULDN'T, SHEPHERD."
PAC TEL
"THAT'S SMART, GRAVES. AS FOR THE GIRL?"
"FOR MY SAKE, YOURS, AND WHAT'S COMING...
"...SHE WENT WHERE SHE HAD TO."
END

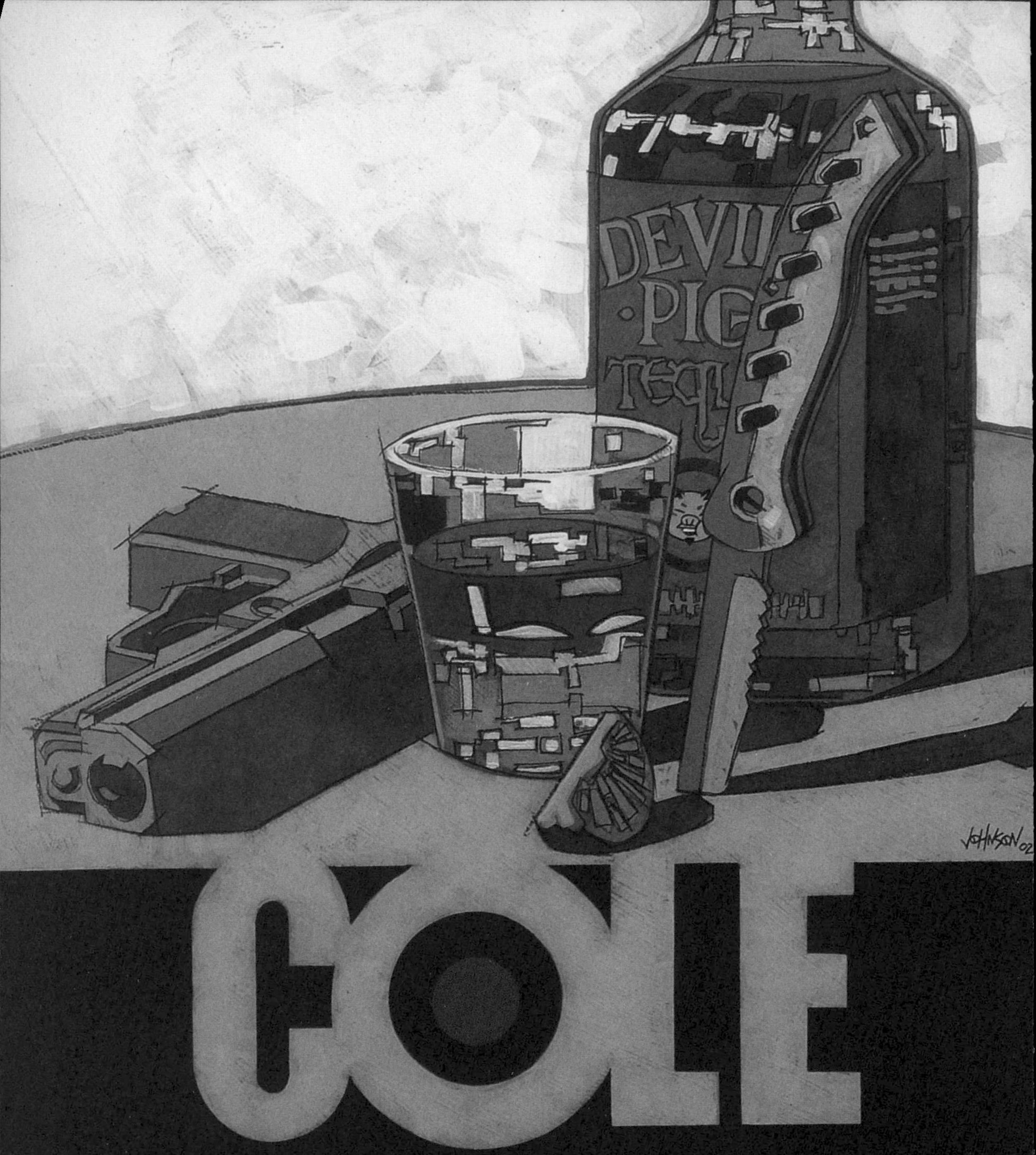
JOHNSON 02
COLE

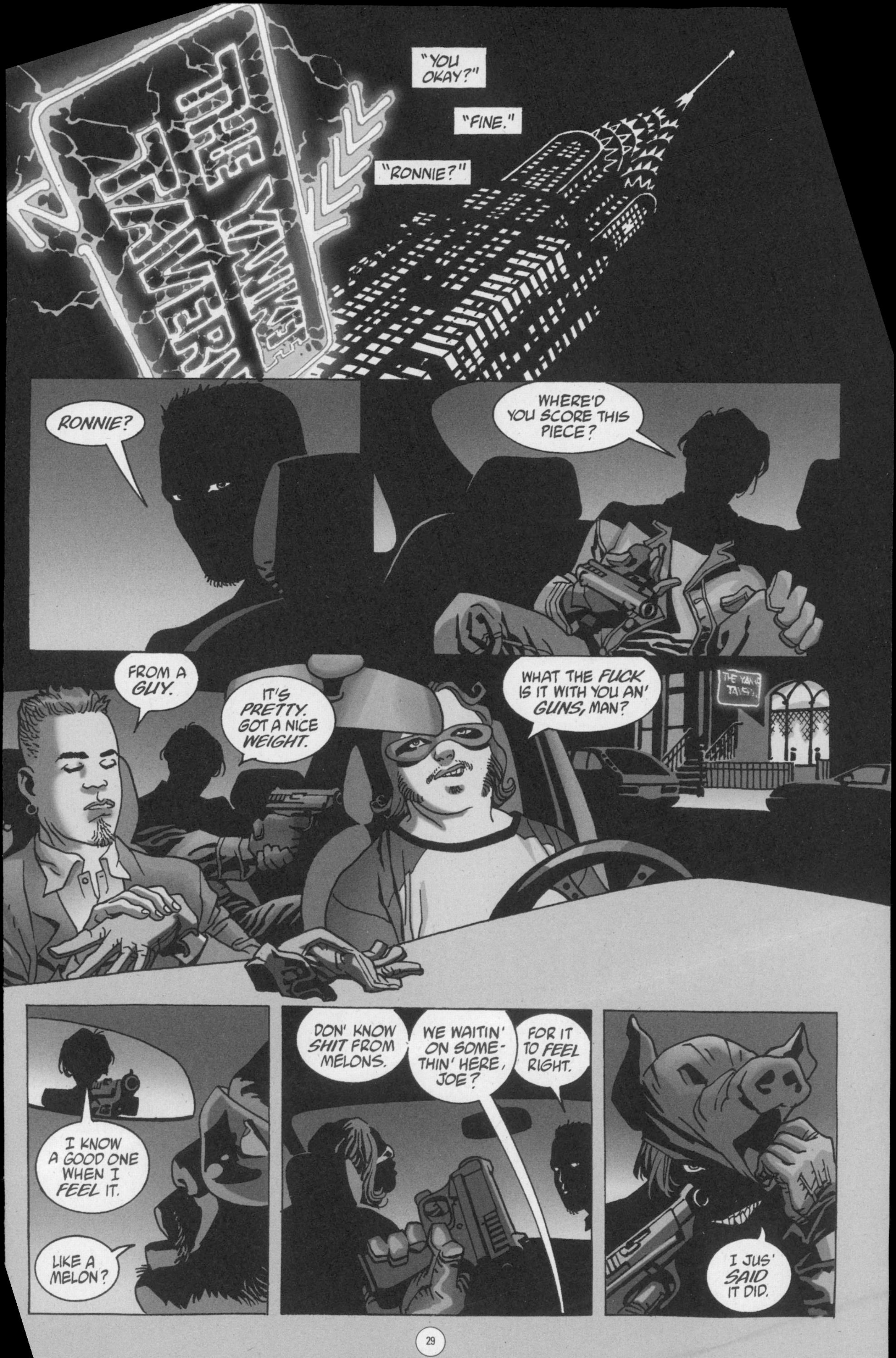
THE YANKS TAVERN
"YOU OKAY?"
"FINE."
"RONNIE?"
RONNIE?
WHERE'D YOU SCORE THIS PIECE?
FROM A *GUY*.
IT'S *PRETTY*. GOT A NICE *WEIGHT*.
WHAT THE *FUCK* IS IT WITH YOU AN' *GUNS*, MAN?
I KNOW A GOOD ONE WHEN I *FEEL* IT.
LIKE A MELON?
DON' KNOW *SHIT* FROM MELONS.
WE WAITIN' ON SOME-THIN' HERE, JOE?
FOR IT TO *FEEL* RIGHT.
I JUS' *SAID* IT DID.

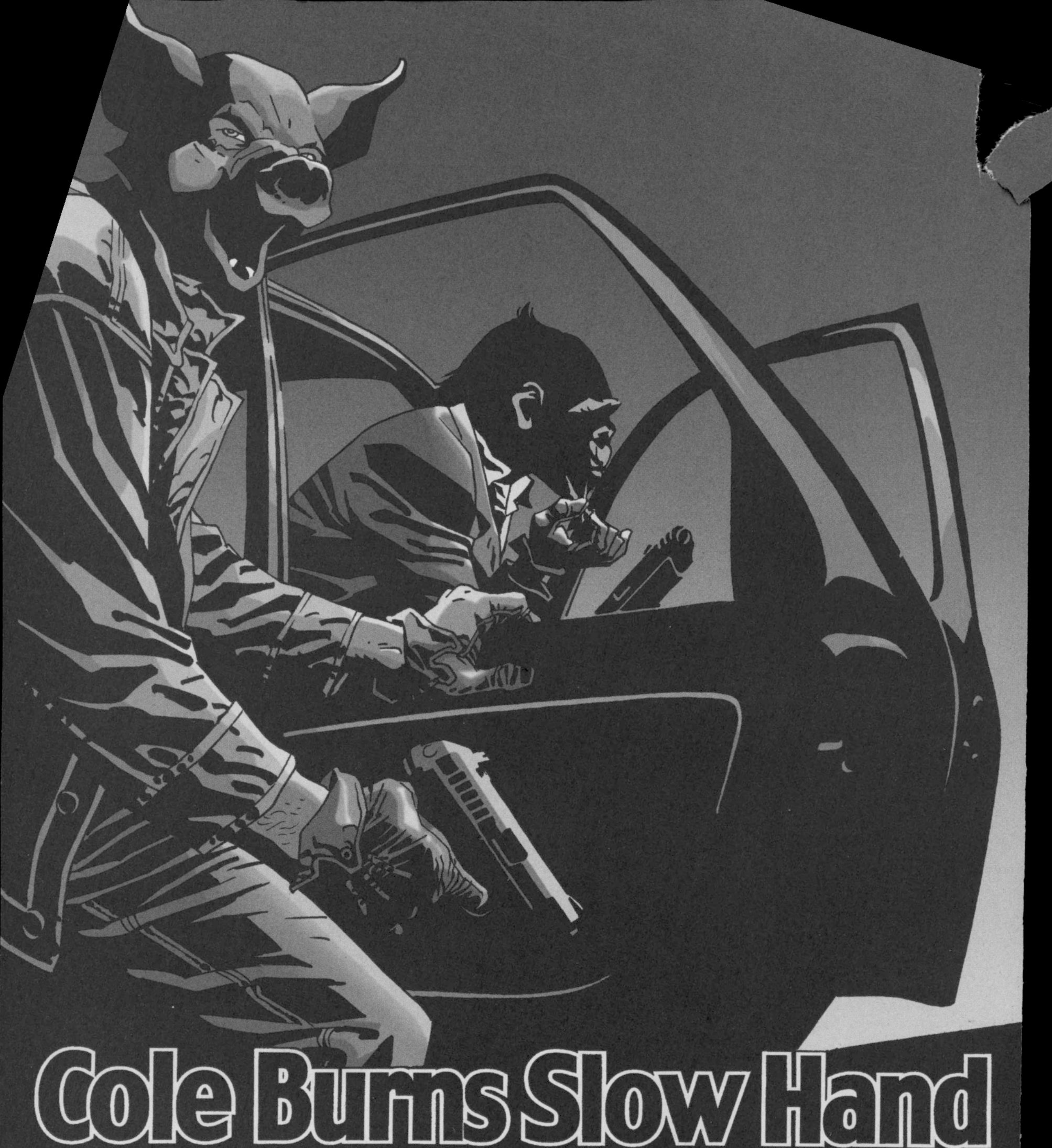

Cole Burns Slow Hand

BRIAN AZZARELLO, writer
PATRICIA MULVIHILL, colorist
DIGITAL CHAMELEON, separations
ZACHARY RAU, assistant editor

EDUARDO RISSO, artist
CLEM ROBINS, letterer
DAVE JOHNSON, cover artist
WILL DENNIS, editor

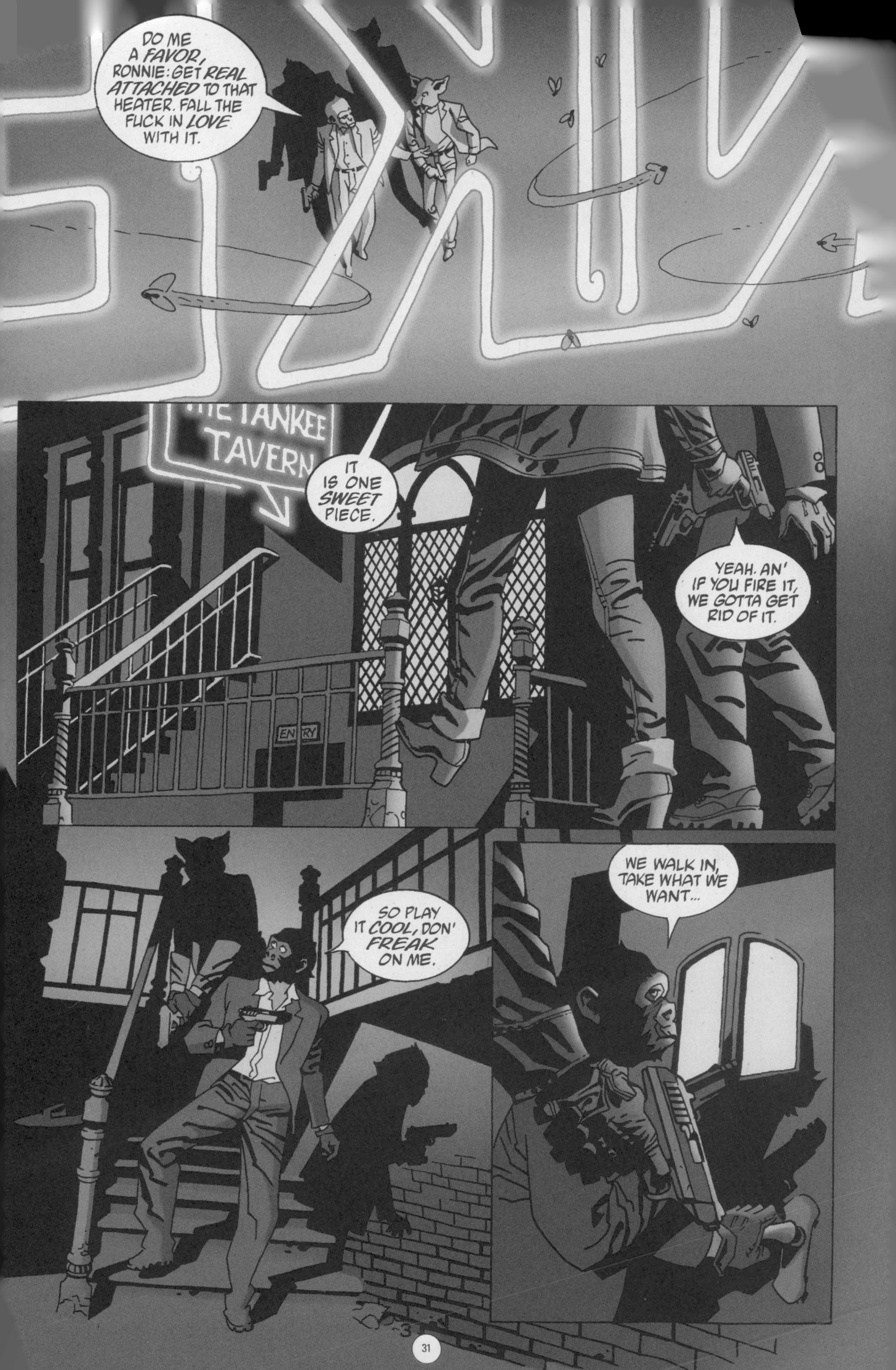
DO ME A FAVOR, RONNIE: GET REAL ATTACHED TO THAT HEATER. FALL THE FUCK IN LOVE WITH IT.
THE YANKEE TAVERN
IT IS ONE SWEET PIECE.
YEAH. AN' IF YOU FIRE IT, WE GOTTA GET RID OF IT.
ENTRY
SO PLAY IT COOL, DON' FREAK ON ME.
WE WALK IN, TAKE WHAT WE WANT...

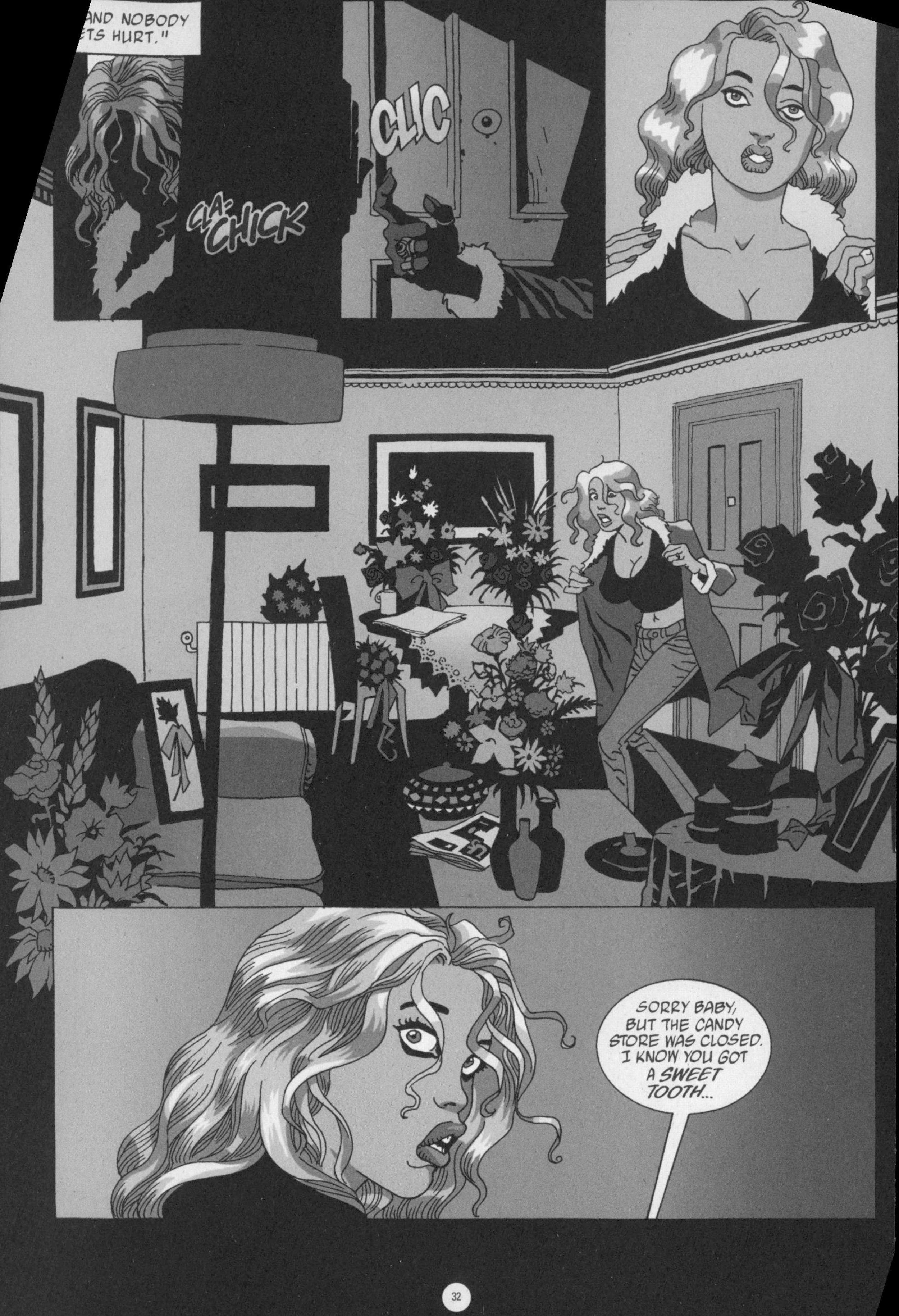
AND NOBODY
GETS HURT."
CLA-CHICK
CLIC
SORRY BABY, BUT THE CANDY STORE WAS CLOSED. I KNOW YOU GOT A *SWEET TOOTH*...

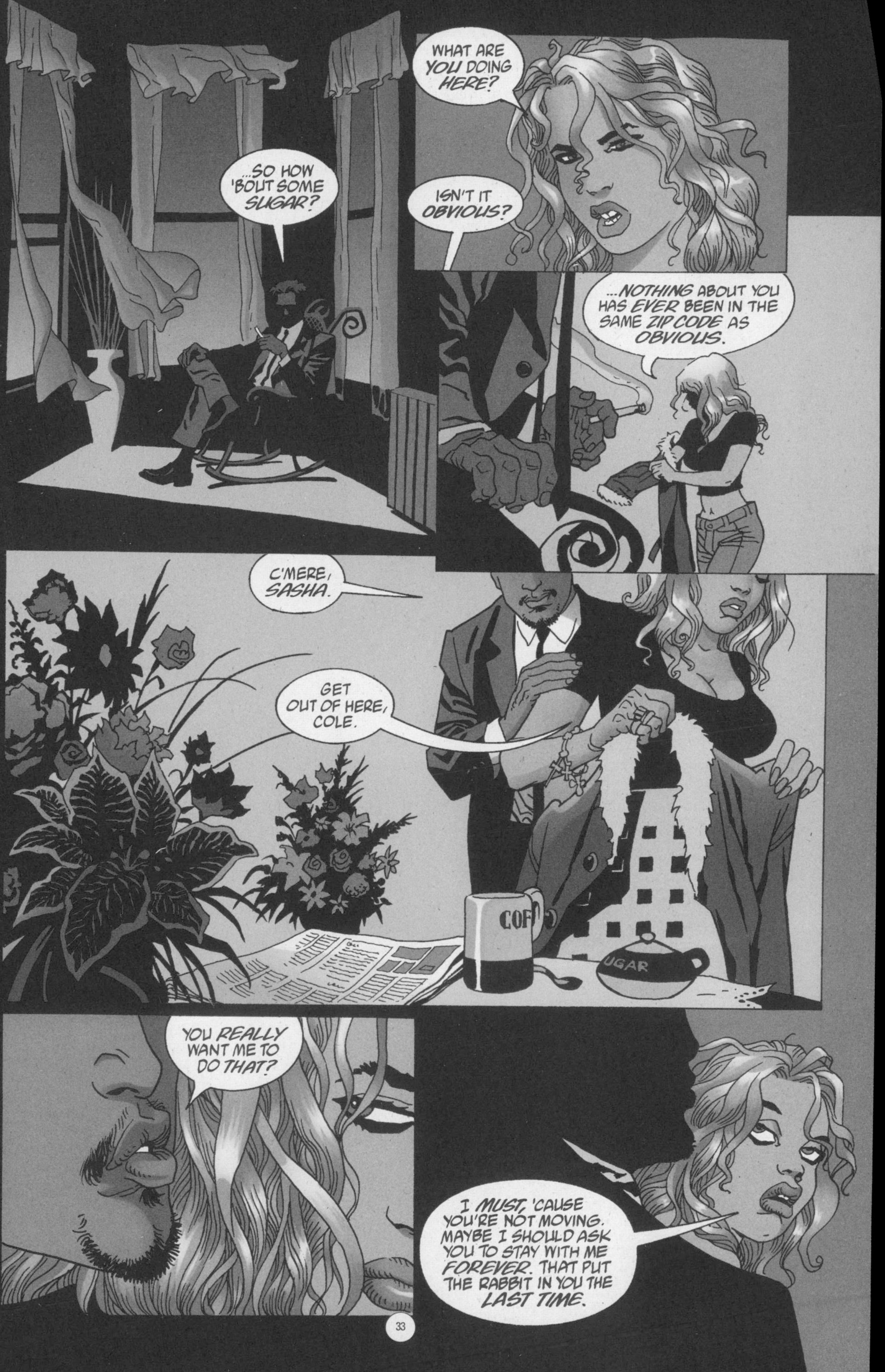
...SO HOW 'BOUT SOME SUGAR?
WHAT ARE YOU DOING HERE?
ISN'T IT OBVIOUS?
...NOTHING ABOUT YOU HAS EVER BEEN IN THE SAME ZIP CODE AS OBVIOUS.
C'MERE, SASHA.
GET OUT OF HERE, COLE.
COF
UGAR
YOU REALLY WANT ME TO DO THAT?
I MUST, 'CAUSE YOU'RE NOT MOVING. MAYBE I SHOULD ASK YOU TO STAY WITH ME FOREVER. THAT PUT THE RABBIT IN YOU THE LAST TIME.

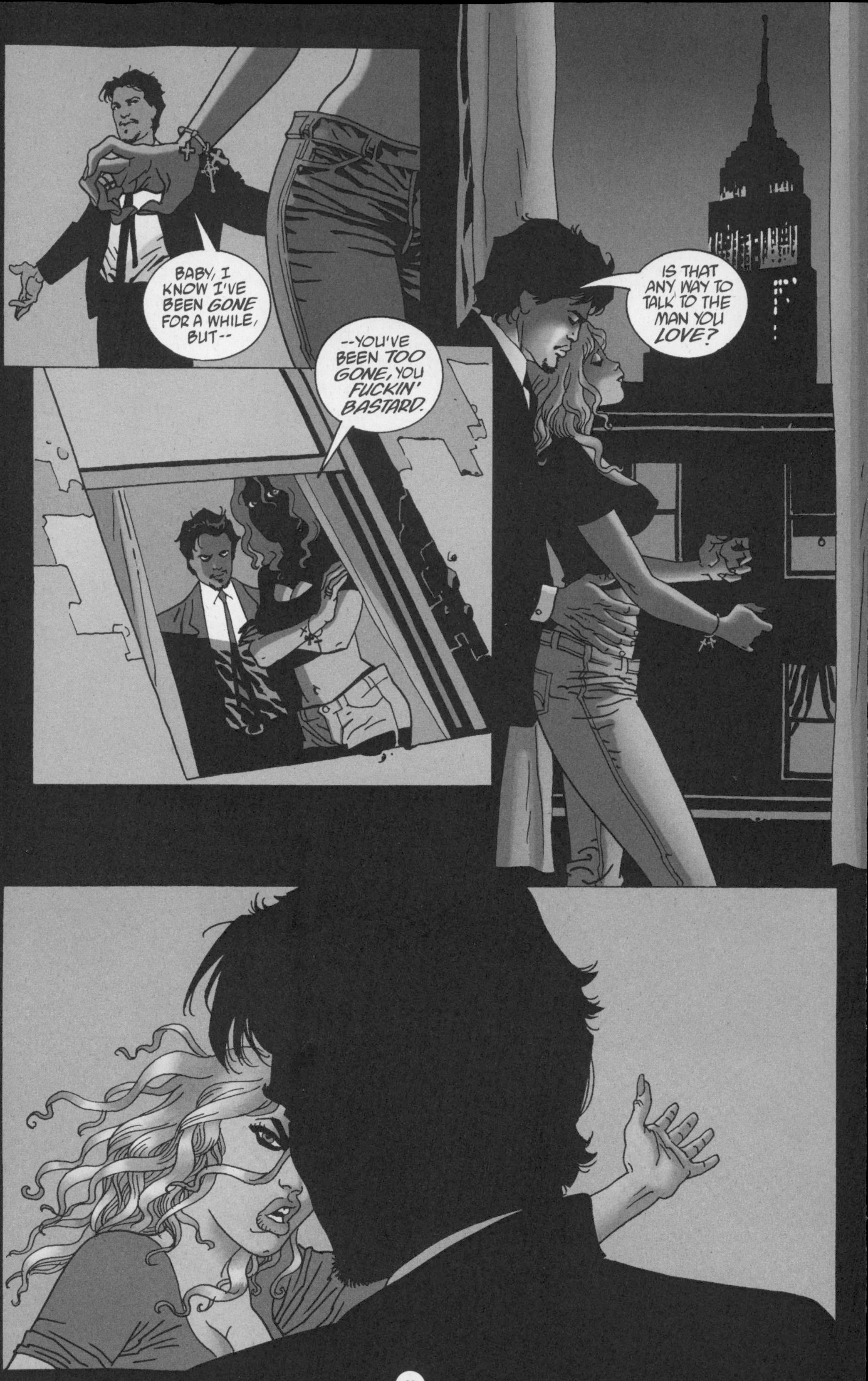
BABY, I KNOW I'VE BEEN GONE FOR A WHILE, BUT--
--YOU'VE BEEN TOO GONE, YOU FUCKIN' BASTARD.
IS THAT ANY WAY TO TALK TO THE MAN YOU LOVE?

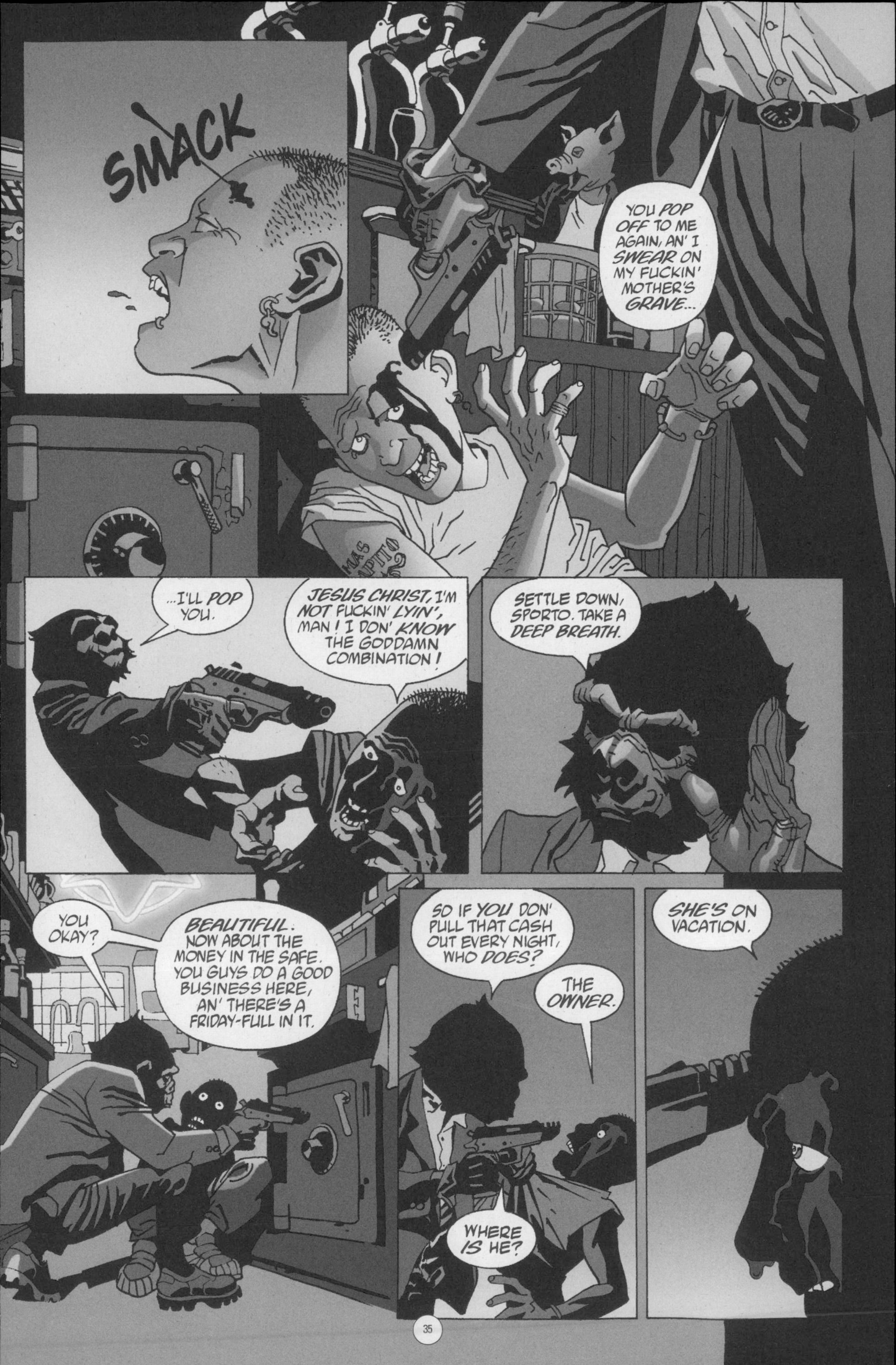
SMACK
YOU POP OFF TO ME AGAIN, AN' I SWEAR ON MY FUCKIN' MOTHER'S GRAVE...
...I'LL POP YOU.
JESUS CHRIST, I'M NOT FUCKIN' LYIN', MAN! I DON' KNOW THE GODDAMN COMBINATION!
SETTLE DOWN, SPORTO. TAKE A DEEP BREATH.
YOU OKAY?
BEAUTIFUL. NOW ABOUT THE MONEY IN THE SAFE. YOU GUYS DO A GOOD BUSINESS HERE, AN' THERE'S A FRIDAY-FULL IN IT.
SO IF YOU DON' PULL THAT CASH OUT EVERY NIGHT, WHO DOES?
THE OWNER.
WHERE IS HE?
SHE'S ON VACATION.

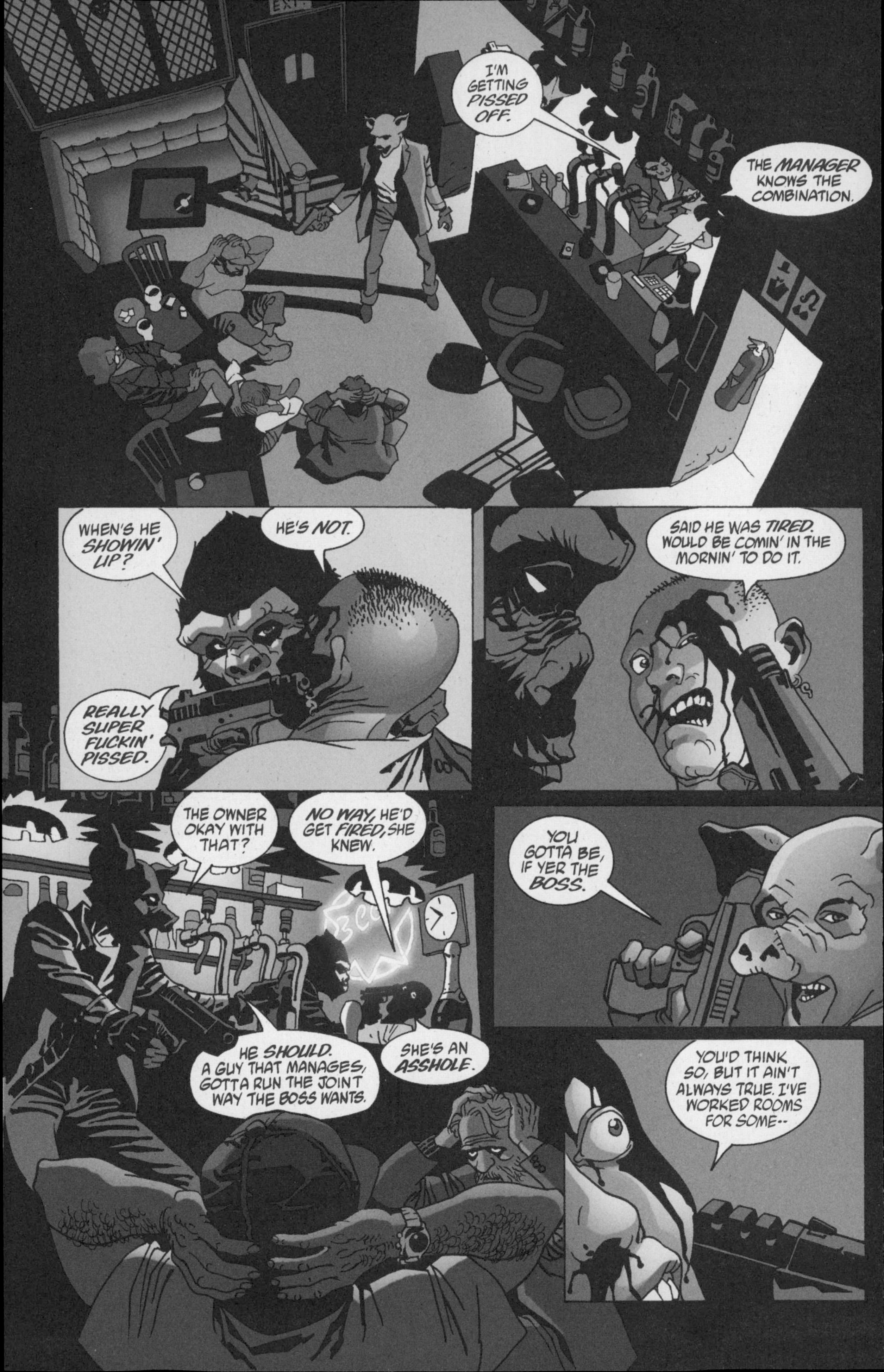
EXIT
I'M GETTING PISSED OFF.
THE MANAGER KNOWS THE COMBINATION.
WHEN'S HE SHOWIN' UP?
HE'S NOT.
REALLY SUPER FUCKIN' PISSED.
SAID HE WAS TIRED. WOULD BE COMIN' IN THE MORNIN' TO DO IT.
THE OWNER OKAY WITH THAT?
NO WAY, HE'D GET FIRED, SHE KNEW.
YOU GOTTA BE, IF YER THE BOSS.
HE SHOULD. A GUY THAT MANAGES, GOTTA RUN THE JOINT WAY THE BOSS WANTS.
SHE'S AN ASSHOLE.
YOU'D THINK SO, BUT IT AIN'T ALWAYS TRUE. I'VE WORKED ROOMS FOR SOME--

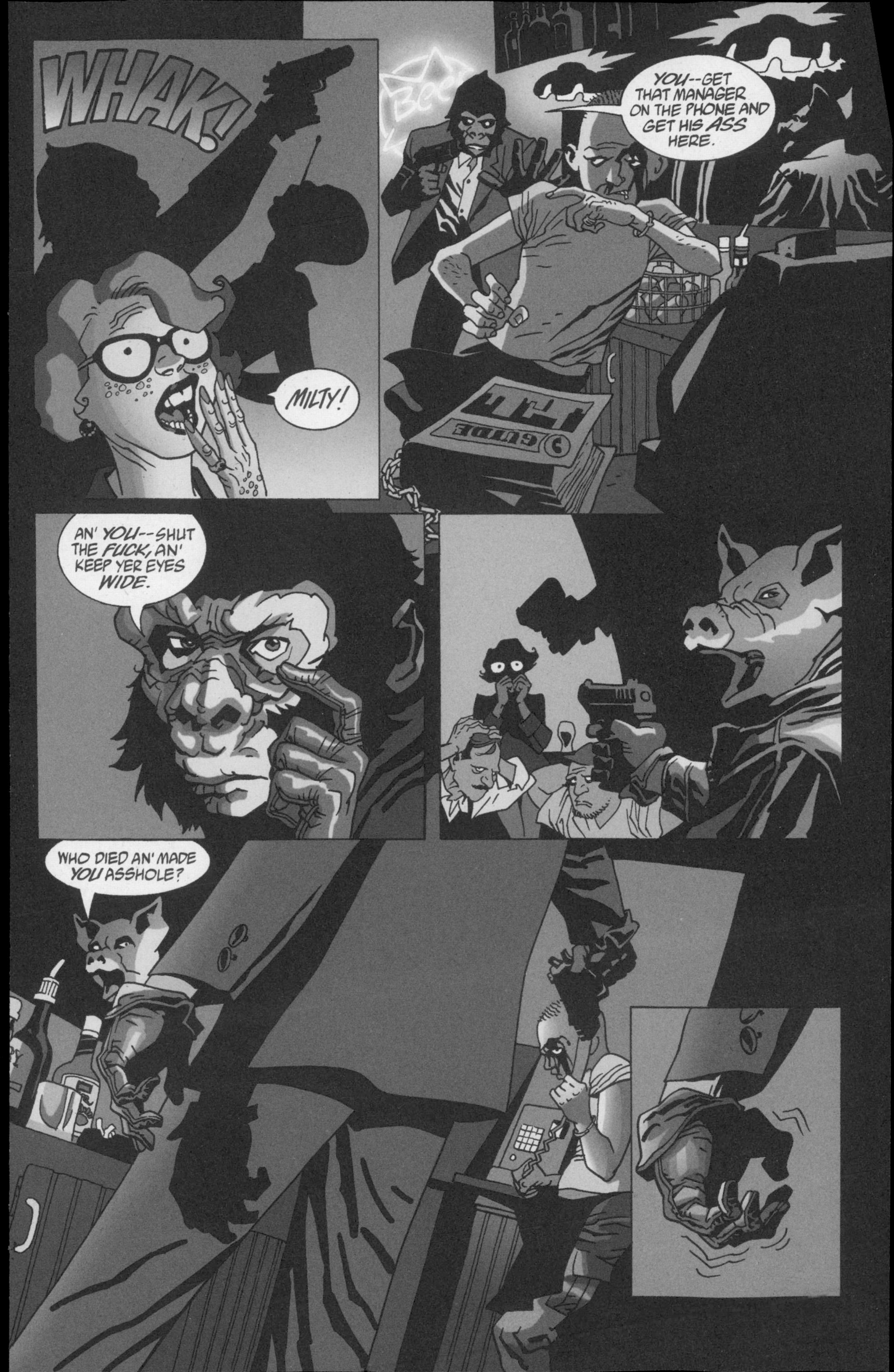
WHAK!
MILTY!
YOU--GET THAT MANAGER ON THE PHONE AND GET HIS ASS HERE.
AN' YOU--SHUT THE FUCK, AN' KEEP YER EYES WIDE.
WHO DIED AN' MADE YOU ASSHOLE?

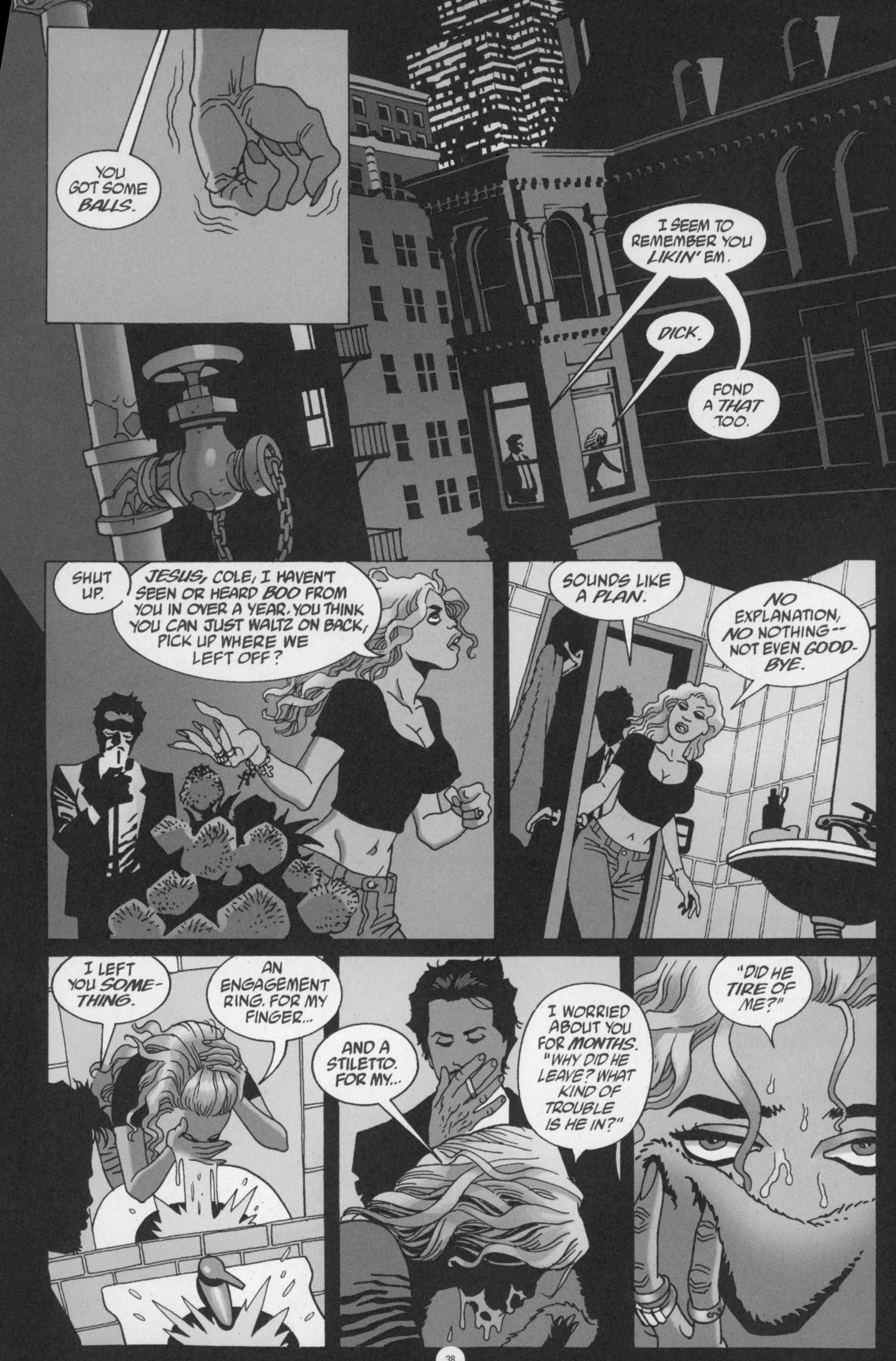
YOU GOT SOME BALLS.
I SEEM TO REMEMBER YOU LIKIN' EM.
DICK.
FOND A THAT TOO.
SHUT UP.
JESUS, COLE, I HAVEN'T SEEN OR HEARD BOO FROM YOU IN OVER A YEAR. YOU THINK YOU CAN JUST WALTZ ON BACK, PICK UP WHERE WE LEFT OFF?
SOUNDS LIKE A PLAN.
NO EXPLANATION, NO NOTHING-- NOT EVEN GOOD-BYE.
I LEFT YOU SOME-THING.
AN ENGAGEMENT RING. FOR MY FINGER...
AND A STILETTO. FOR MY...
I WORRIED ABOUT YOU FOR MONTHS. "WHY DID HE LEAVE? WHAT KIND OF TROUBLE IS HE IN?"
"DID HE TIRE OF ME?"

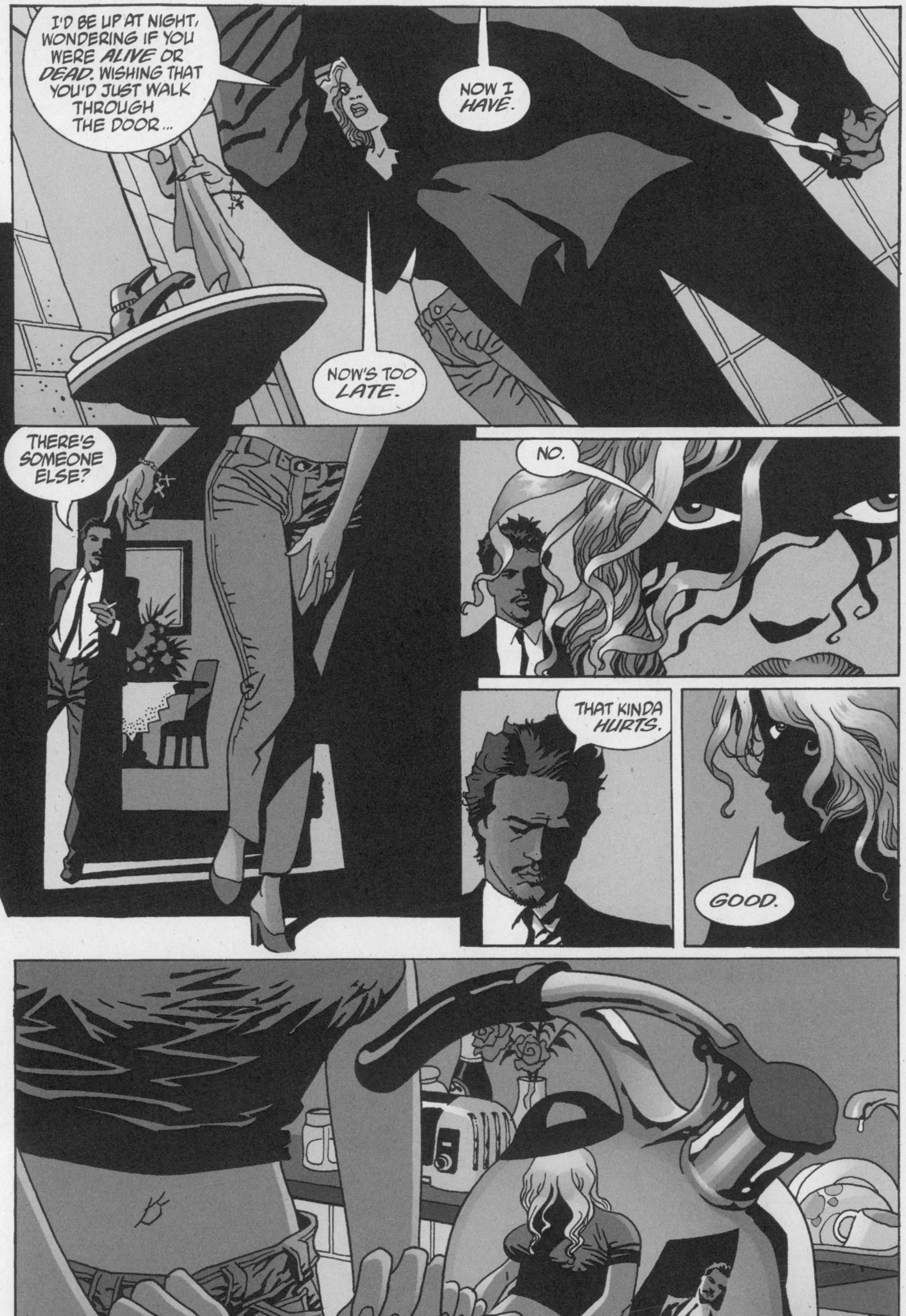
I'D BE UP AT NIGHT, WONDERING IF YOU WERE ALIVE OR DEAD. WISHING THAT YOU'D JUST WALK THROUGH THE DOOR...
NOW I HAVE.
NOW'S TOO LATE.
THERE'S SOMEONE ELSE?
NO.
THAT KINDA HURTS.
GOOD.

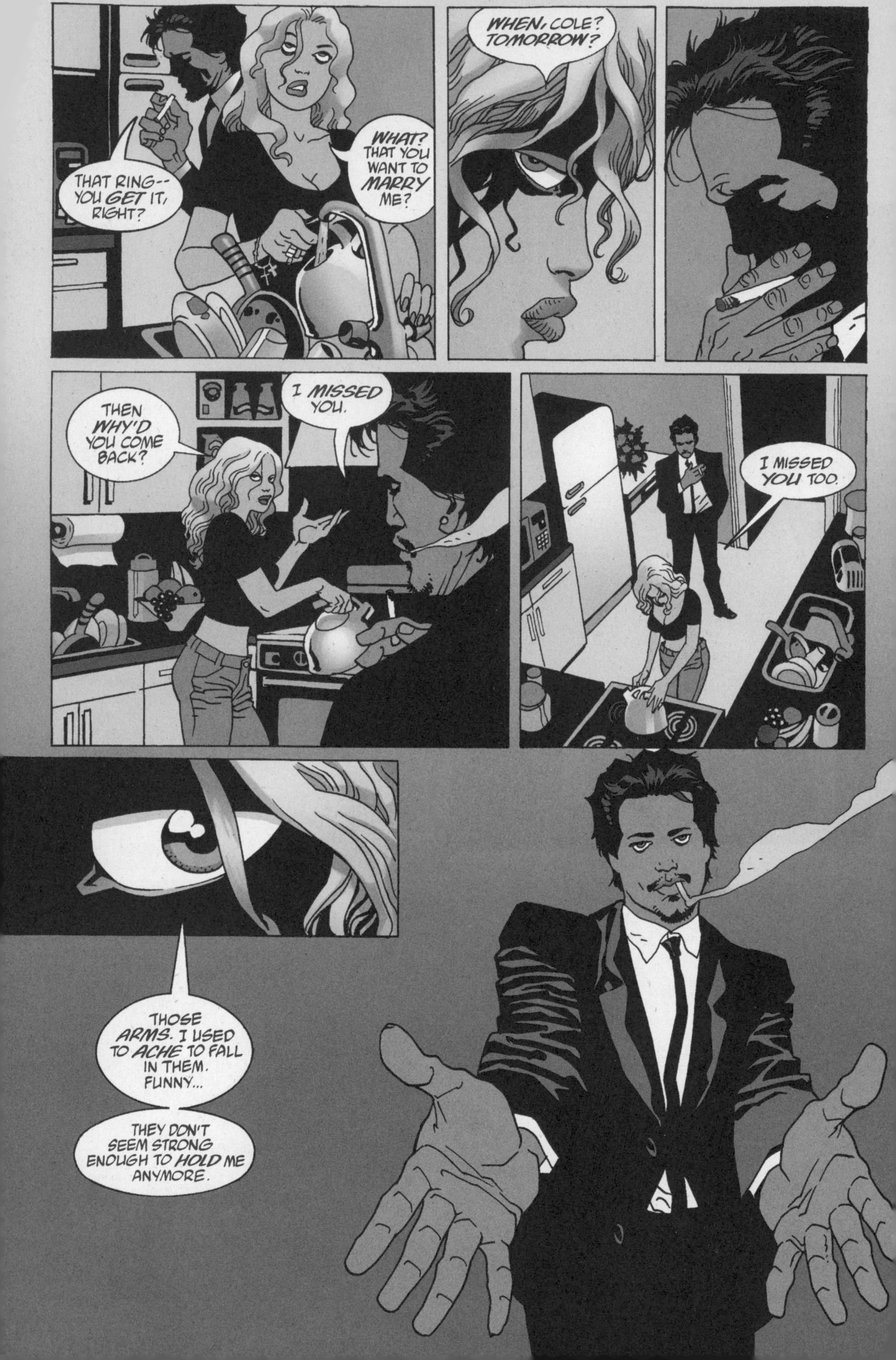
THAT RING-- YOU GET IT, RIGHT?
WHAT? THAT YOU WANT TO MARRY ME?
WHEN, COLE? TOMORROW?
THEN WHY'D YOU COME BACK?
I MISSED YOU.
I MISSED YOU TOO.
THOSE ARMS. I USED TO ACHE TO FALL IN THEM. FUNNY...
THEY DON'T SEEM STRONG ENOUGH TO HOLD ME ANYMORE.

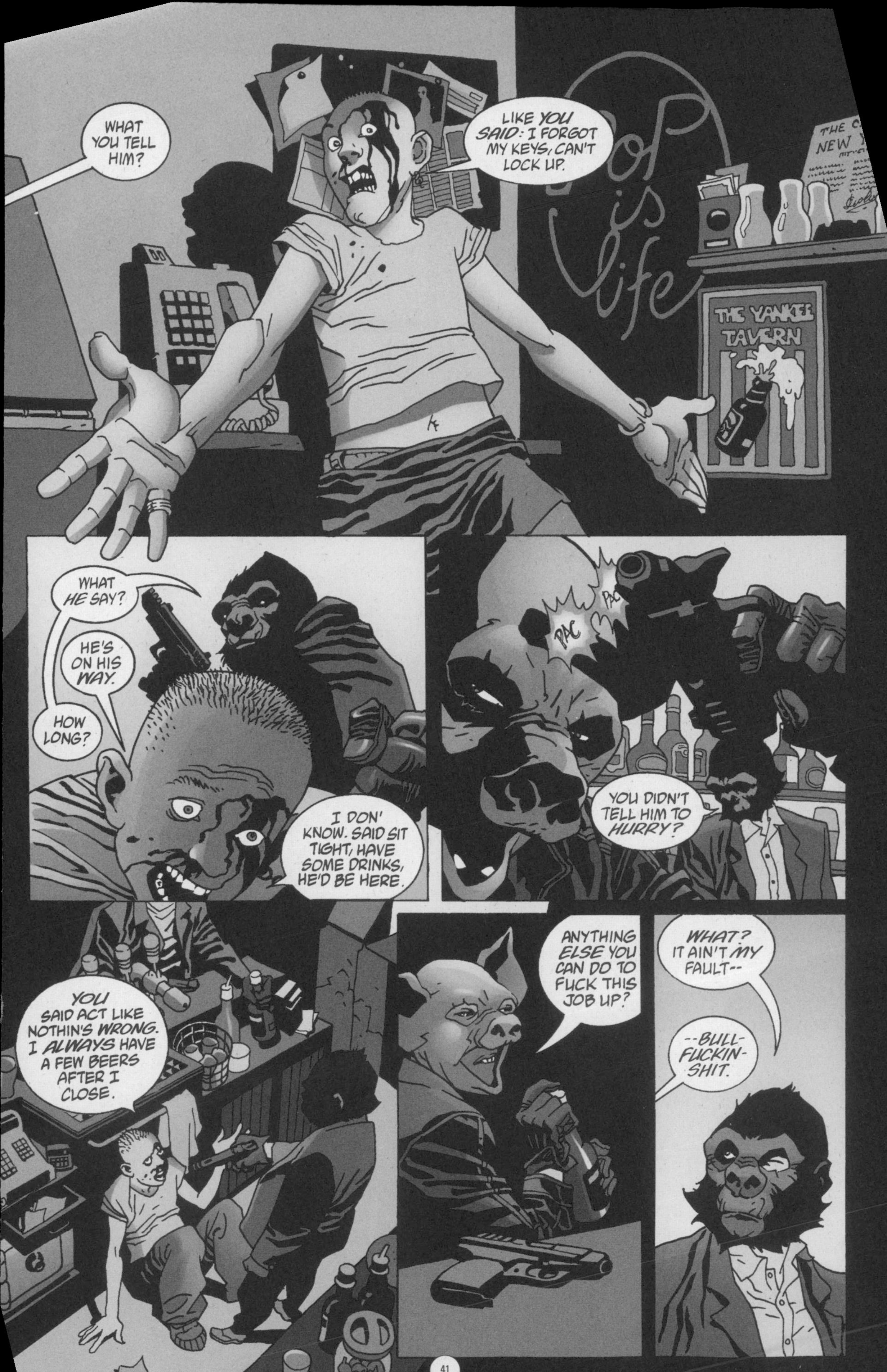
WHAT YOU TELL HIM?
LIKE YOU SAID: I FORGOT MY KEYS, CAN'T LOCK UP.
THE YANKEE TAVERN
WHAT HE SAY?
HE'S ON HIS WAY.
HOW LONG?
I DON' KNOW. SAID SIT TIGHT, HAVE SOME DRINKS, HE'D BE HERE.
PAC
PAC
YOU DIDN'T TELL HIM TO HURRY?
YOU SAID ACT LIKE NOTHIN'S WRONG. I ALWAYS HAVE A FEW BEERS AFTER I CLOSE.
ANYTHING ELSE YOU CAN DO TO FUCK THIS JOB UP?
WHAT? IT AIN'T MY FAULT--
--BULL-FUCKIN-SHIT.

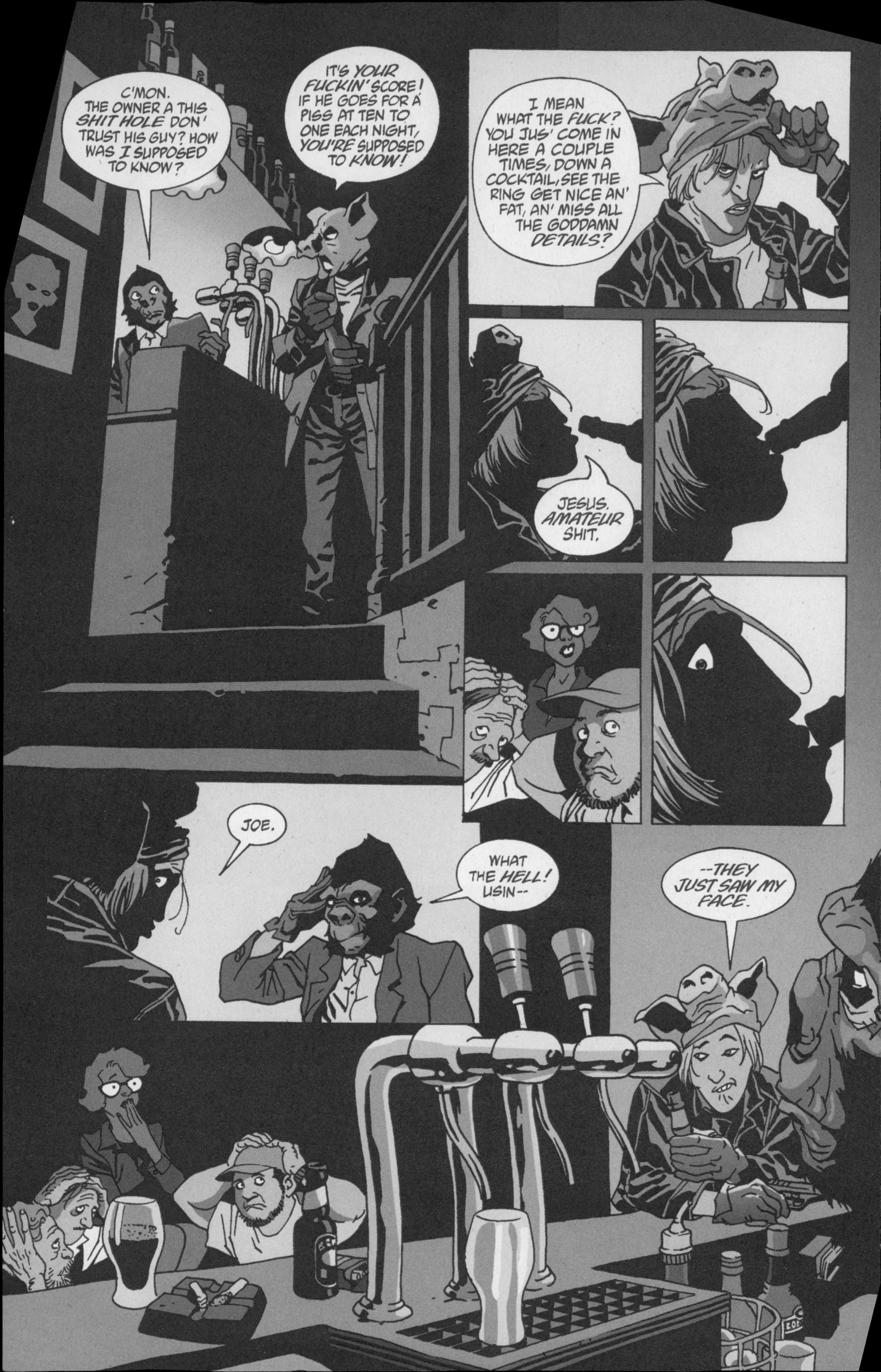
C'MON. THE OWNER A THIS SHIT HOLE DON' TRUST HIS GUY? HOW WAS I SUPPOSED TO KNOW?
IT'S YOUR FUCKIN' SCORE! IF HE GOES FOR A PISS AT TEN TO ONE EACH NIGHT, YOU'RE SUPPOSED TO KNOW!
I MEAN WHAT THE FUCK? YOU JUS' COME IN HERE A COUPLE TIMES, DOWN A COCKTAIL, SEE THE RING GET NICE AN' FAT, AN' MISS ALL THE GODDAMN DETAILS?
JESUS. AMATEUR SHIT.
JOE.
WHAT THE HELL! USIN--
--THEY JUST SAW MY FACE.

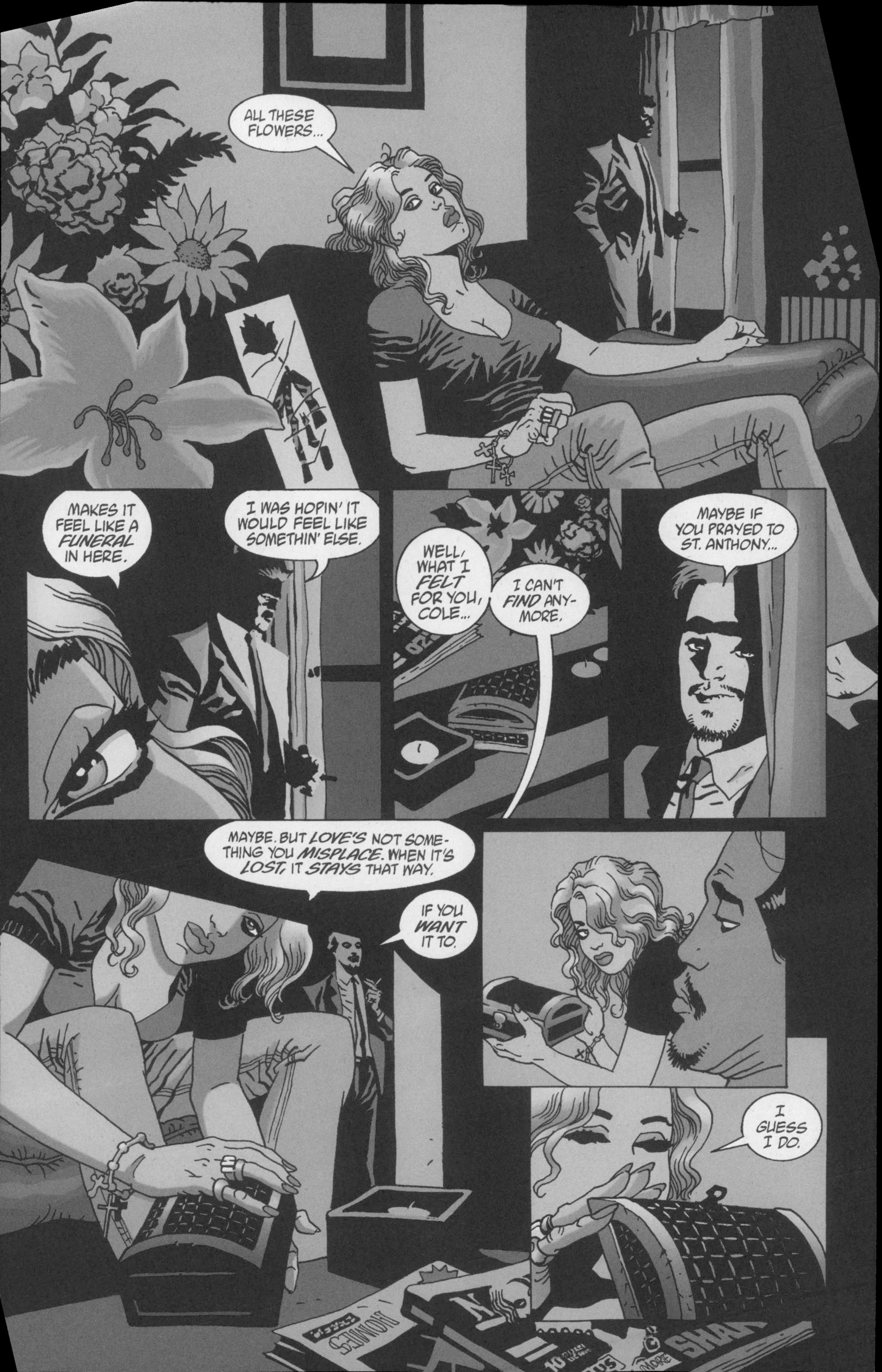
ALL THESE FLOWERS...
MAKES IT FEEL LIKE A *FUNERAL* IN HERE.
I WAS HOPIN' IT WOULD FEEL LIKE SOMETHIN' ELSE.
WELL, WHAT I *FELT* FOR YOU, COLE...
I CAN'T *FIND* ANY-MORE.
MAYBE IF YOU PRAYED TO ST. ANTHONY...
MAYBE. BUT *LOVE'S* NOT SOME-THING YOU *MISPLACE*. WHEN IT'S *LOST*, IT *STAYS* THAT WAY.
IF YOU *WANT* IT TO.
I GUESS I DO.

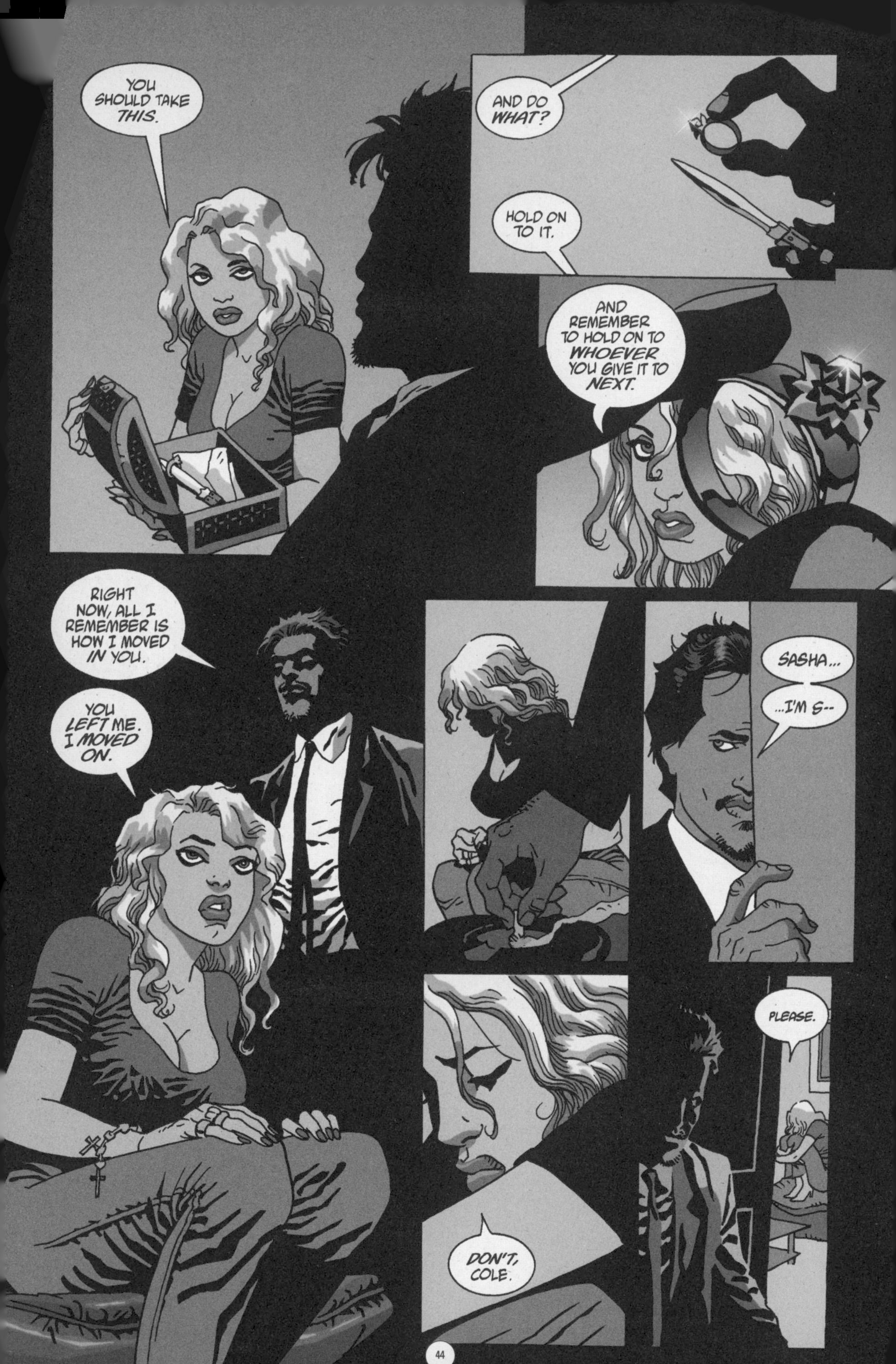
YOU SHOULD TAKE THIS.
AND DO WHAT?
HOLD ON TO IT.
AND REMEMBER TO HOLD ON TO WHOEVER YOU GIVE IT TO NEXT.
RIGHT NOW, ALL I REMEMBER IS HOW I MOVED IN YOU.
YOU LEFT ME. I MOVED ON.
SASHA...
...I'M S--
DON'T, COLE.
PLEASE.

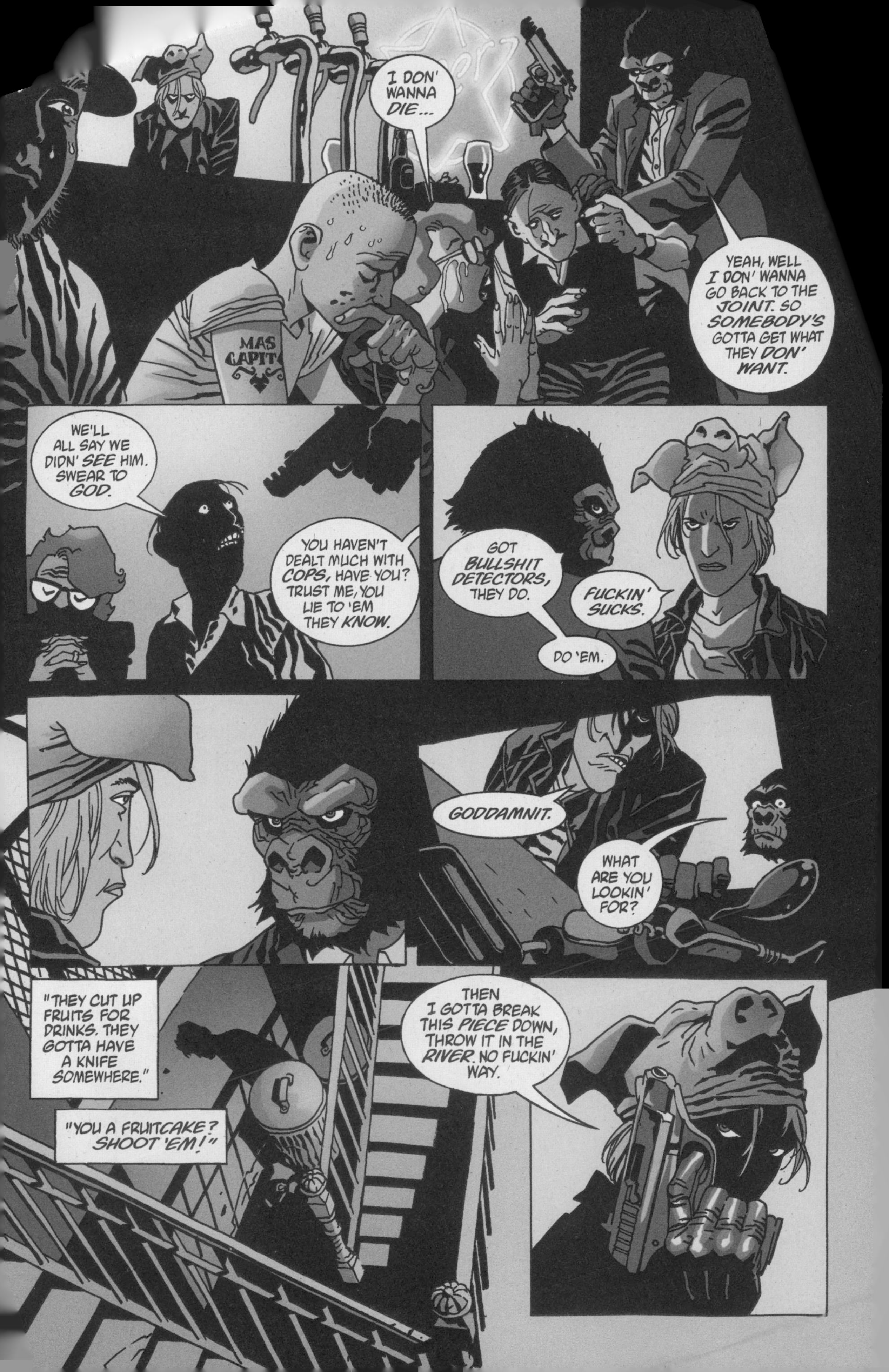

I DON' WANNA DIE...
YEAH, WELL I DON' WANNA GO BACK TO THE JOINT. SO SOMEBODY'S GOTTA GET WHAT THEY DON' WANT.
WE'LL ALL SAY WE DIDN' SEE HIM. SWEAR TO GOD.
YOU HAVEN'T DEALT MUCH WITH COPS, HAVE YOU? TRUST ME, YOU LIE TO 'EM THEY KNOW.
GOT BULLSHIT DETECTORS, THEY DO.
FUCKIN' SUCKS.
DO 'EM.
GODDAMNIT.
WHAT ARE YOU LOOKIN' FOR?
"THEY CUT UP FRUITS FOR DRINKS. THEY GOTTA HAVE A KNIFE SOMEWHERE."
"YOU A FRUITCAKE? SHOOT 'EM!"
THEN I GOTTA BREAK THIS PIECE DOWN, THROW IT IN THE RIVER. NO FUCKIN' WAY.

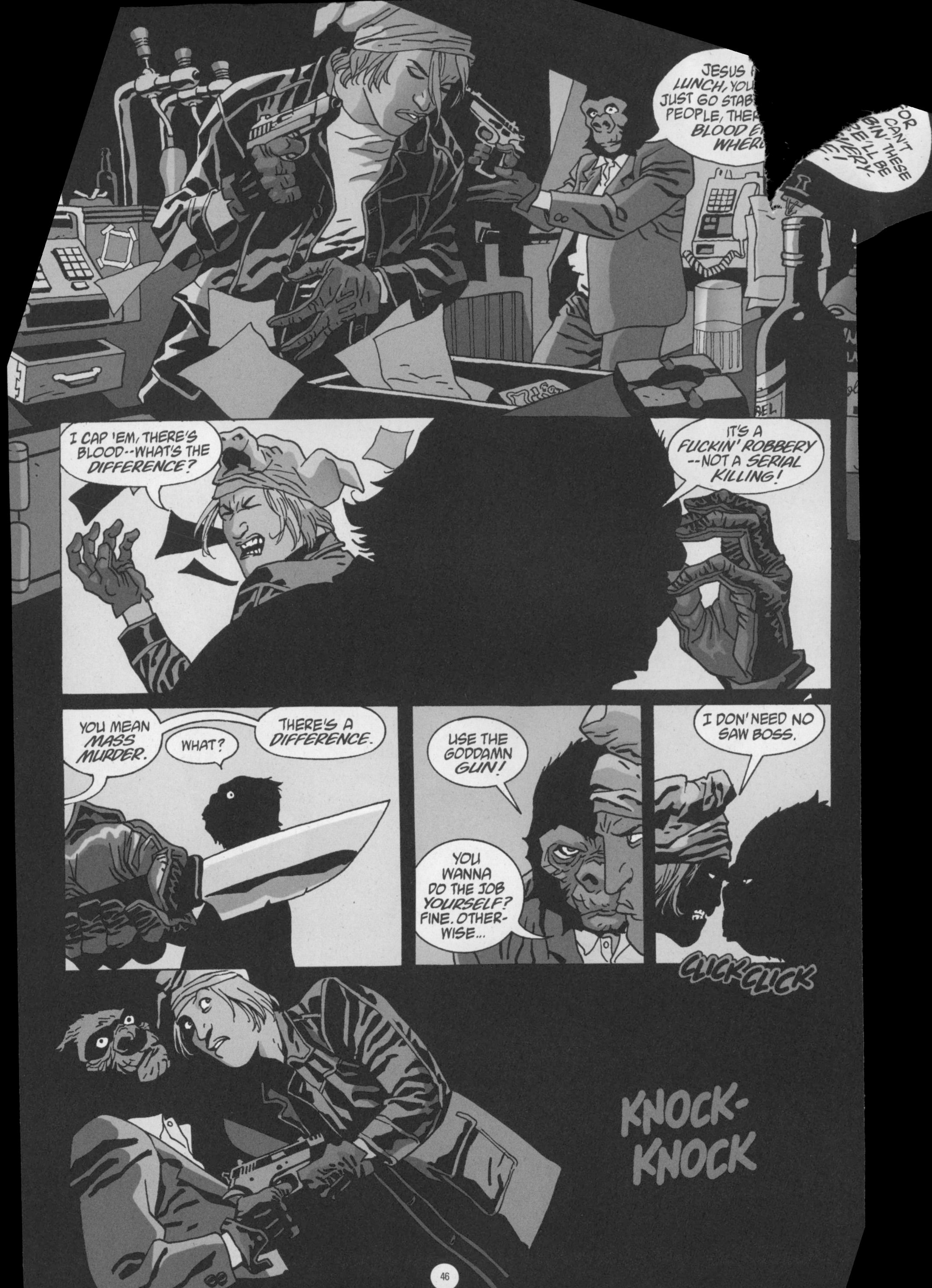

I CAP 'EM, THERE'S BLOOD--WHAT'S THE DIFFERENCE?
IT'S A FUCKIN' ROBBERY --NOT A SERIAL KILLING!
YOU MEAN MASS MURDER.
WHAT?
THERE'S A DIFFERENCE.
USE THE GODDAMN GUN!
YOU WANNA DO THE JOB YOURSELF? FINE. OTHER-WISE...
I DON' NEED NO SAW BOSS.
CLICK CLICK
KNOCK-KNOCK

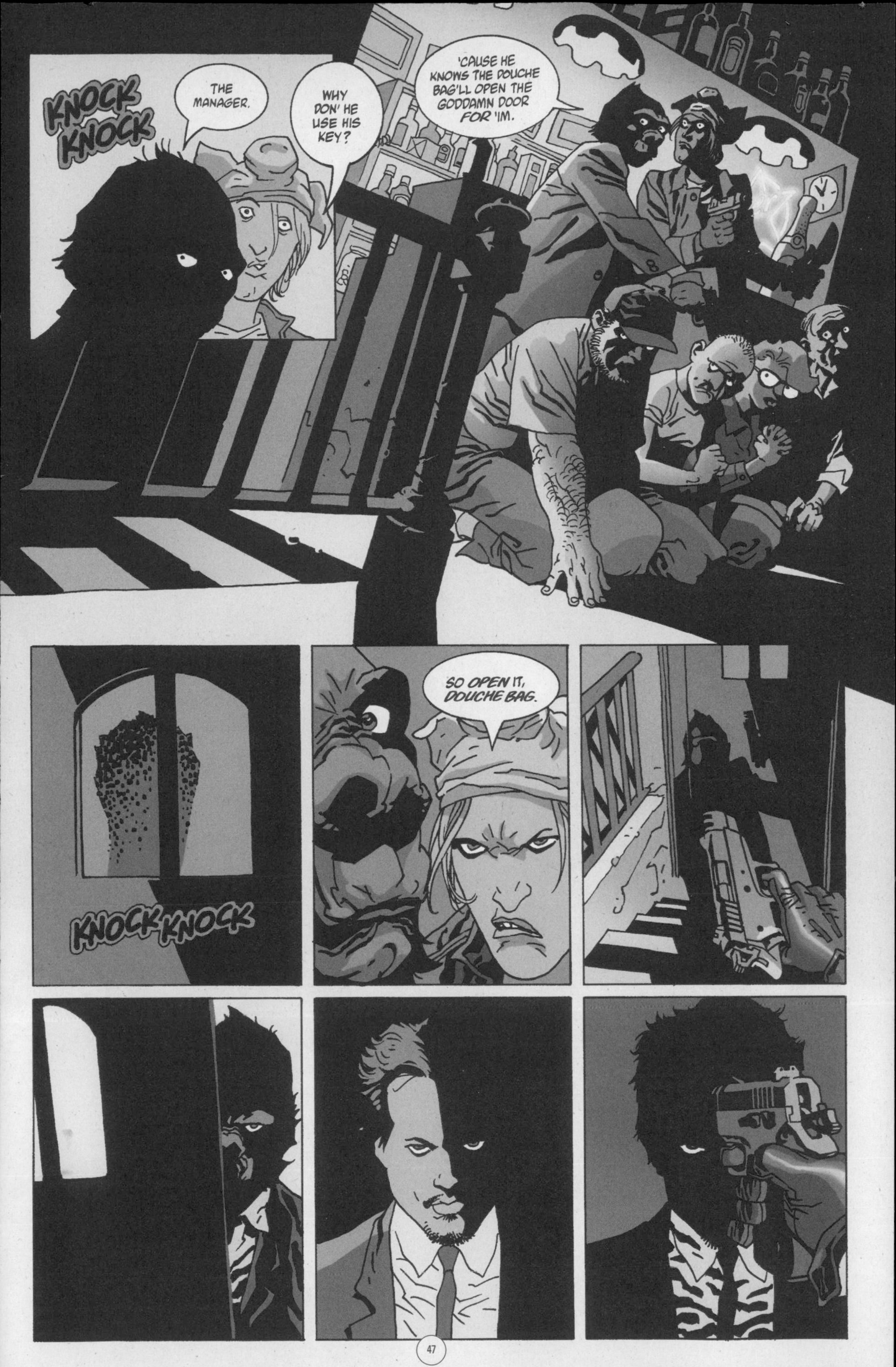
KNOCK KNOCK
THE MANAGER.
WHY DON' HE USE HIS KEY?
'CAUSE HE KNOWS THE DOUCHE BAG'LL OPEN THE GODDAMN DOOR FOR 'IM.
KNOCK KNOCK
SO OPEN IT, DOUCHE BAG.

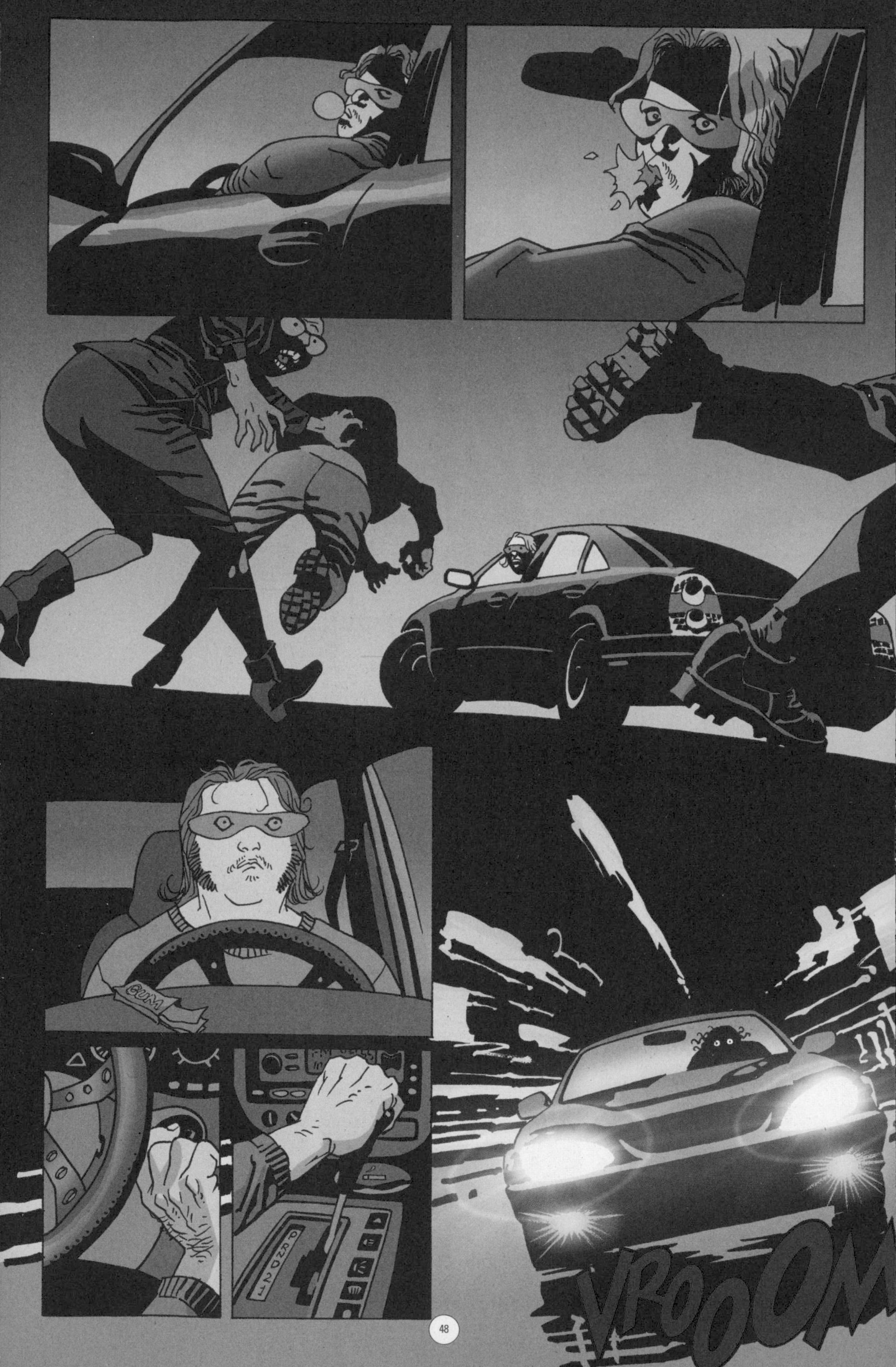
GUM
VROOOOM

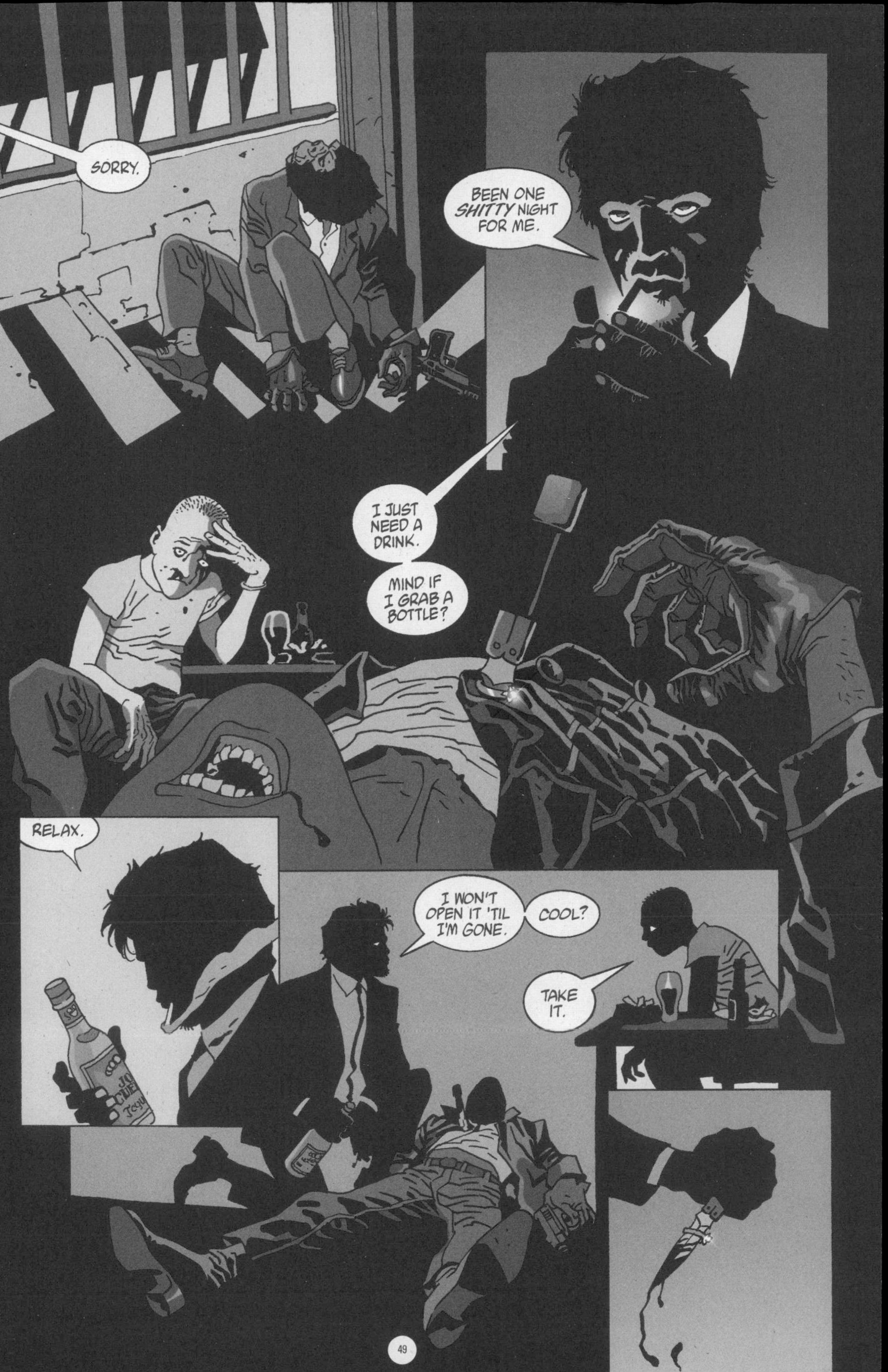
SORRY.
BEEN ONE SHITTY NIGHT FOR ME.
I JUST NEED A DRINK.
MIND IF I GRAB A BOTTLE?
RELAX.
I WON'T OPEN IT 'TIL I'M GONE.
COOL?
TAKE IT.

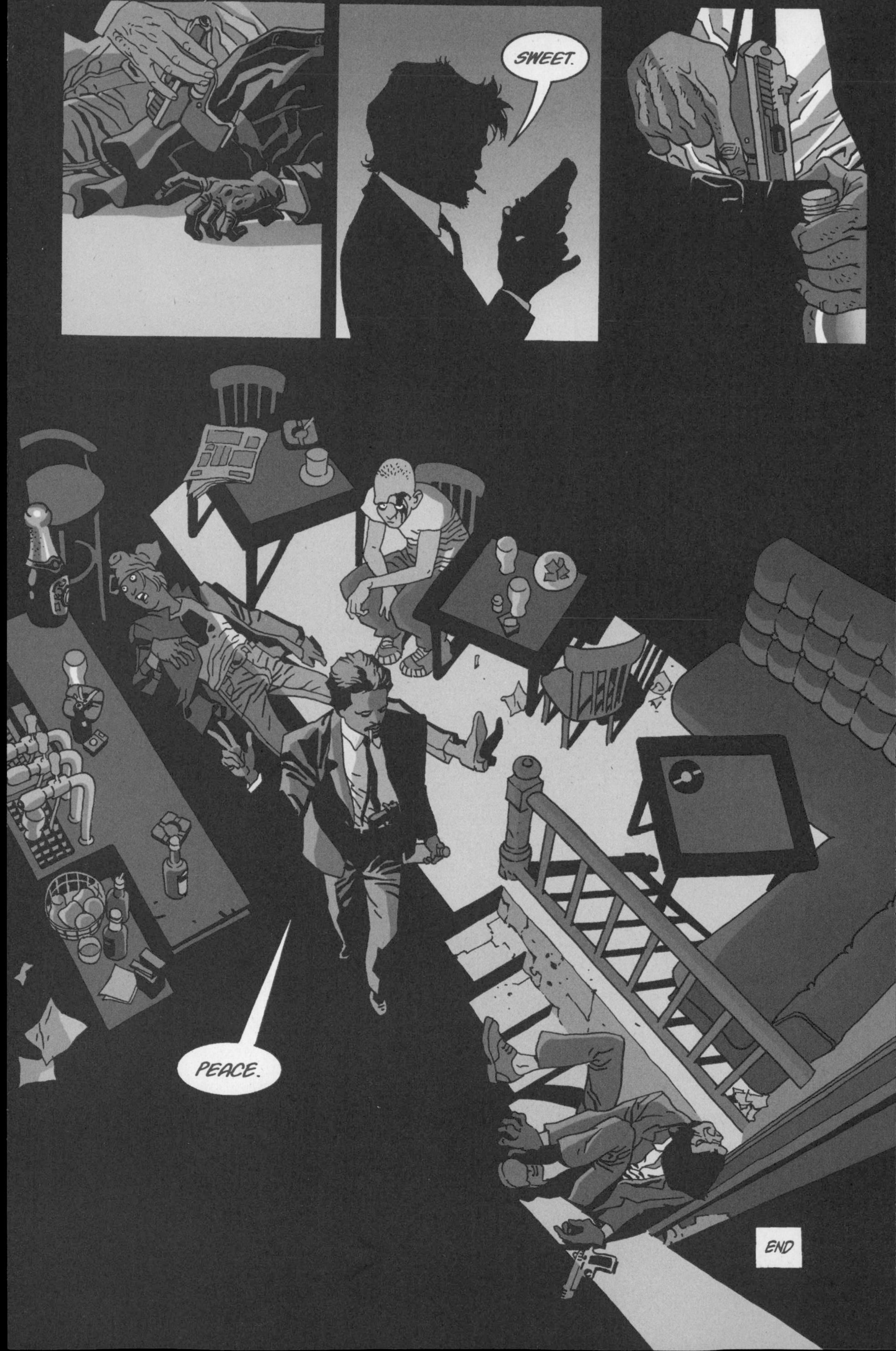
SWEET.
PEACE.
END

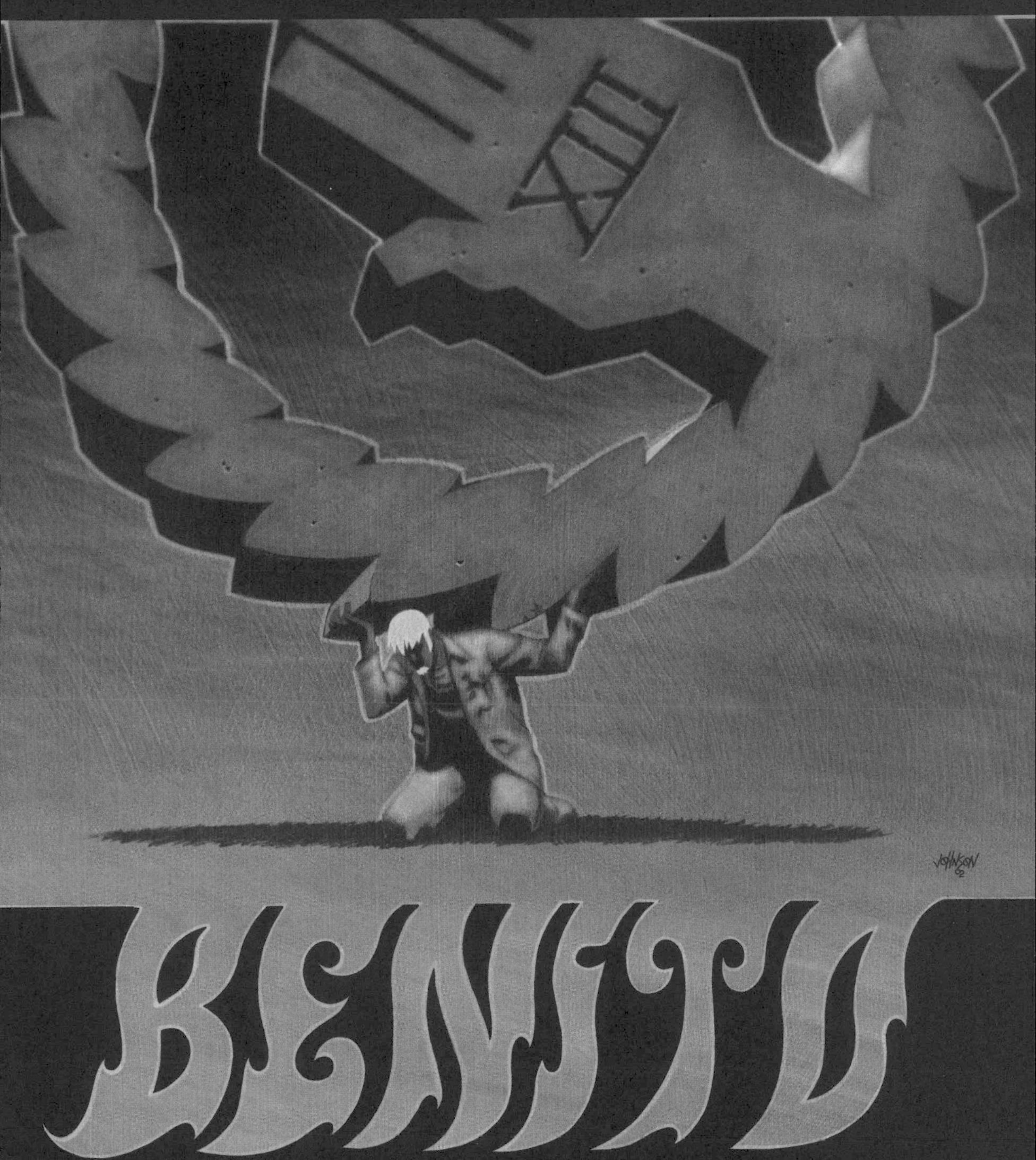
JOHNSON
02

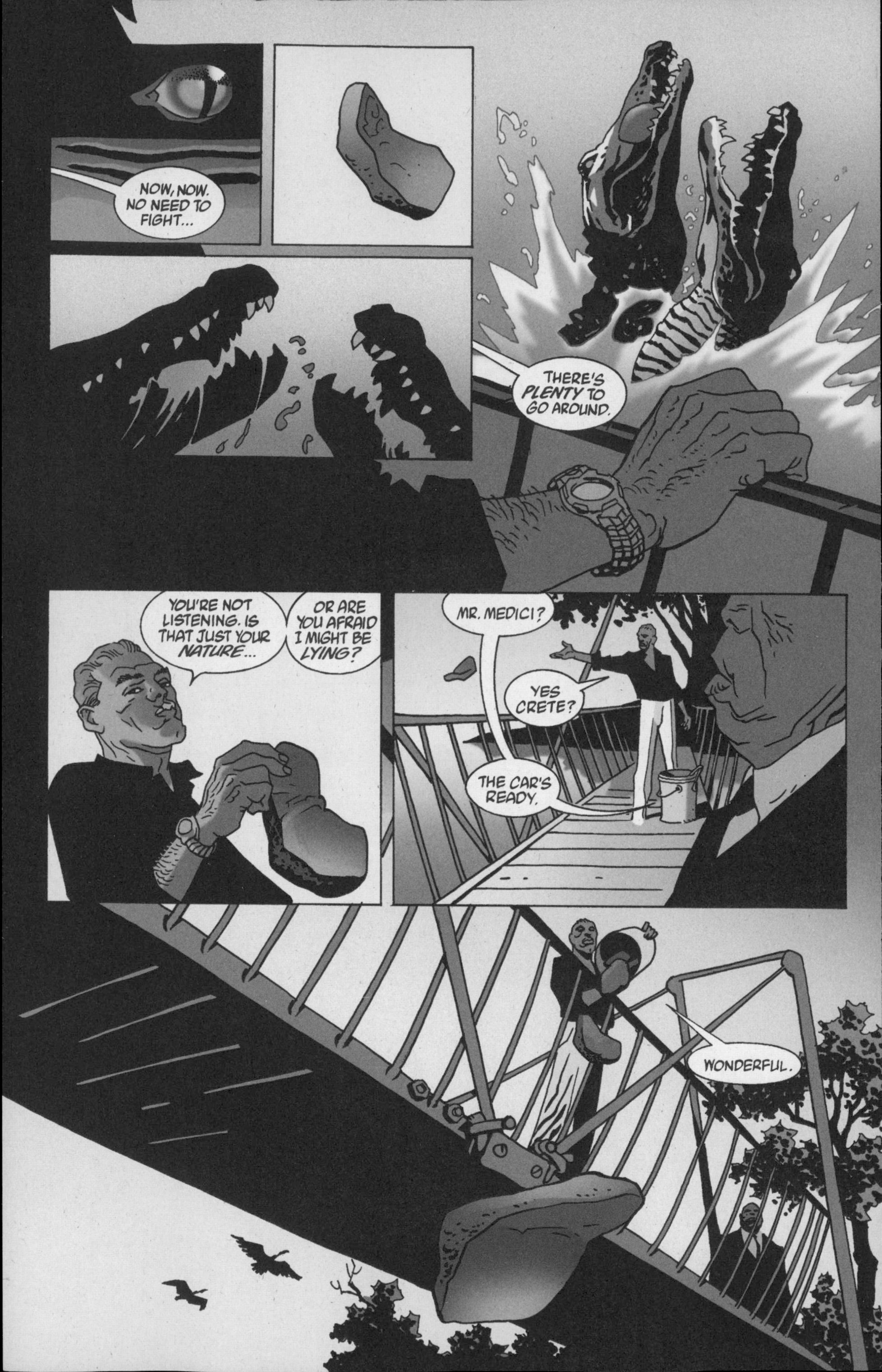
NOW, NOW. NO NEED TO FIGHT...
THERE'S *PLENTY* TO GO AROUND.
YOU'RE NOT LISTENING. IS THAT JUST YOUR *NATURE*...
OR ARE YOU AFRAID I MIGHT BE *LYING*?
MR. MEDICI?
YES CRETE?
THE CAR'S READY.
WONDERFUL.

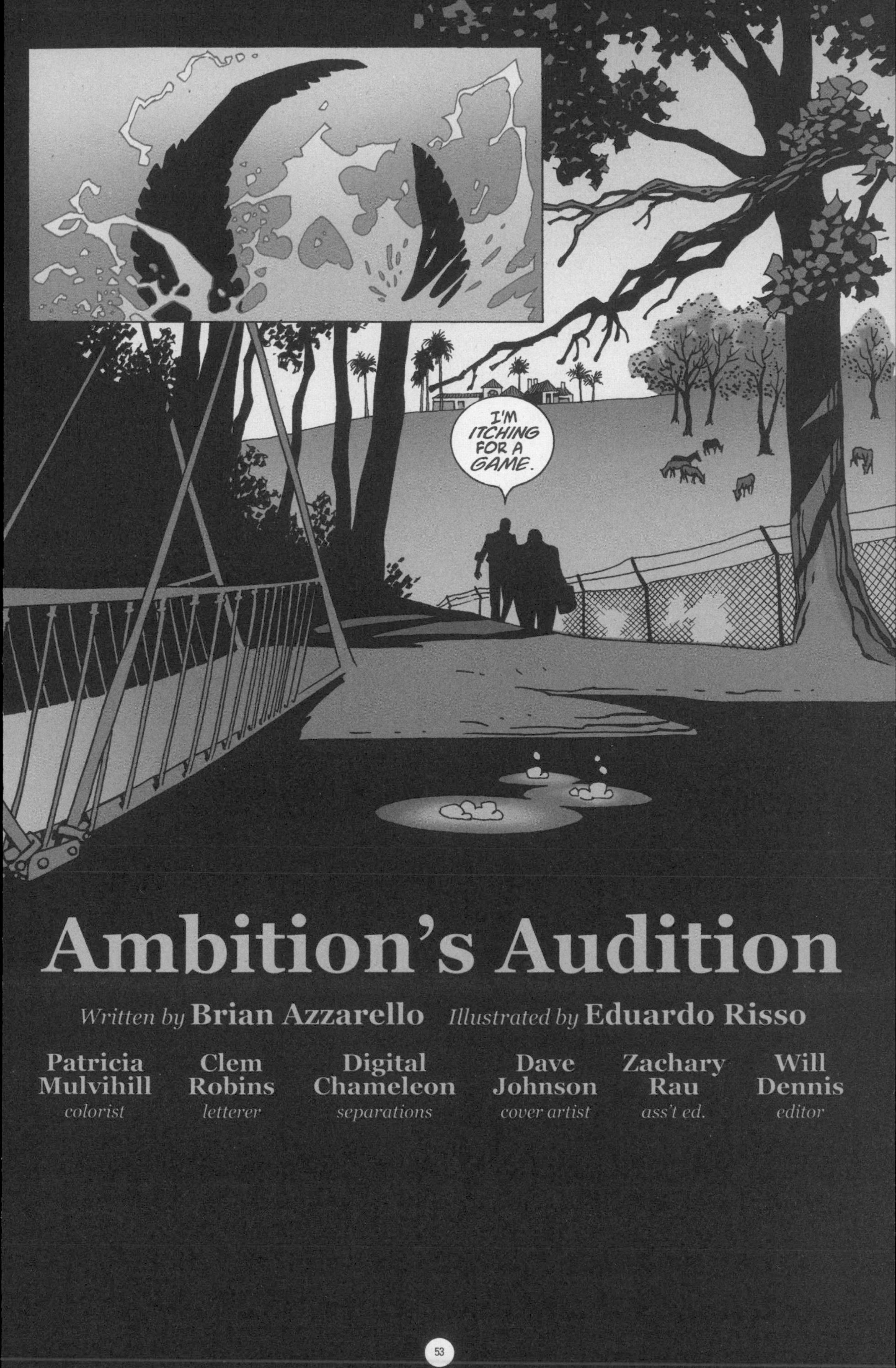
I'M ITCHING FOR A GAME.

Ambition's Audition

Written by **Brian Azzarello** *Illustrated by* **Eduardo Risso**

Patricia Mulvihill *colorist*
Clem Robins *letterer*
Digital Chameleon *separations*
Dave Johnson *cover artist*
Zachary Rau *ass't ed.*
Will Dennis *editor*

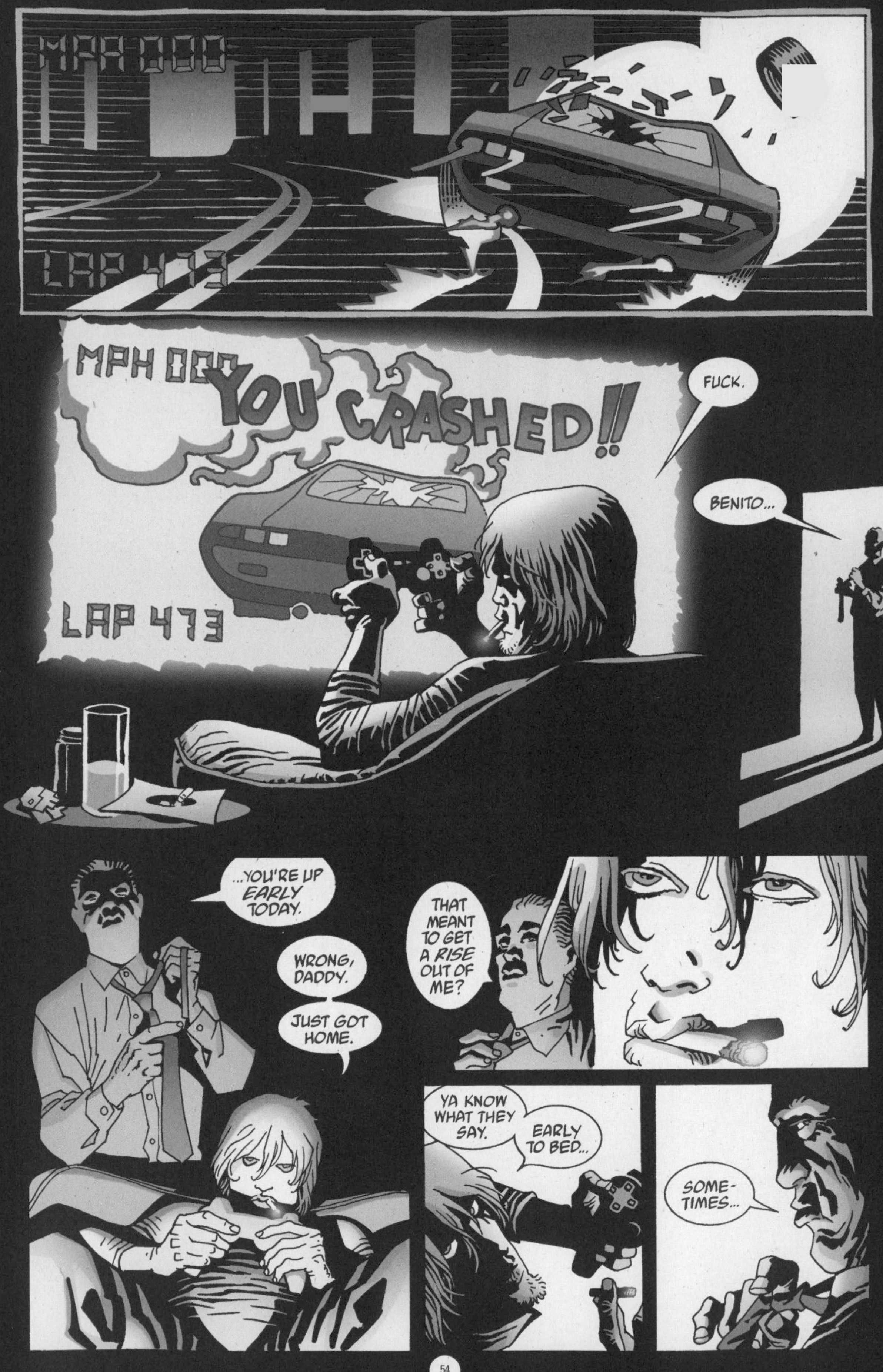
MPH 000
LAP 473
MPH 000
YOU CRASHED!!
LAP 473
FUCK.
BENITO...
...YOU'RE UP EARLY TODAY.
WRONG, DADDY.
JUST GOT HOME.
THAT MEANT TO GET A RISE OUT OF ME?
YA KNOW WHAT THEY SAY.
EARLY TO BED...
SOME-TIMES...

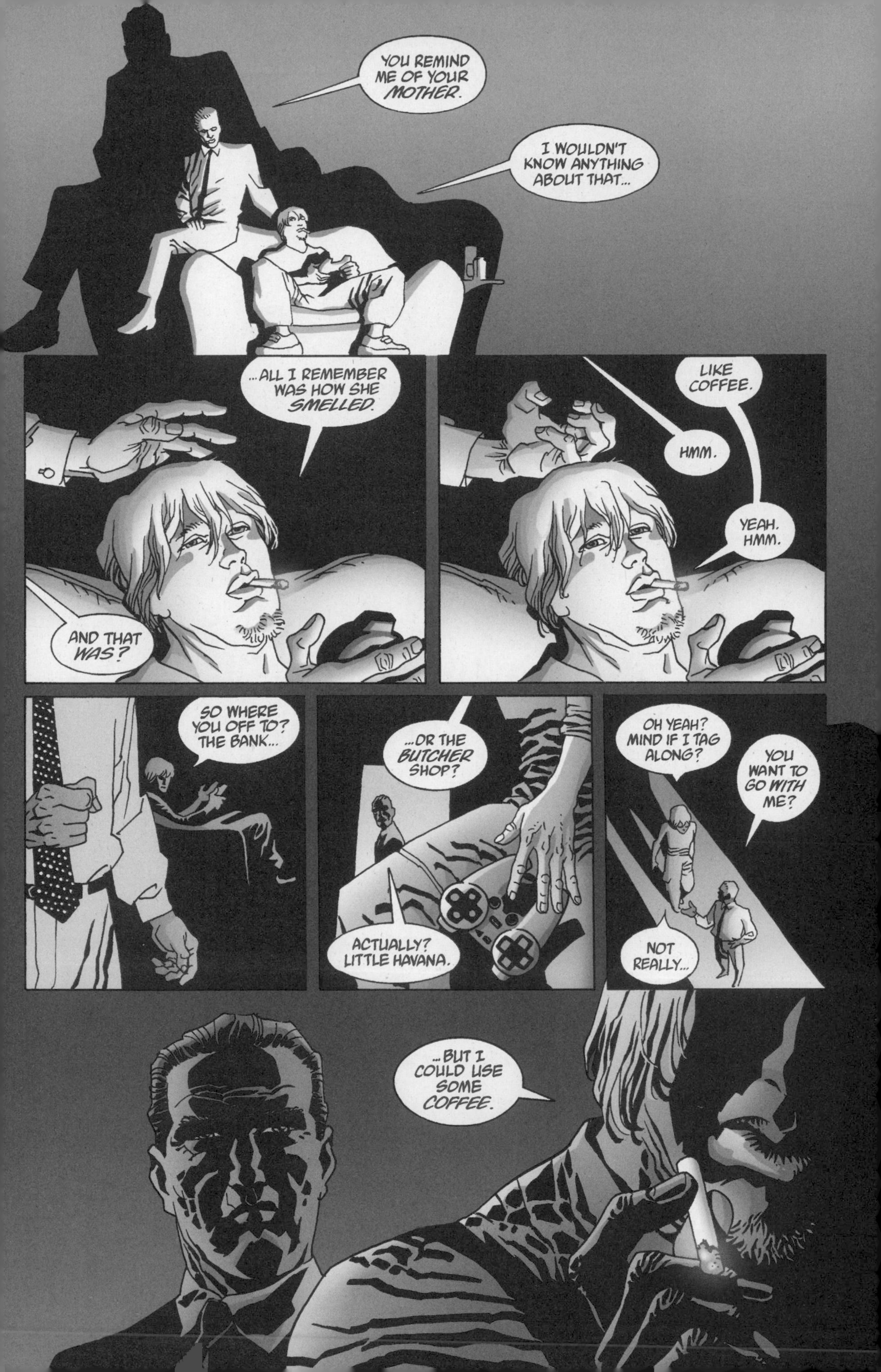
YOU REMIND ME OF YOUR MOTHER.
I WOULDN'T KNOW ANYTHING ABOUT THAT...
...ALL I REMEMBER WAS HOW SHE SMELLED.
AND THAT WAS?
LIKE COFFEE.
HMM.
YEAH. HMM.
SO WHERE YOU OFF TO? THE BANK...
...OR THE BUTCHER SHOP?
ACTUALLY? LITTLE HAVANA.
OH YEAH? MIND IF I TAG ALONG?
YOU WANT TO GO WITH ME?
NOT REALLY...
...BUT I COULD USE SOME COFFEE.

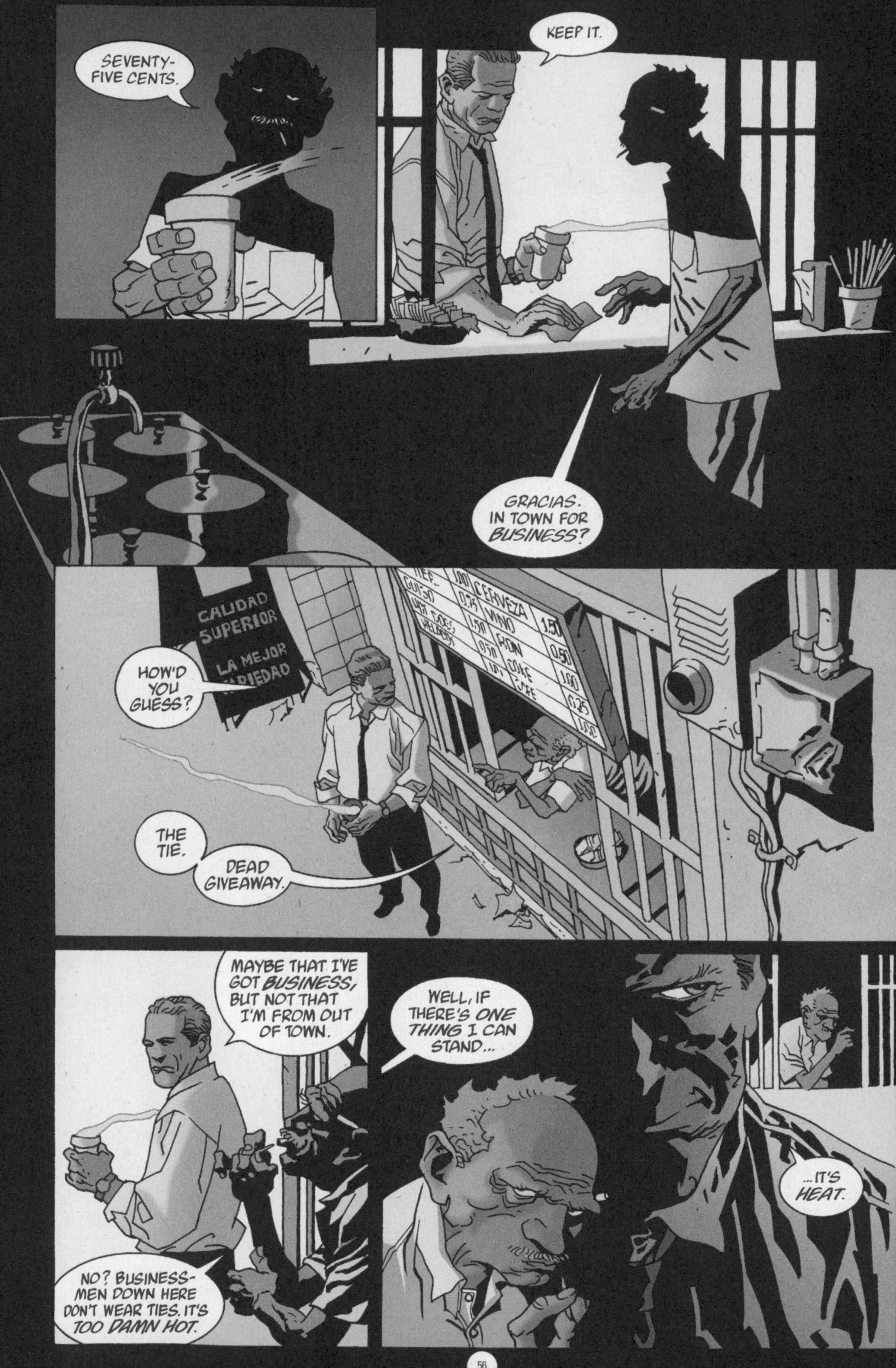

SEVENTY-FIVE CENTS.
KEEP IT.
GRACIAS. IN TOWN FOR BUSINESS?
CALIDAD SUPERIOR
LA MEJOR VARIEDAD
CERVEZA
VINO
RON
COKE
HOW'D YOU GUESS?
THE TIE.
DEAD GIVEAWAY.
MAYBE THAT I'VE GOT BUSINESS, BUT NOT THAT I'M FROM OUT OF TOWN.
NO? BUSINESS-MEN DOWN HERE DON'T WEAR TIES. IT'S TOO DAMN HOT.
WELL, IF THERE'S ONE THING I CAN STAND...
...IT'S HEAT.

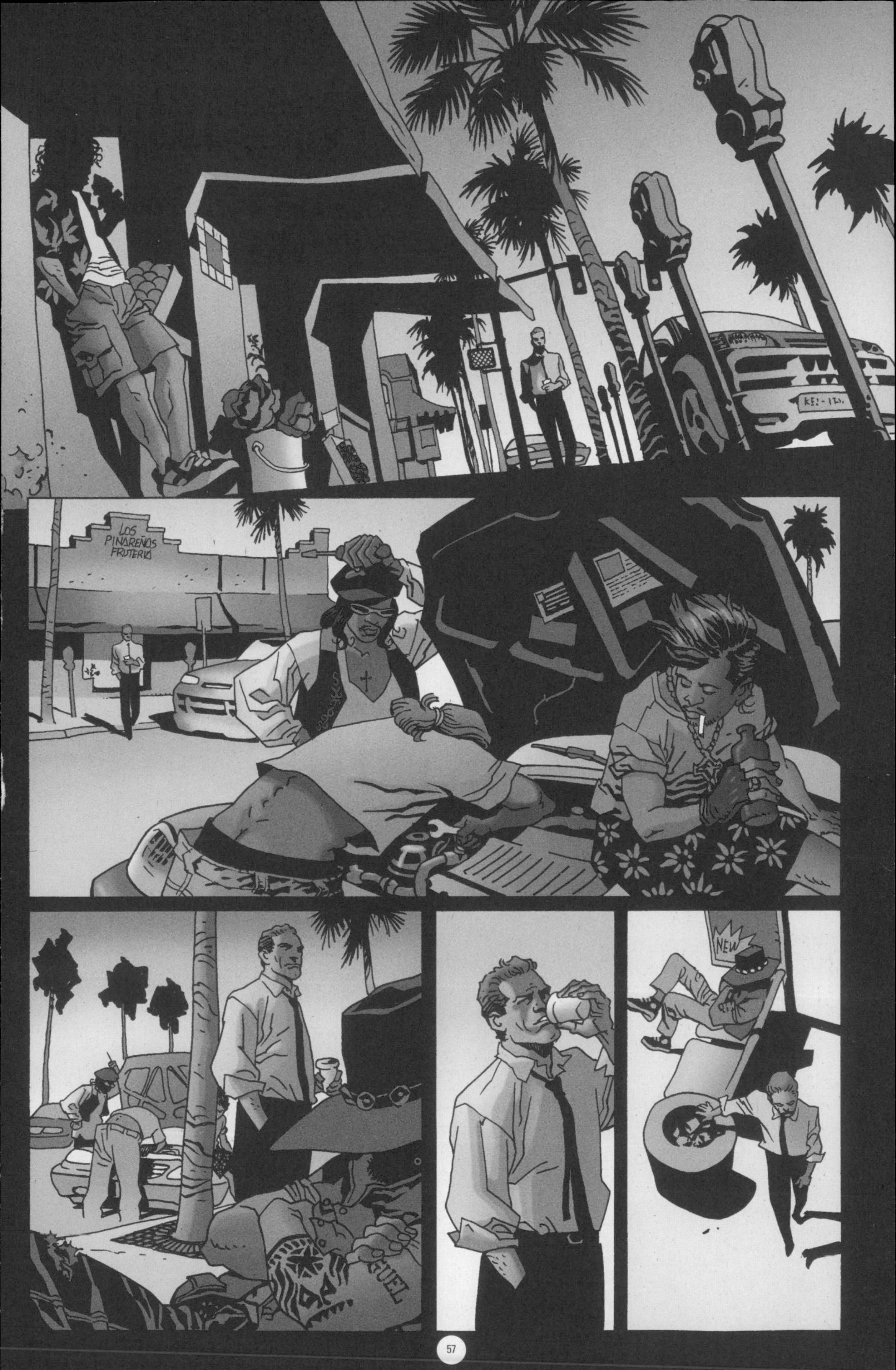
LOS PINAREÑOS FRUTERIA
NEW

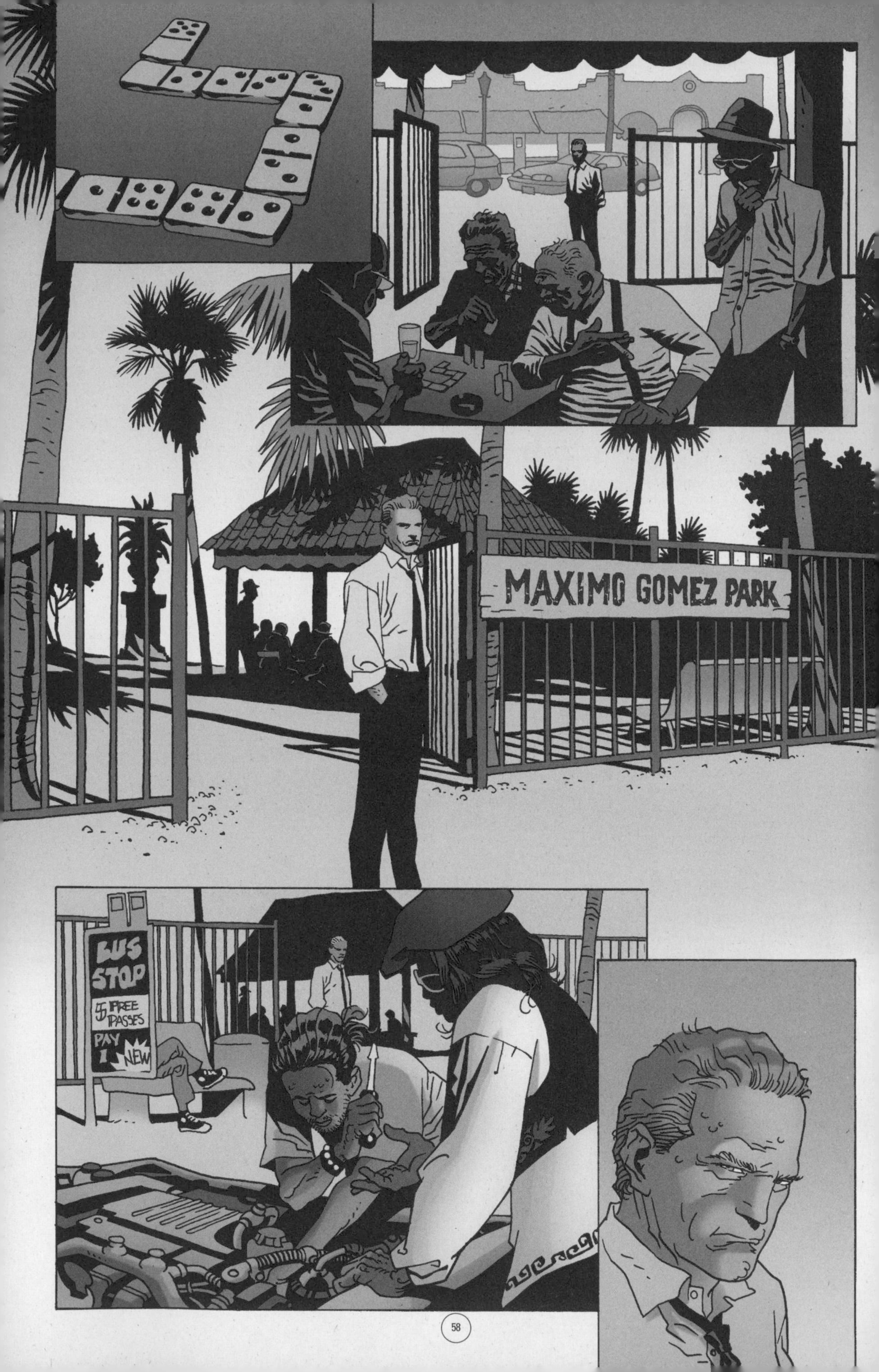
MAXIMO GOMEZ PARK
BUS STOP
5 FREE PASSES
PAY 1
NEW

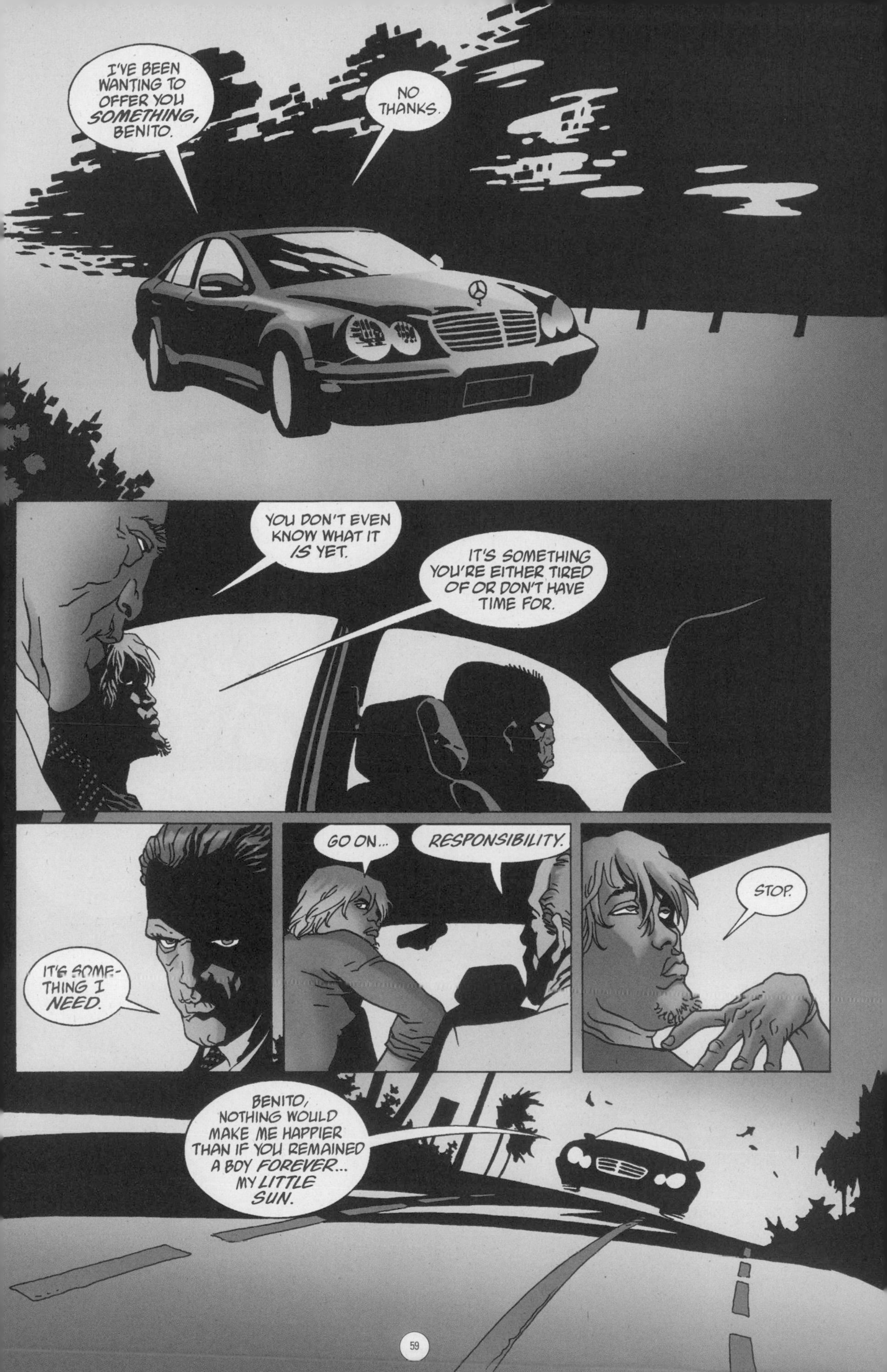
I'VE BEEN WANTING TO OFFER YOU SOMETHING, BENITO.
NO THANKS.
YOU DON'T EVEN KNOW WHAT IT IS YET.
IT'S SOMETHING YOU'RE EITHER TIRED OF OR DON'T HAVE TIME FOR.
IT'S SOMETHING I NEED.
GO ON...
RESPONSIBILITY.
STOP.
BENITO, NOTHING WOULD MAKE ME HAPPIER THAN IF YOU REMAINED A BOY FOREVER... MY LITTLE SUN.

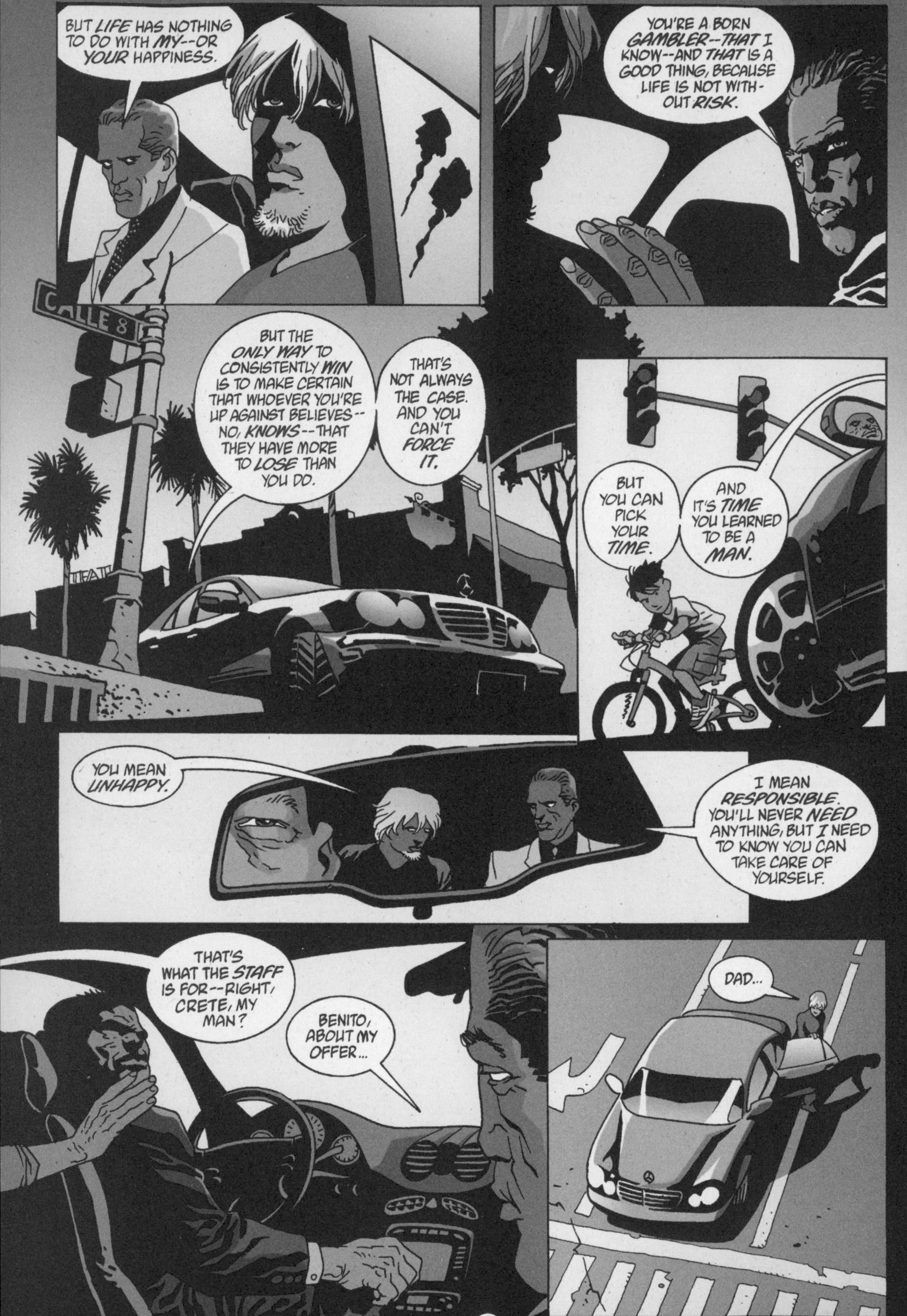
BUT LIFE HAS NOTHING TO DO WITH MY--OR YOUR HAPPINESS.
YOU'RE A BORN GAMBLER--THAT I KNOW--AND THAT IS A GOOD THING, BECAUSE LIFE IS NOT WITH-OUT RISK.
CALLE 8
BUT THE ONLY WAY TO CONSISTENTLY WIN IS TO MAKE CERTAIN THAT WHOEVER YOU'RE UP AGAINST BELIEVES--NO, KNOWS--THAT THEY HAVE MORE TO LOSE THAN YOU DO.
THAT'S NOT ALWAYS THE CASE. AND YOU CAN'T FORCE IT.
BUT YOU CAN PICK YOUR TIME.
AND IT'S TIME YOU LEARNED TO BE A MAN.
YOU MEAN UNHAPPY.
I MEAN RESPONSIBLE. YOU'LL NEVER NEED ANYTHING, BUT I NEED TO KNOW YOU CAN TAKE CARE OF YOURSELF.
THAT'S WHAT THE STAFF IS FOR--RIGHT, CRETE, MY MAN?
BENITO, ABOUT MY OFFER...
DAD...

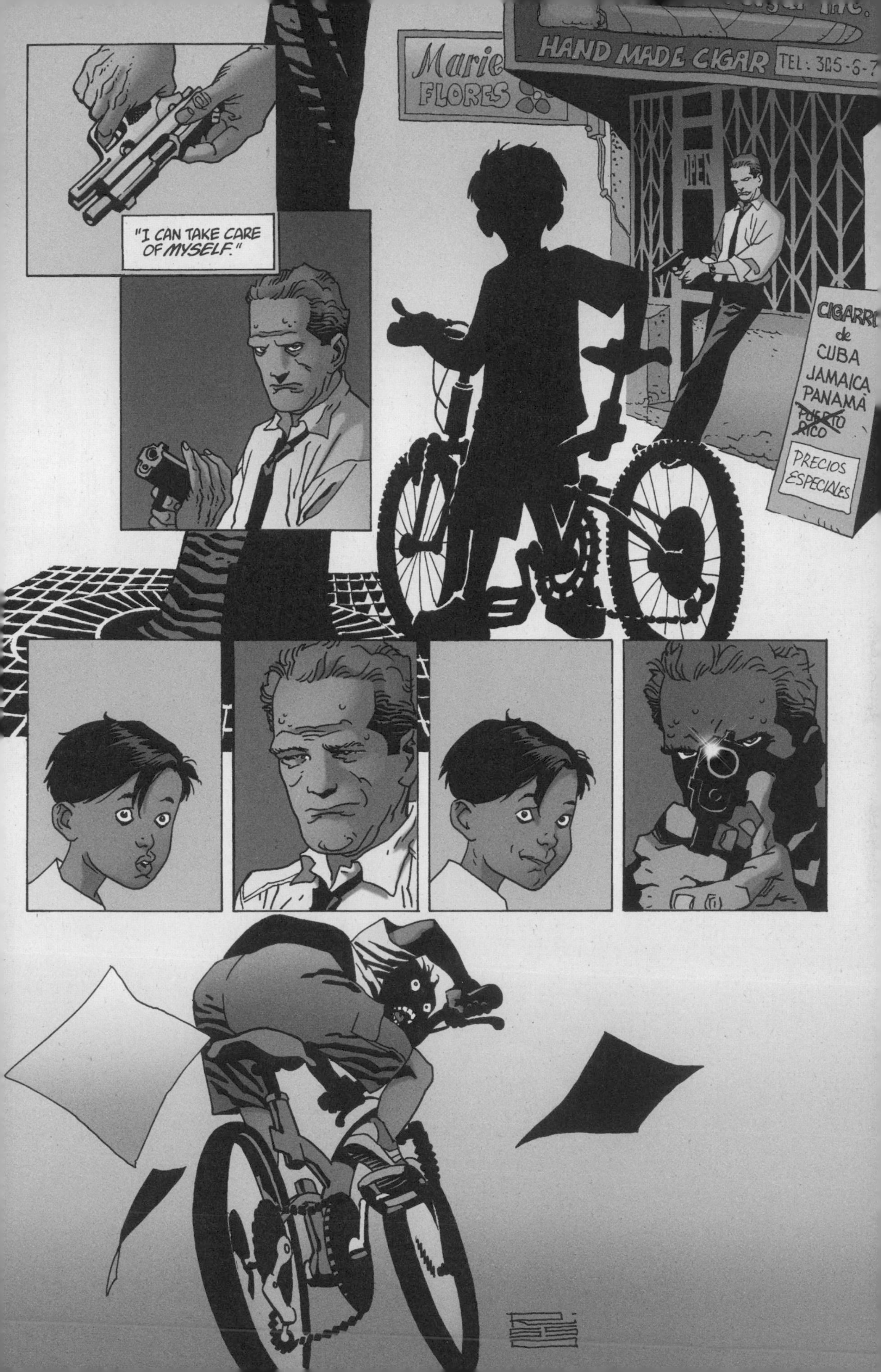
HAND MADE CIGAR
TEL: 305-6-7
Marie
FLORES
"I CAN TAKE CARE OF MYSELF."
OPEN
CIGARRO
de
CUBA
JAMAICA
PANAMÁ
PUERTO RICO
PRECIOS ESPECIALES

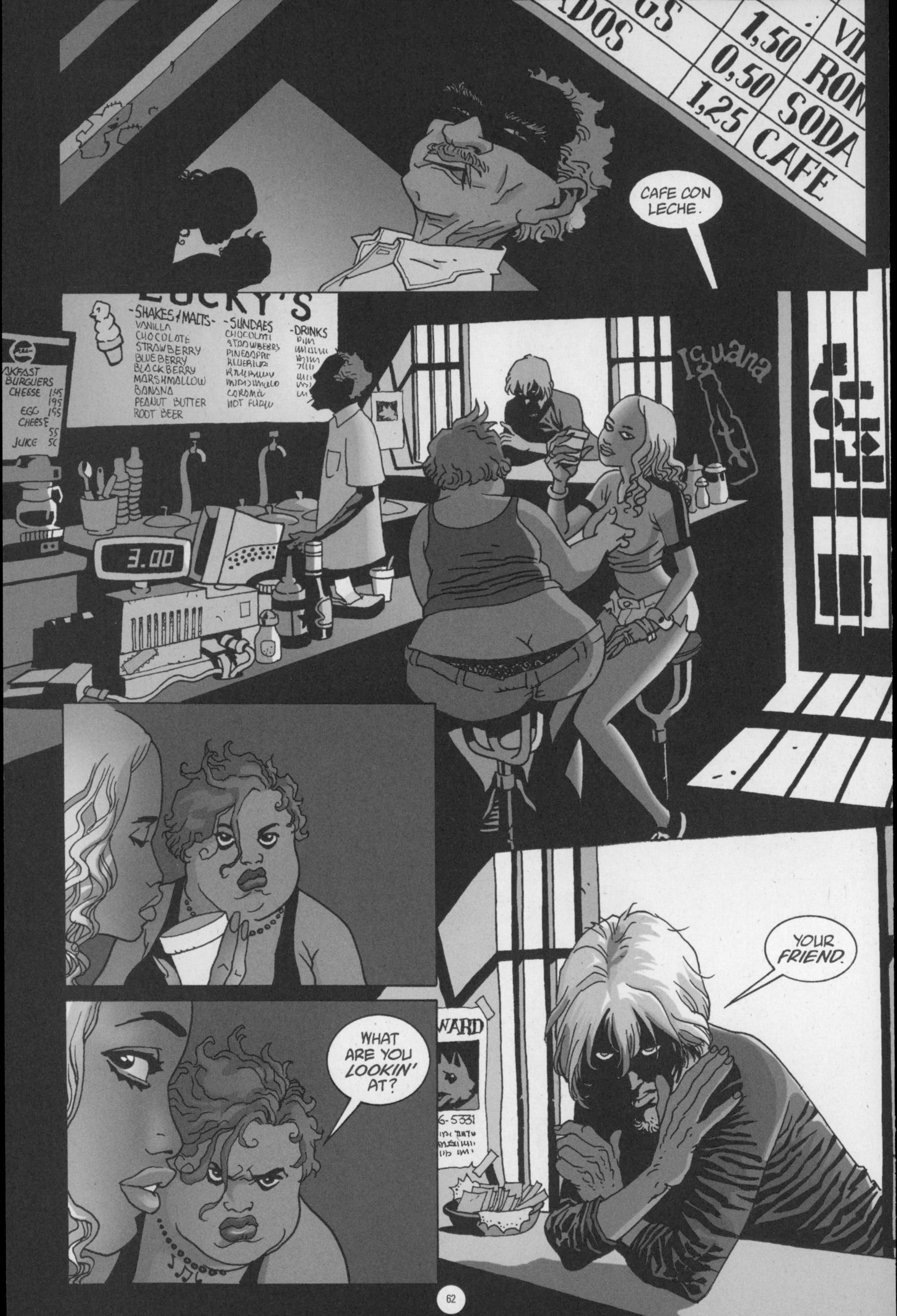
1,50
0,50
1,25 SODA
CAFE
CAFE CON LECHE.
-SHAKES & MALTS-
VANILLA
CHOCOLATE
STRAWBERRY
BLUEBERRY
BLACKBERRY
MARSHMALLOW
BANANA
PEANUT BUTTER
ROOT BEER
-SUNDAES
PINEAPPLE
-DRINKS
BURGUERS
CHEESE 1.45
EGG 1.95
JUICE
3.00
Iguana
YOUR FRIEND.
WHAT ARE YOU LOOKIN' AT?

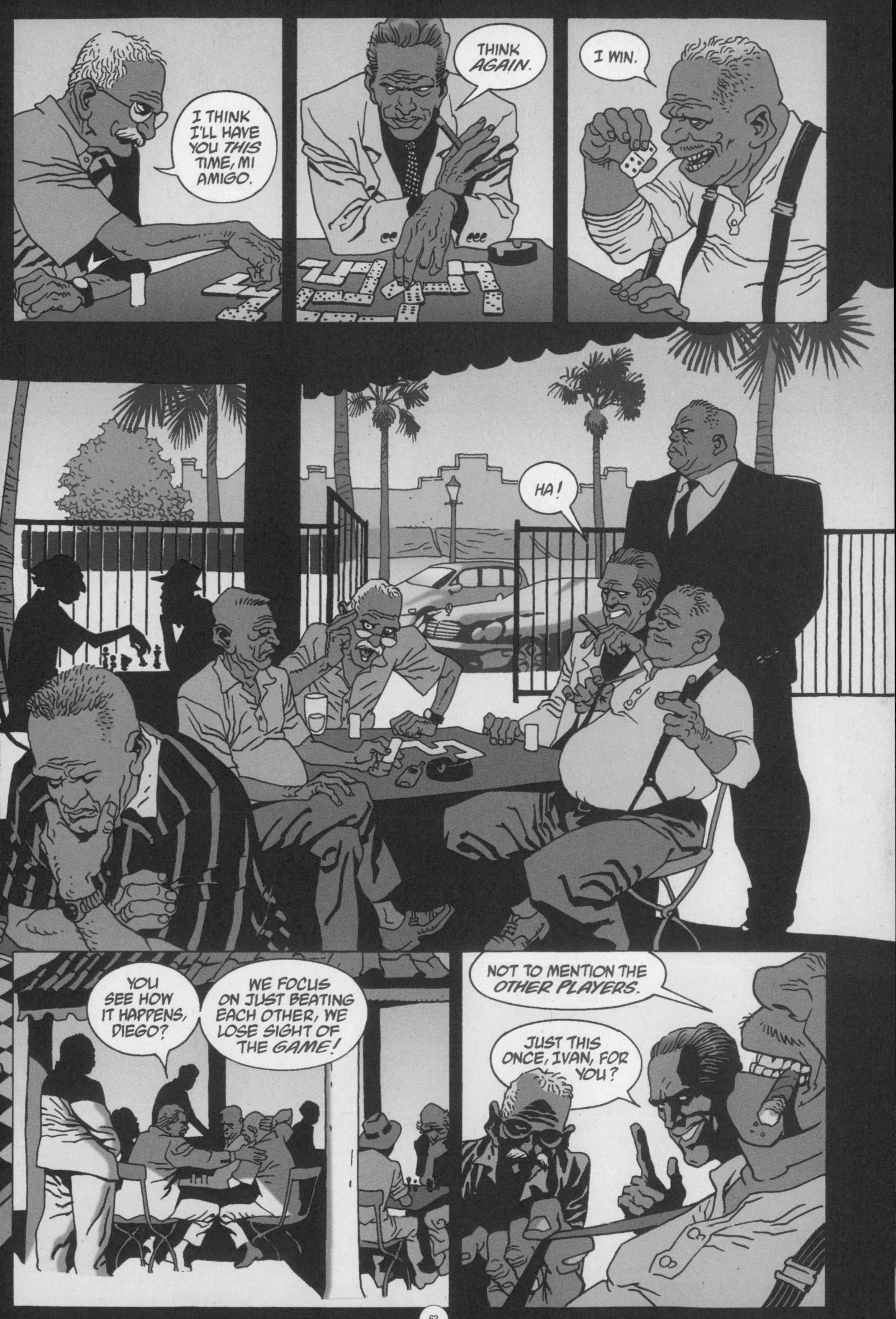
I THINK I'LL HAVE YOU THIS TIME, MI AMIGO.
THINK AGAIN.
I WIN.
HA!
YOU SEE HOW IT HAPPENS, DIEGO?
WE FOCUS ON JUST BEATING EACH OTHER, WE LOSE SIGHT OF THE GAME!
NOT TO MENTION THE OTHER PLAYERS.
JUST THIS ONCE, IVAN, FOR YOU?

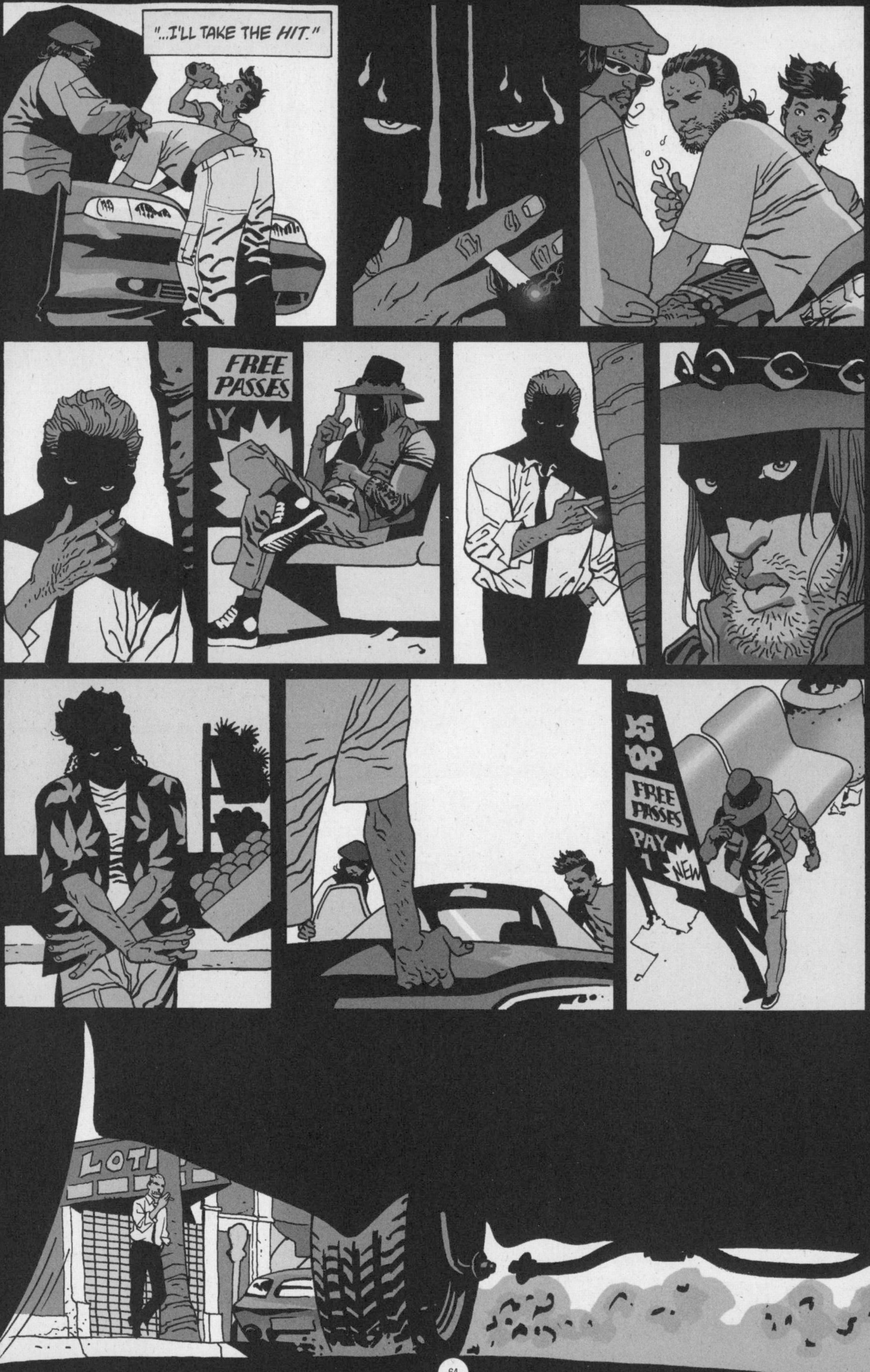

"...I'LL TAKE THE HIT."
FREE PASSES
FREE PASSES
PAY 1
NEW
LOT

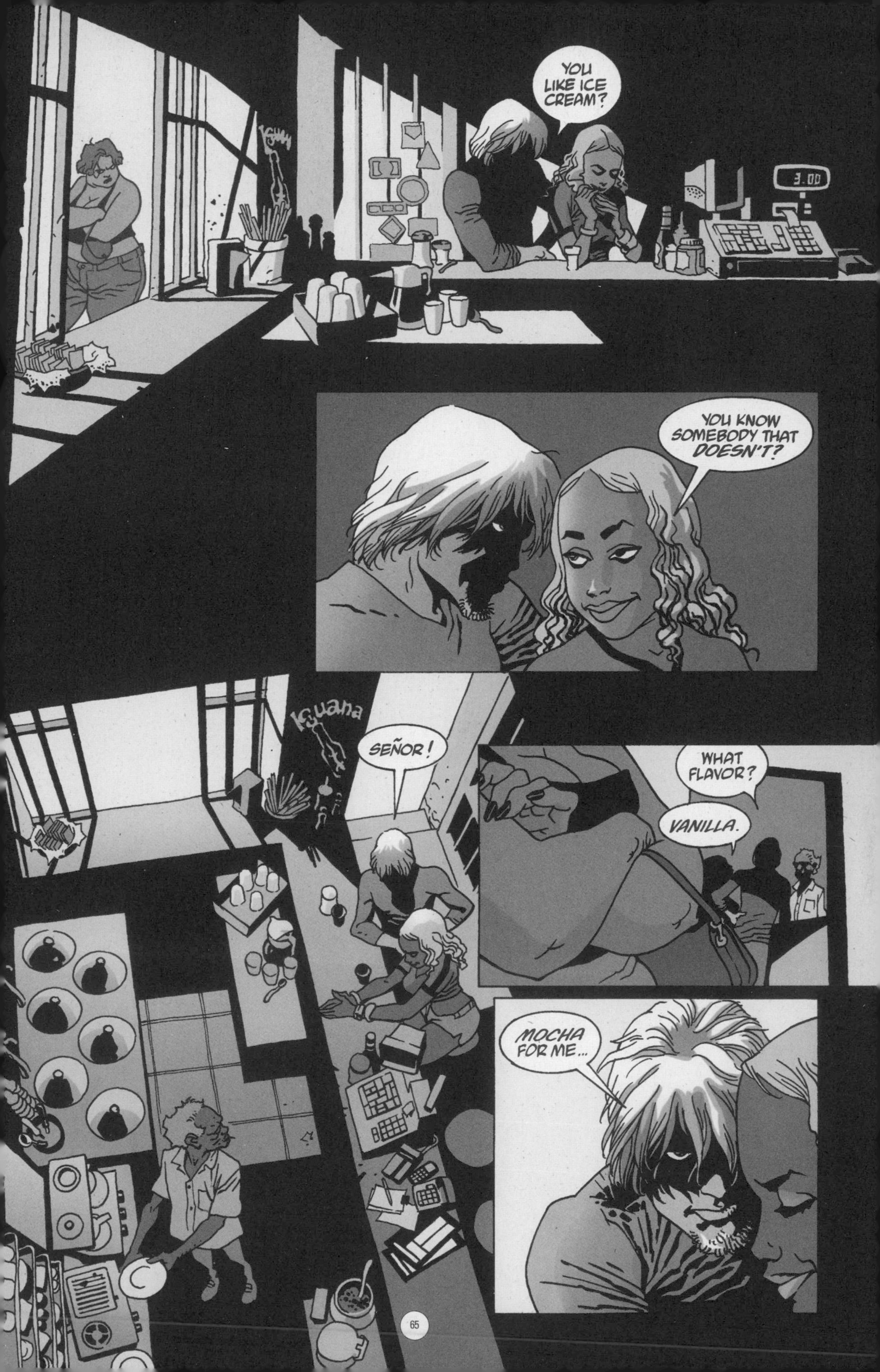
YOU LIKE ICE CREAM?
3.00
YOU KNOW SOMEBODY THAT DOESN'T?
Iguana
SEÑOR!
WHAT FLAVOR?
VANILLA.
MOCHA FOR ME...

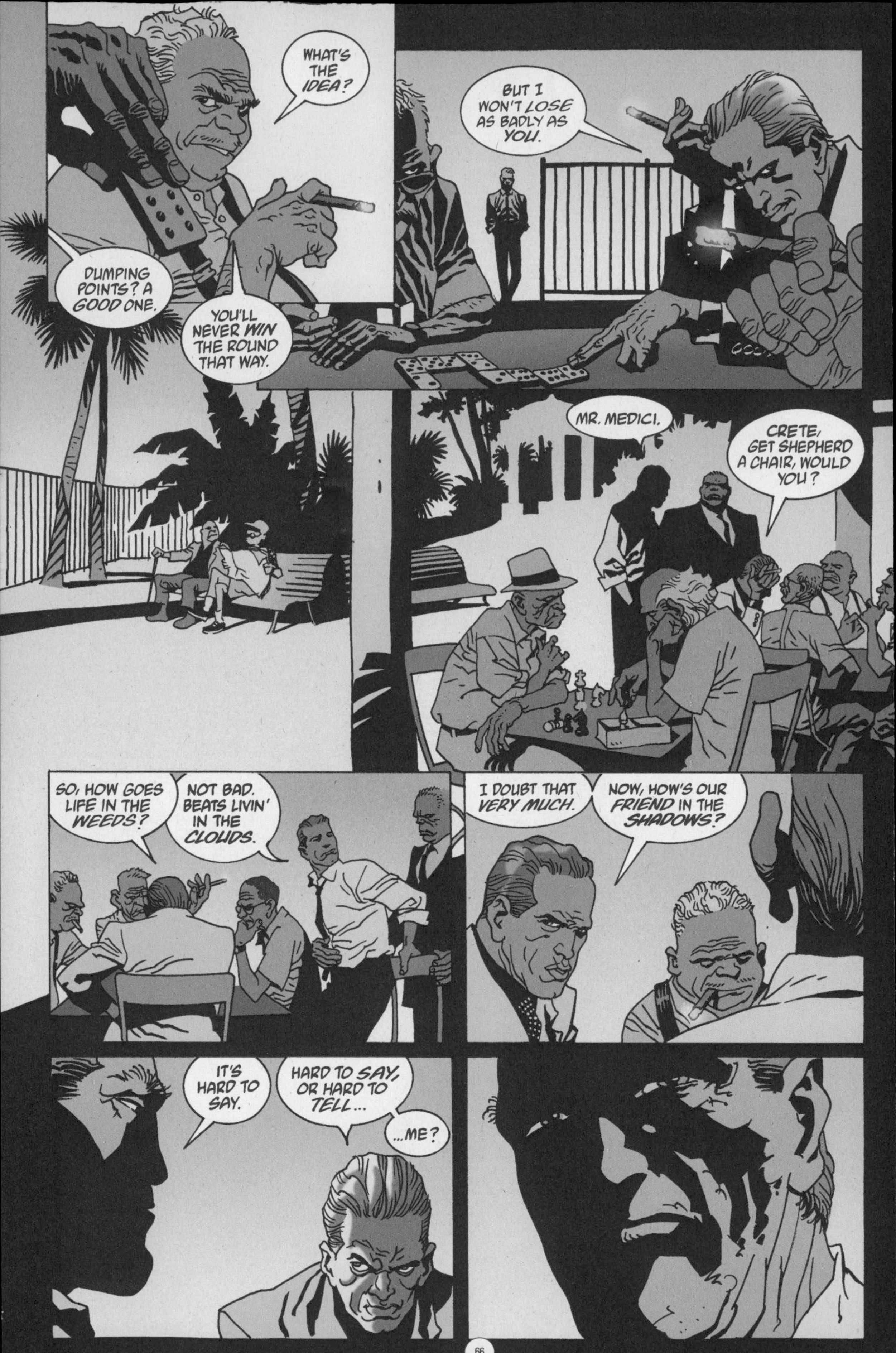

WHAT'S THE IDEA?
DUMPING POINTS? A GOOD ONE.
YOU'LL NEVER WIN THE ROUND THAT WAY.
BUT I WON'T LOSE AS BADLY AS YOU.
MR. MEDICI.
CRETE, GET SHEPHERD A CHAIR, WOULD YOU?
SO, HOW GOES LIFE IN THE WEEDS?
NOT BAD. BEATS LIVIN' IN THE CLOUDS.
I DOUBT THAT VERY MUCH.
NOW, HOW'S OUR FRIEND IN THE SHADOWS?
IT'S HARD TO SAY.
HARD TO SAY, OR HARD TO TELL...
...ME?

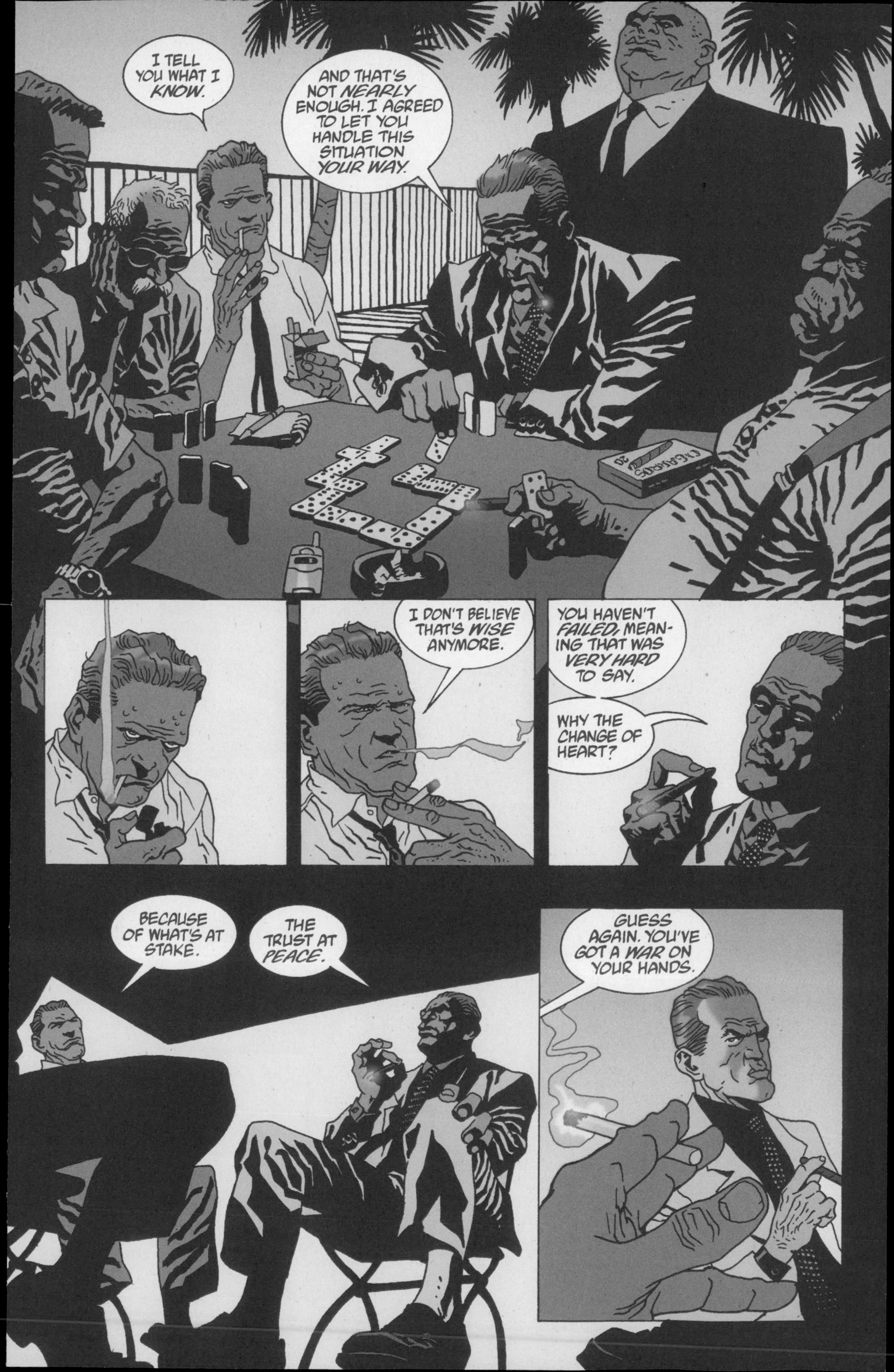
I TELL YOU WHAT I KNOW.
AND THAT'S NOT NEARLY ENOUGH. I AGREED TO LET YOU HANDLE THIS SITUATION YOUR WAY.
I DON'T BELIEVE THAT'S WISE ANYMORE.
YOU HAVEN'T FAILED, MEANING THAT WAS VERY HARD TO SAY.
WHY THE CHANGE OF HEART?
BECAUSE OF WHAT'S AT STAKE.
THE TRUST AT PEACE.
GUESS AGAIN. YOU'VE GOT A WAR ON YOUR HANDS.

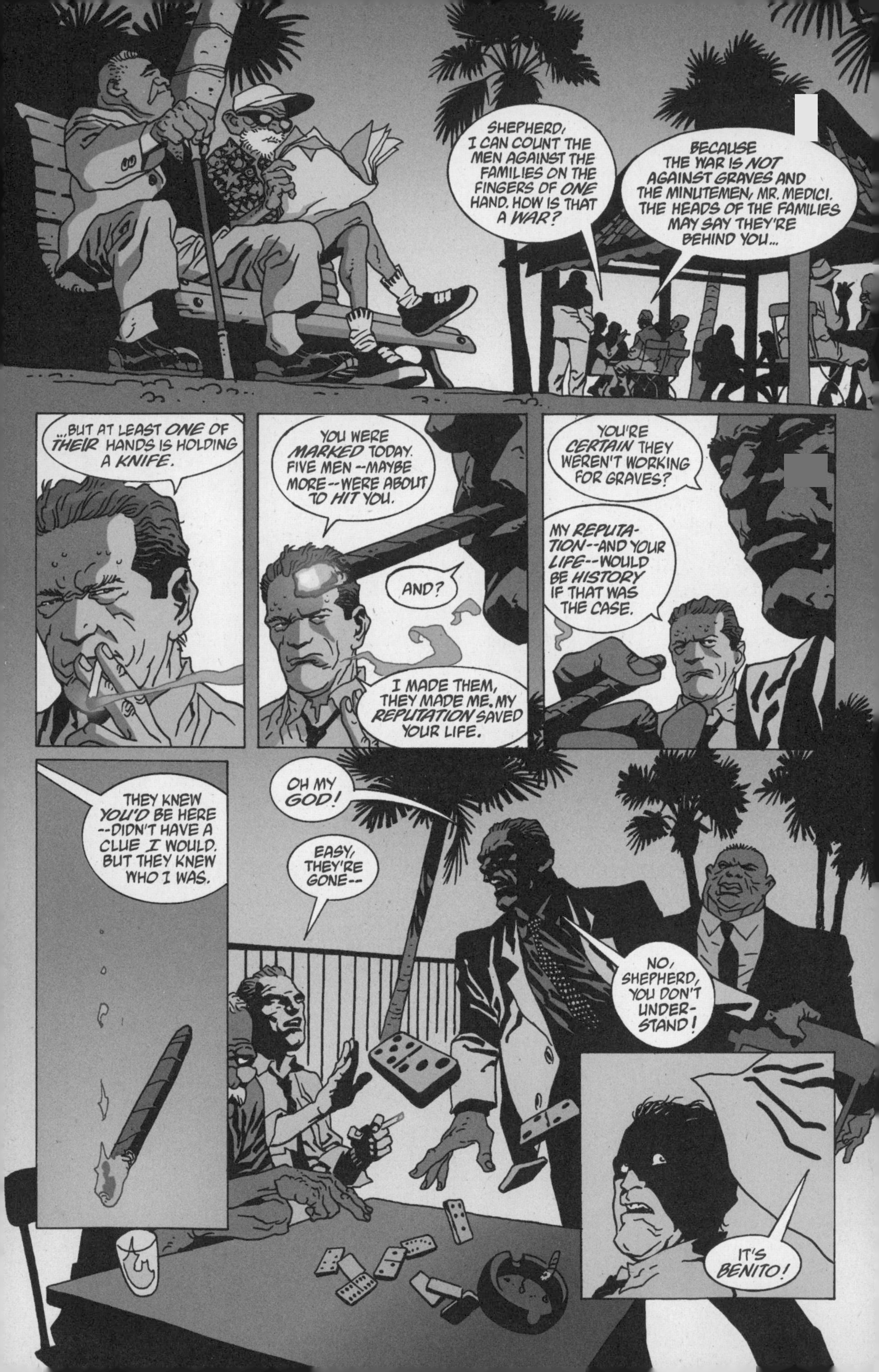
SHEPHERD, I CAN COUNT THE MEN AGAINST THE FAMILIES ON THE FINGERS OF ONE HAND. HOW IS THAT A WAR?
BECAUSE THE WAR IS NOT AGAINST GRAVES AND THE MINUTEMEN, MR. MEDICI. THE HEADS OF THE FAMILIES MAY SAY THEY'RE BEHIND YOU...
...BUT AT LEAST ONE OF THEIR HANDS IS HOLDING A KNIFE.
YOU WERE MARKED TODAY. FIVE MEN --MAYBE MORE--WERE ABOUT TO HIT YOU.
AND?
I MADE THEM, THEY MADE ME. MY REPUTATION SAVED YOUR LIFE.
YOU'RE CERTAIN THEY WEREN'T WORKING FOR GRAVES?
MY REPUTATION--AND YOUR LIFE--WOULD BE HISTORY IF THAT WAS THE CASE.
THEY KNEW YOU'D BE HERE --DIDN'T HAVE A CLUE I WOULD. BUT THEY KNEW WHO I WAS.
OH MY GOD!
EASY, THEY'RE GONE--
NO, SHEPHERD, YOU DON'T UNDERSTAND!
IT'S BENITO!

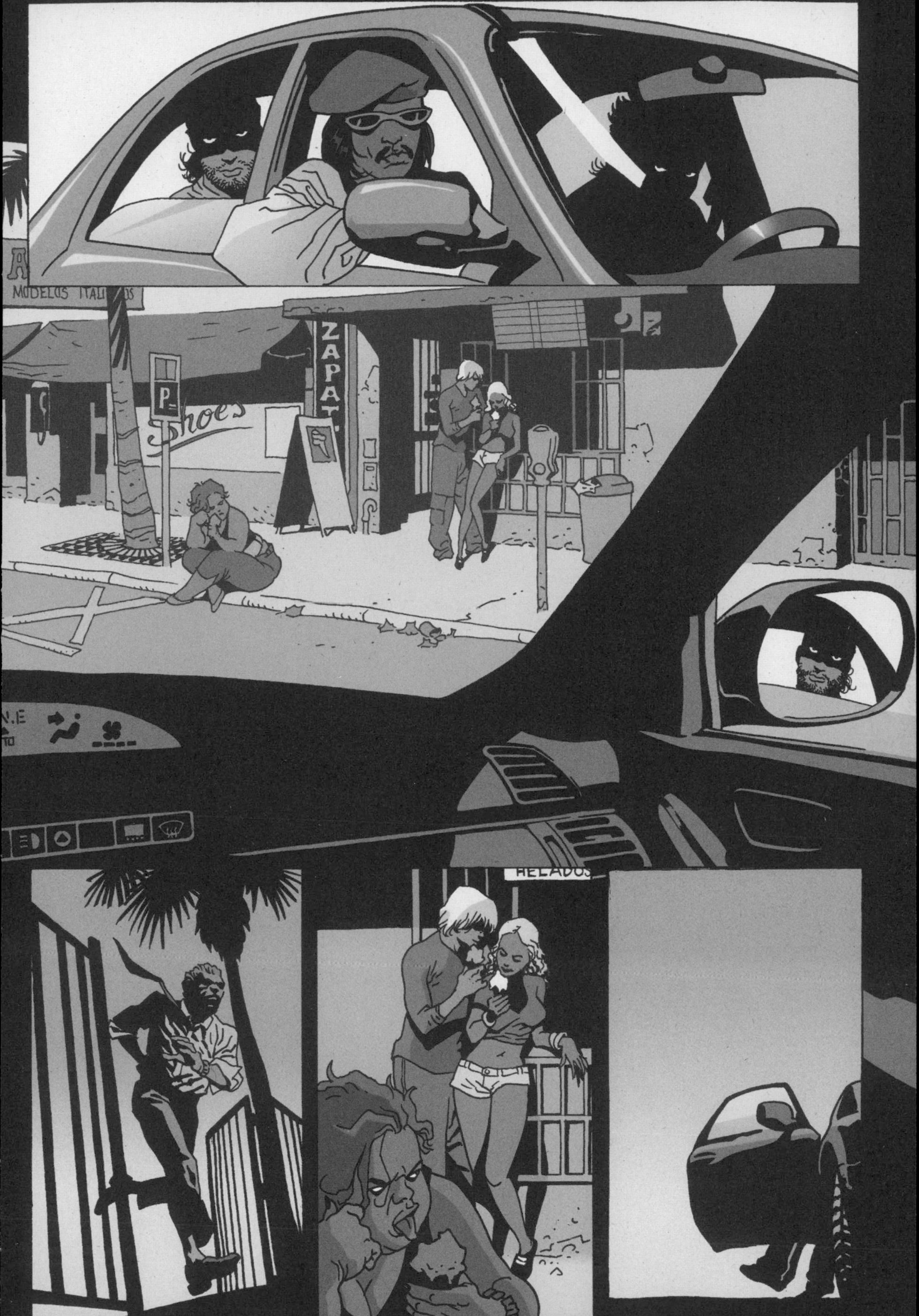
ZAPAT
Shoes
HELADOS

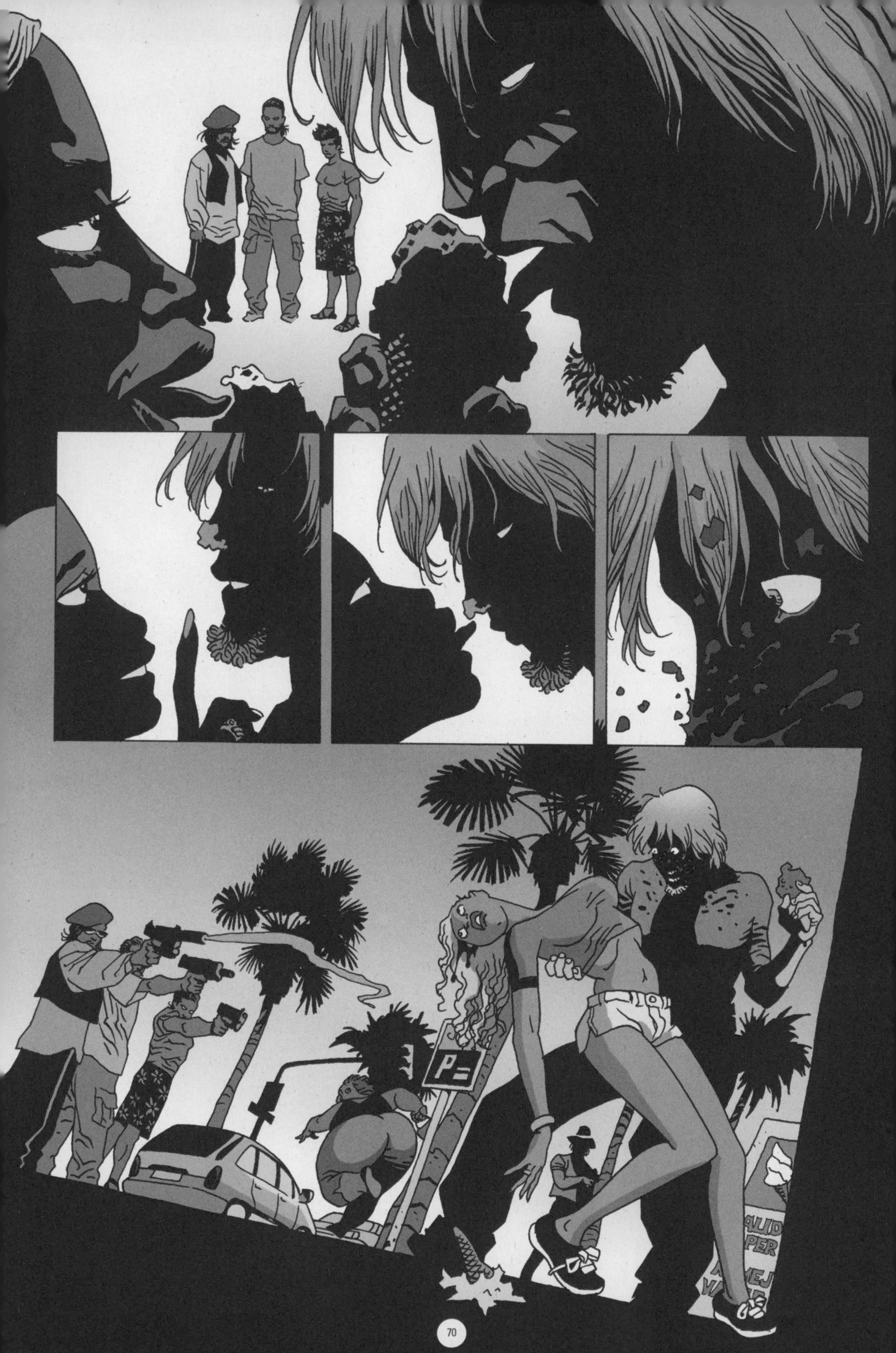

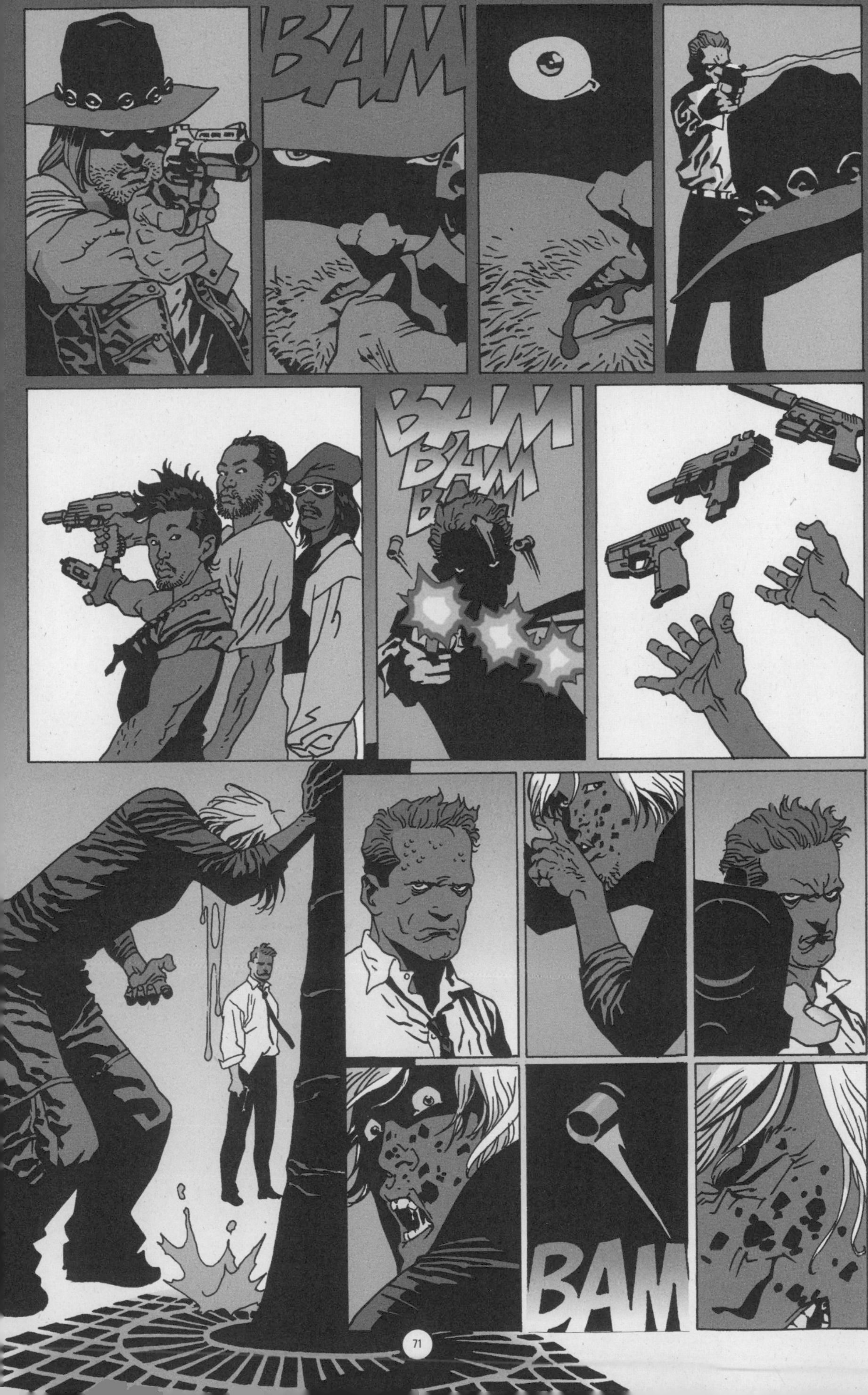
BAM
BAM
BAM
BAM
BAM

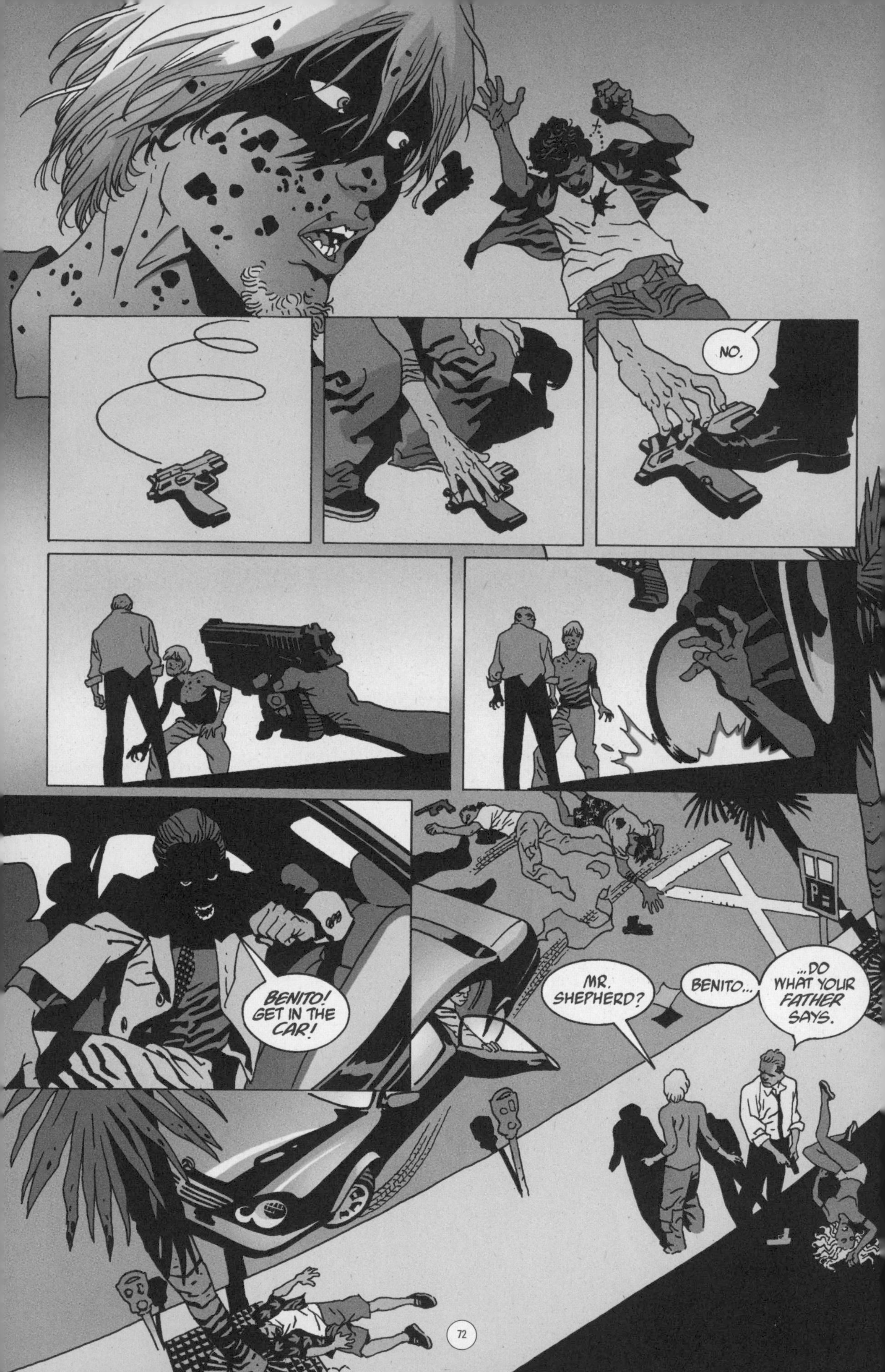
NO.
BENITO! GET IN THE CAR!
MR. SHEPHERD?
BENITO...
...DO WHAT YOUR FATHER SAYS.

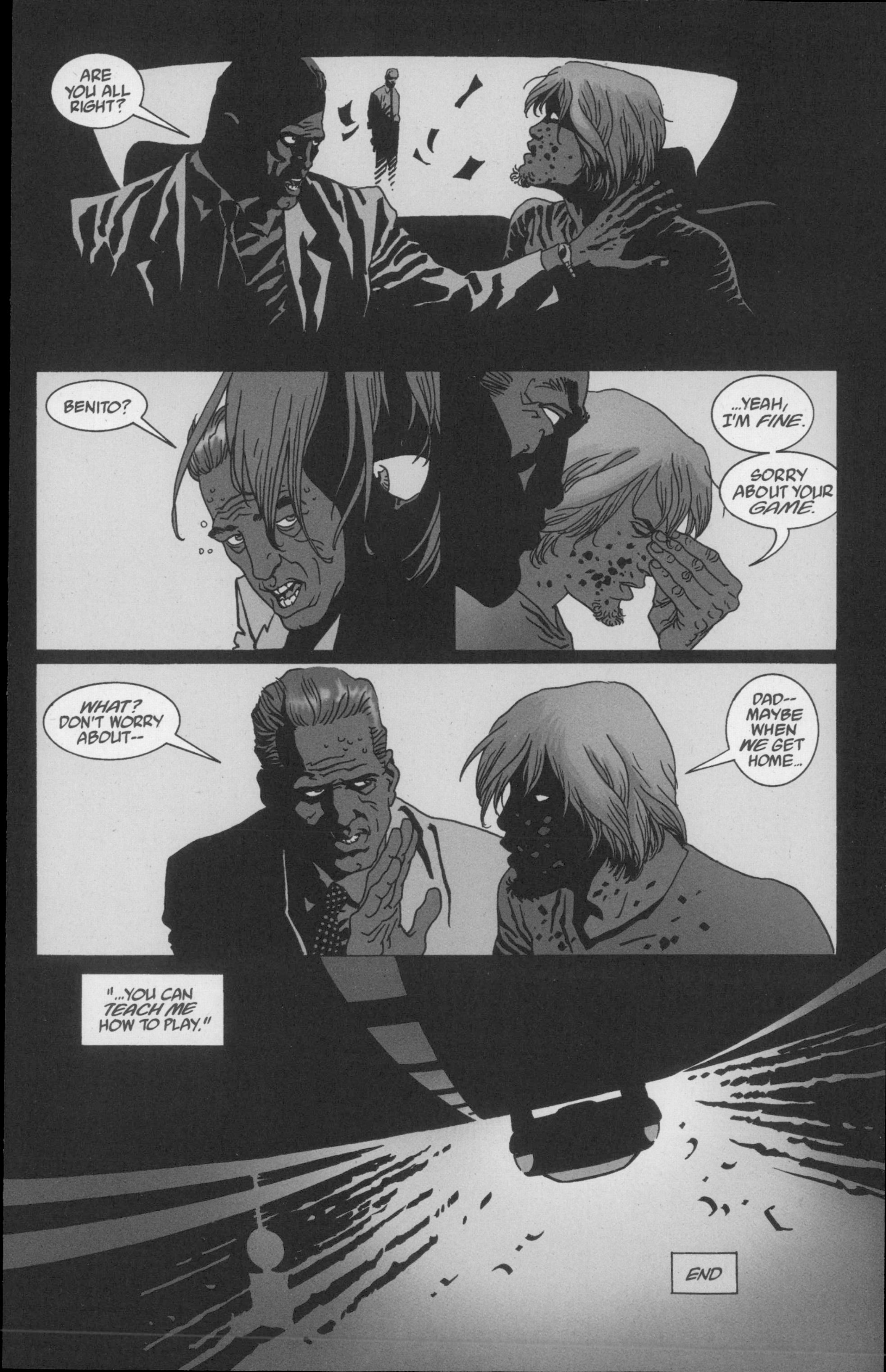
ARE YOU ALL RIGHT?
BENITO?
...YEAH, I'M *FINE*.
SORRY ABOUT YOUR *GAME*.
WHAT? DON'T WORRY ABOUT--
DAD-- MAYBE WHEN *WE* GET HOME...
"...YOU CAN *TEACH ME* HOW TO PLAY."
END

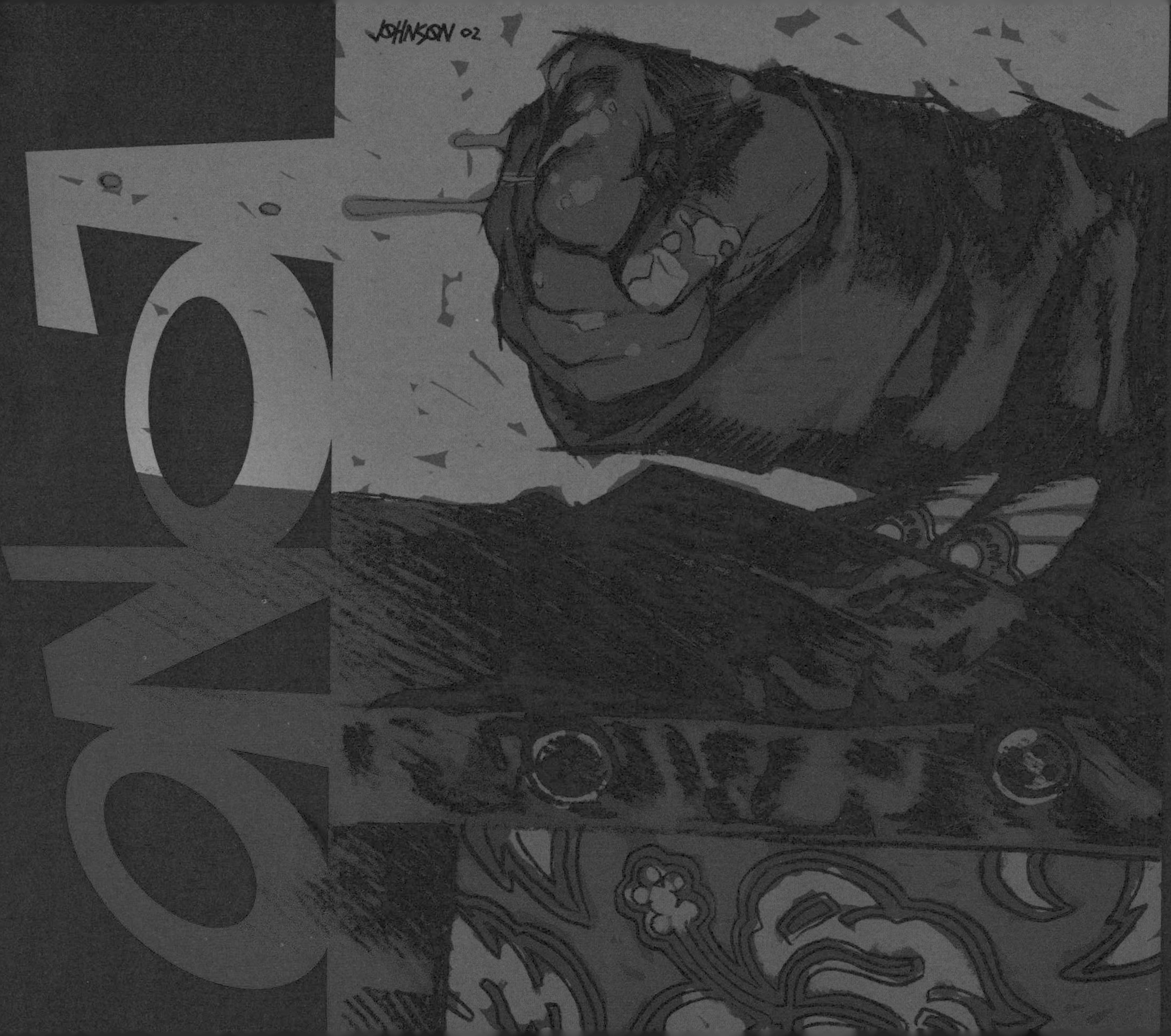
JOHNSON 02
LONO

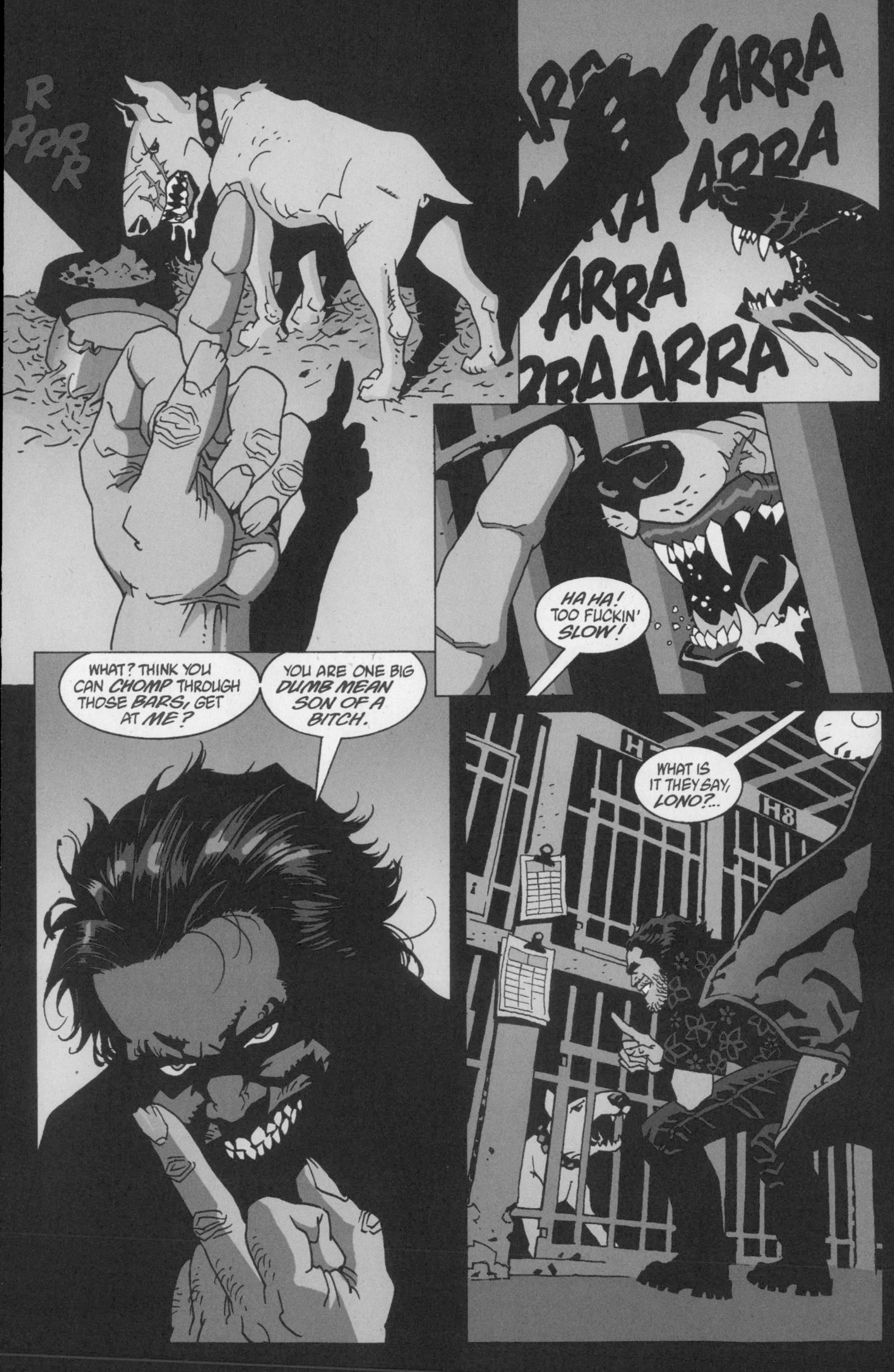

RRRRR
ARRA ARRA ARRA ARRA ARRA ARRA ARRA ARRA
HA HA! TOO FUCKIN' SLOW!
WHAT? THINK YOU CAN CHOMP THROUGH THOSE BARS, GET AT ME?
YOU ARE ONE BIG DUMB MEAN SON OF A BITCH.
WHAT IS IT THEY SAY, LONO?...
H7
H8

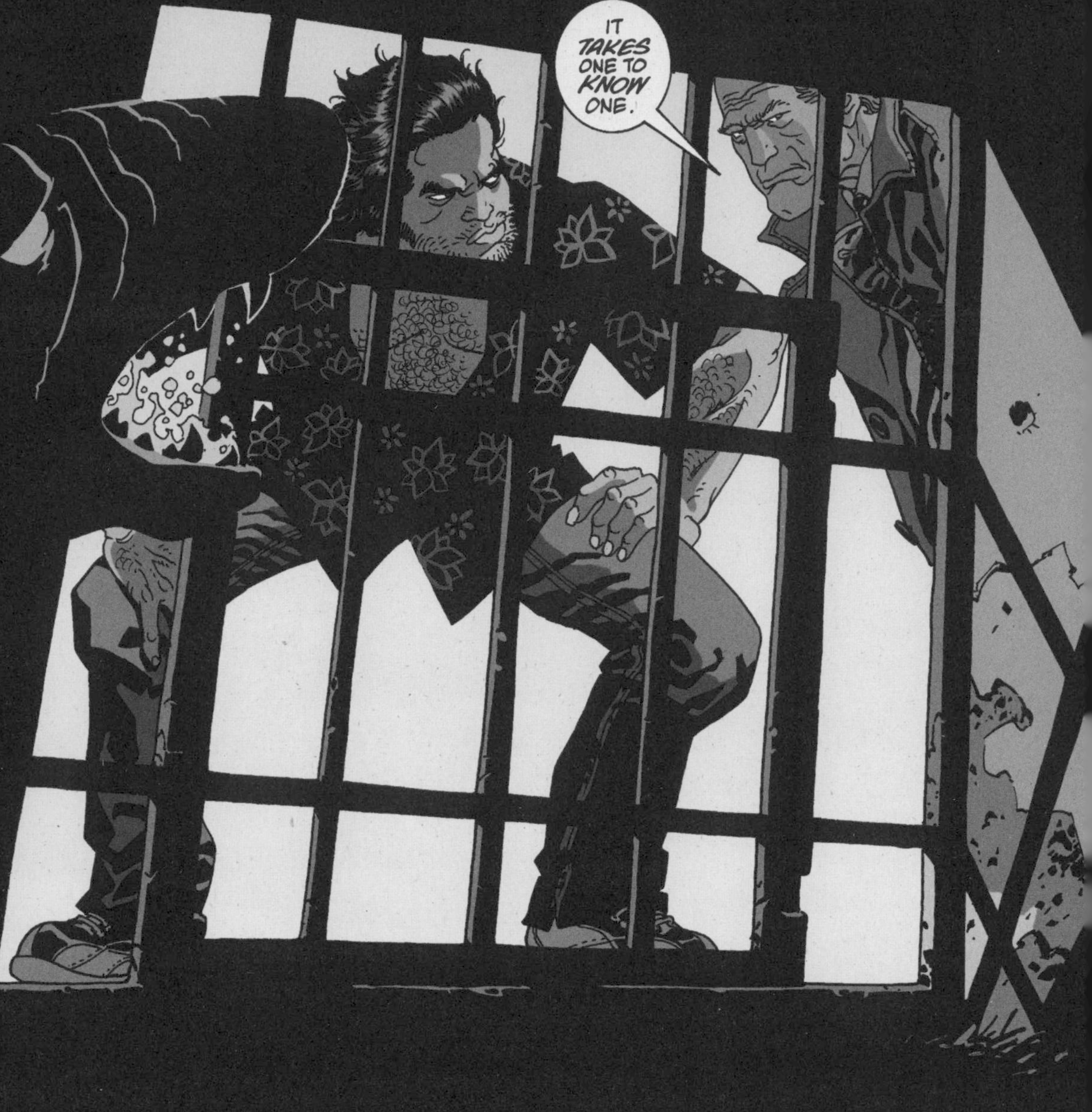
IT TAKES ONE TO KNOW ONE.

NIGHT of the PAYDAY

BRIAN AZZARELLO *writer*
EDUARDO RISSO *artist*
PATRICIA MULVIHILL *colorist*
CLEM ROBINS *letterer*
DIGITAL CHAMELEON *separations*
DAVE JOHNSON *cover*
ZACHARY RAU *ass't ed*
WILL DENNIS *editor*

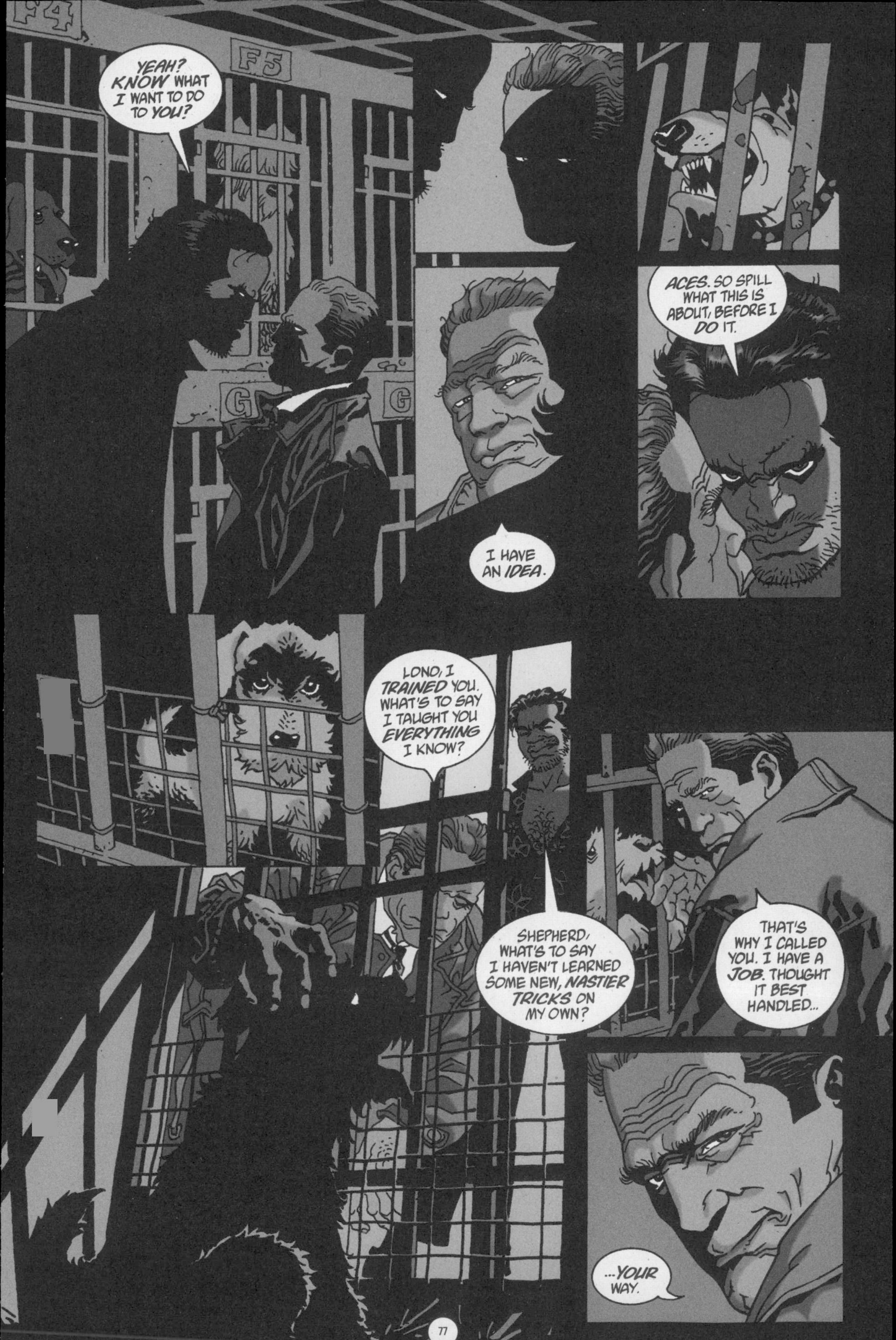
F4
F5
YEAH? KNOW WHAT I WANT TO DO TO YOU?
G
G
I HAVE AN IDEA.
ACES. SO SPILL WHAT THIS IS ABOUT, BEFORE I DO IT.
LONO, I TRAINED YOU. WHAT'S TO SAY I TAUGHT YOU EVERYTHING I KNOW?
SHEPHERD, WHAT'S TO SAY I HAVEN'T LEARNED SOME NEW, NASTIER TRICKS ON MY OWN?
THAT'S WHY I CALLED YOU. I HAVE A JOB. THOUGHT IT BEST HANDLED...
...YOUR WAY.

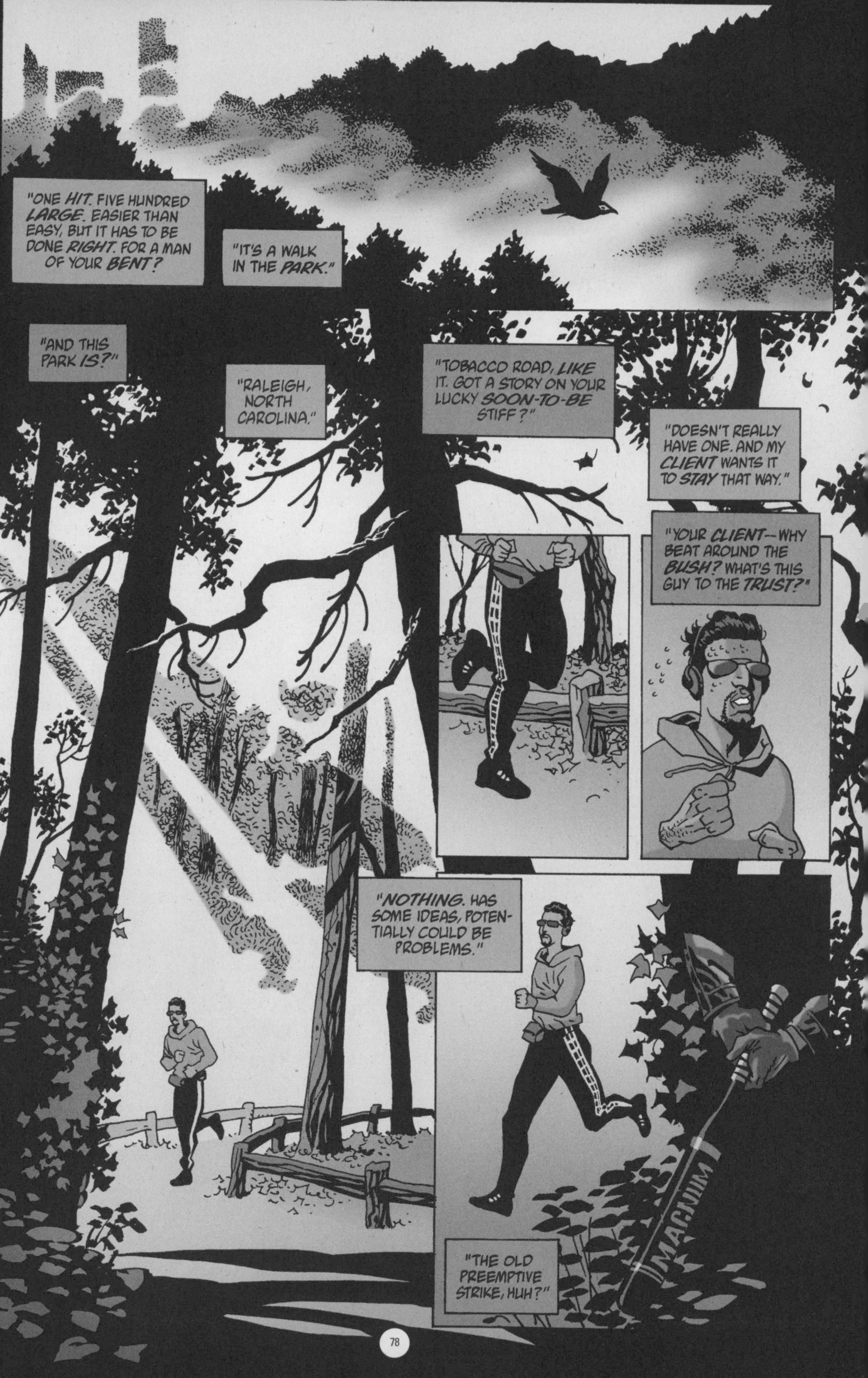
"ONE HIT. FIVE HUNDRED LARGE. EASIER THAN EASY, BUT IT HAS TO BE DONE RIGHT. FOR A MAN OF YOUR BENT?
"IT'S A WALK IN THE PARK."
"AND THIS PARK IS?"
"RALEIGH, NORTH CAROLINA."
"TOBACCO ROAD, LIKE IT. GOT A STORY ON YOUR LUCKY SOON-TO-BE STIFF?"
"DOESN'T REALLY HAVE ONE. AND MY CLIENT WANTS IT TO STAY THAT WAY."
"YOUR CLIENT-- WHY BEAT AROUND THE BUSH? WHAT'S THIS GUY TO THE TRUST?"
"NOTHING. HAS SOME IDEAS, POTENTIALLY COULD BE PROBLEMS."
"THE OLD PREEMPTIVE STRIKE, HUH?"
MAGNUM

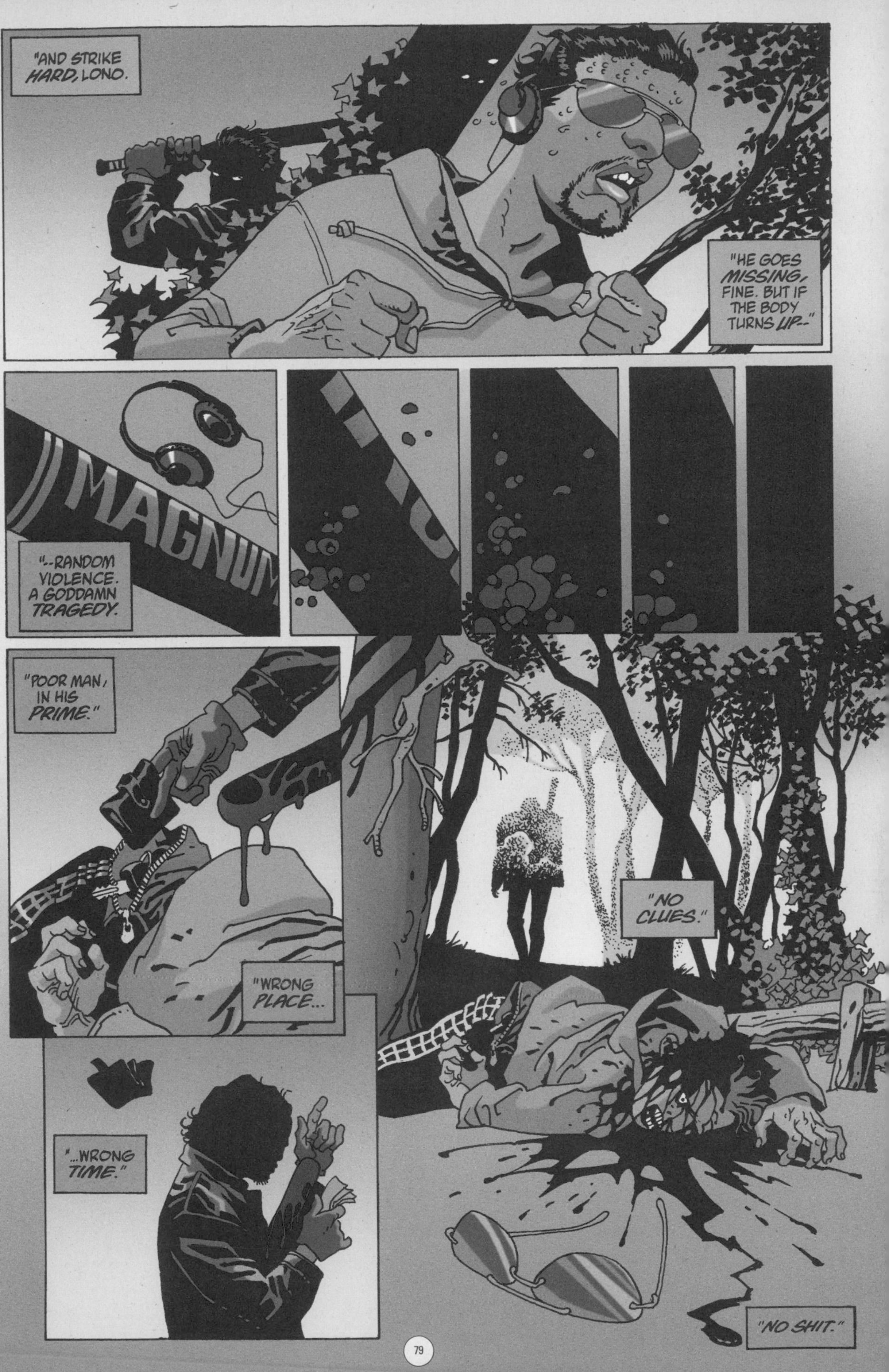
"AND STRIKE HARD, LONO.
"HE GOES MISSING, FINE. BUT IF THE BODY TURNS UP--"
MAGNUM
"--RANDOM VIOLENCE. A GODDAMN TRAGEDY.
"POOR MAN, IN HIS PRIME."
"WRONG PLACE...
"...WRONG TIME."
"NO CLUES."
"NO SHIT."

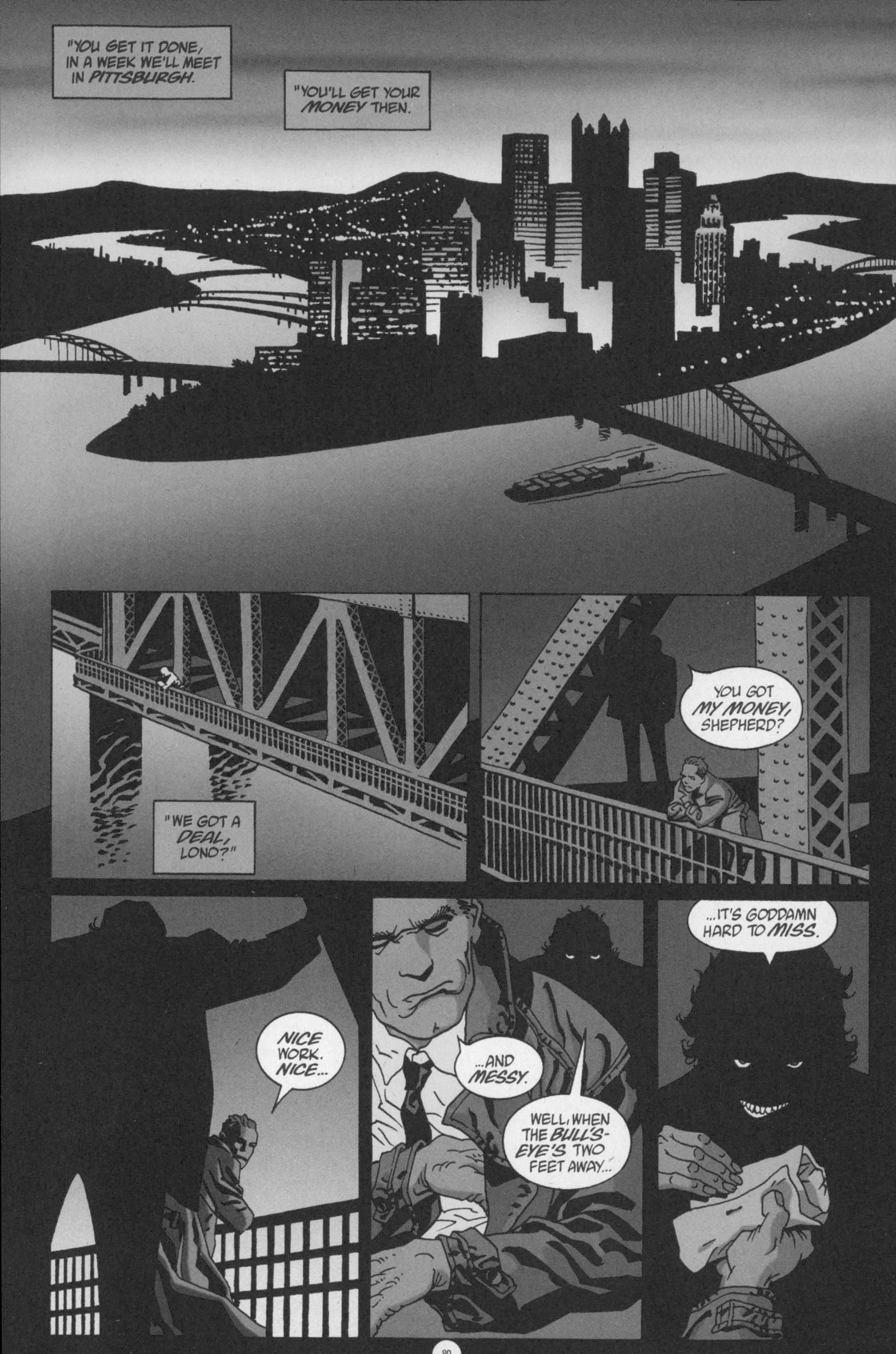
"YOU GET IT DONE, IN A WEEK WE'LL MEET IN PITTSBURGH.
"YOU'LL GET YOUR MONEY THEN.
"WE GOT A DEAL, LONO?"
YOU GOT MY MONEY, SHEPHERD?
NICE WORK. NICE...
...AND MESSY.
WELL, WHEN THE BULL'S-EYE'S TWO FEET AWAY...
...IT'S GODDAMN HARD TO MISS.

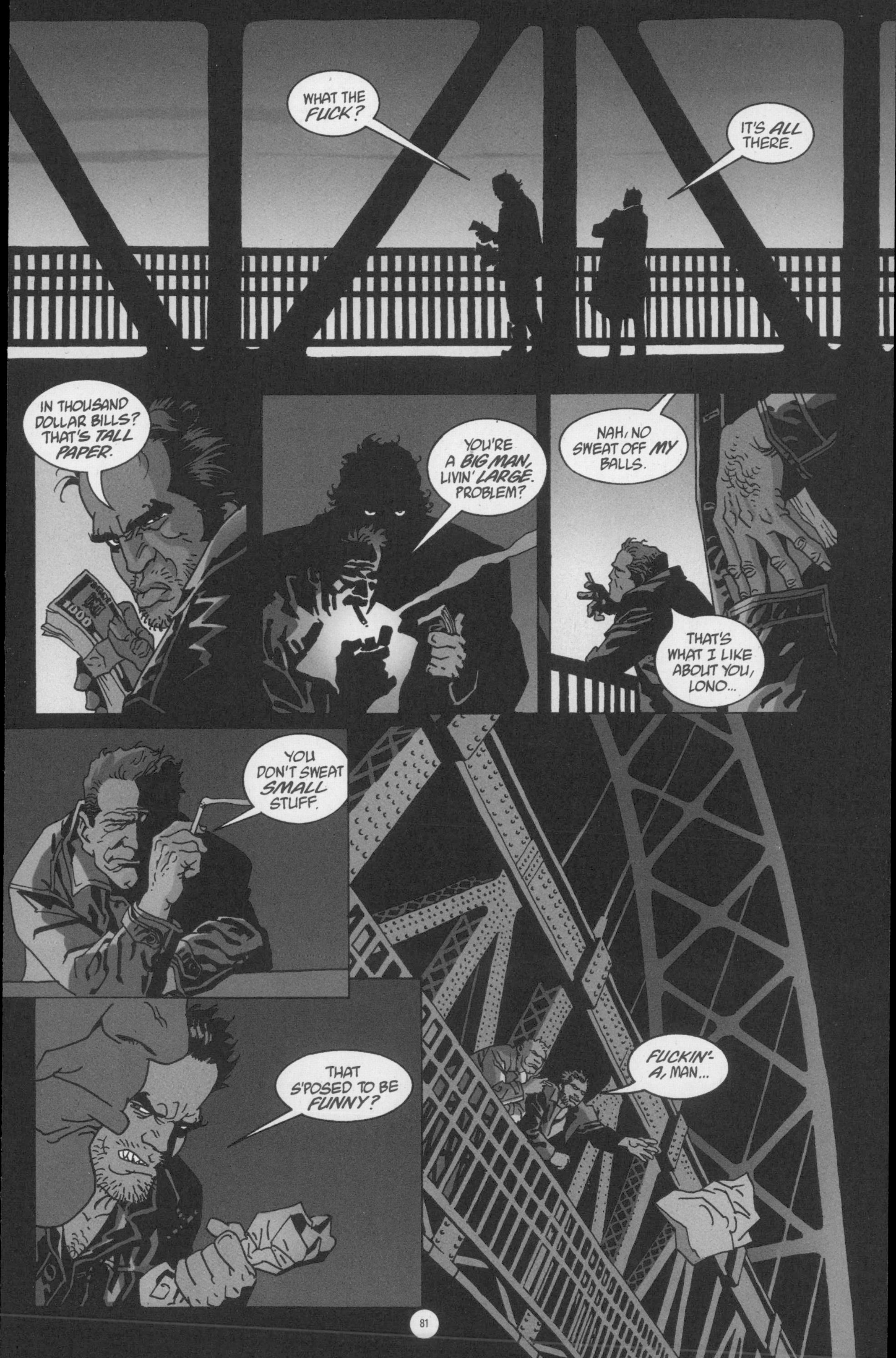

WHAT THE FUCK?
IT'S ALL THERE.
IN THOUSAND DOLLAR BILLS? THAT'S TALL PAPER.
YOU'RE A BIG MAN, LIVIN' LARGE. PROBLEM?
NAH, NO SWEAT OFF MY BALLS.
THAT'S WHAT I LIKE ABOUT YOU, LONO...
YOU DON'T SWEAT SMALL STUFF.
THAT S'POSED TO BE FUNNY?
FUCKIN'-A, MAN...

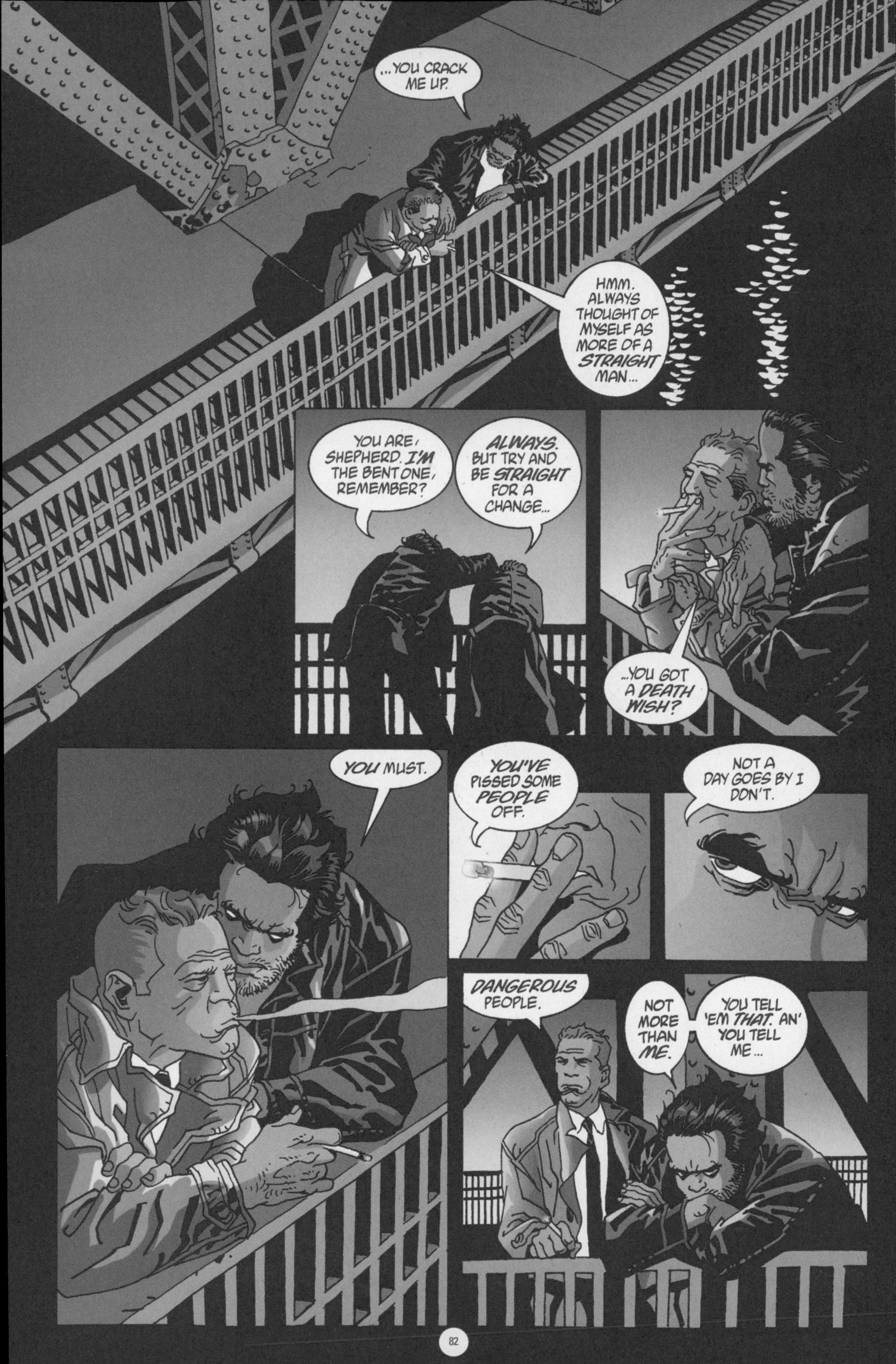
...YOU CRACK ME UP.
HMM. ALWAYS THOUGHT OF MYSELF AS MORE OF A STRAIGHT MAN...
YOU ARE, SHEPHERD. I'M THE BENT ONE, REMEMBER?
ALWAYS. BUT TRY AND BE STRAIGHT FOR A CHANGE...
...YOU GOT A DEATH WISH?
YOU MUST.
YOU'VE PISSED SOME PEOPLE OFF.
NOT A DAY GOES BY I DON'T.
DANGEROUS PEOPLE.
NOT MORE THAN ME.
YOU TELL 'EM THAT. AN' YOU TELL ME ...

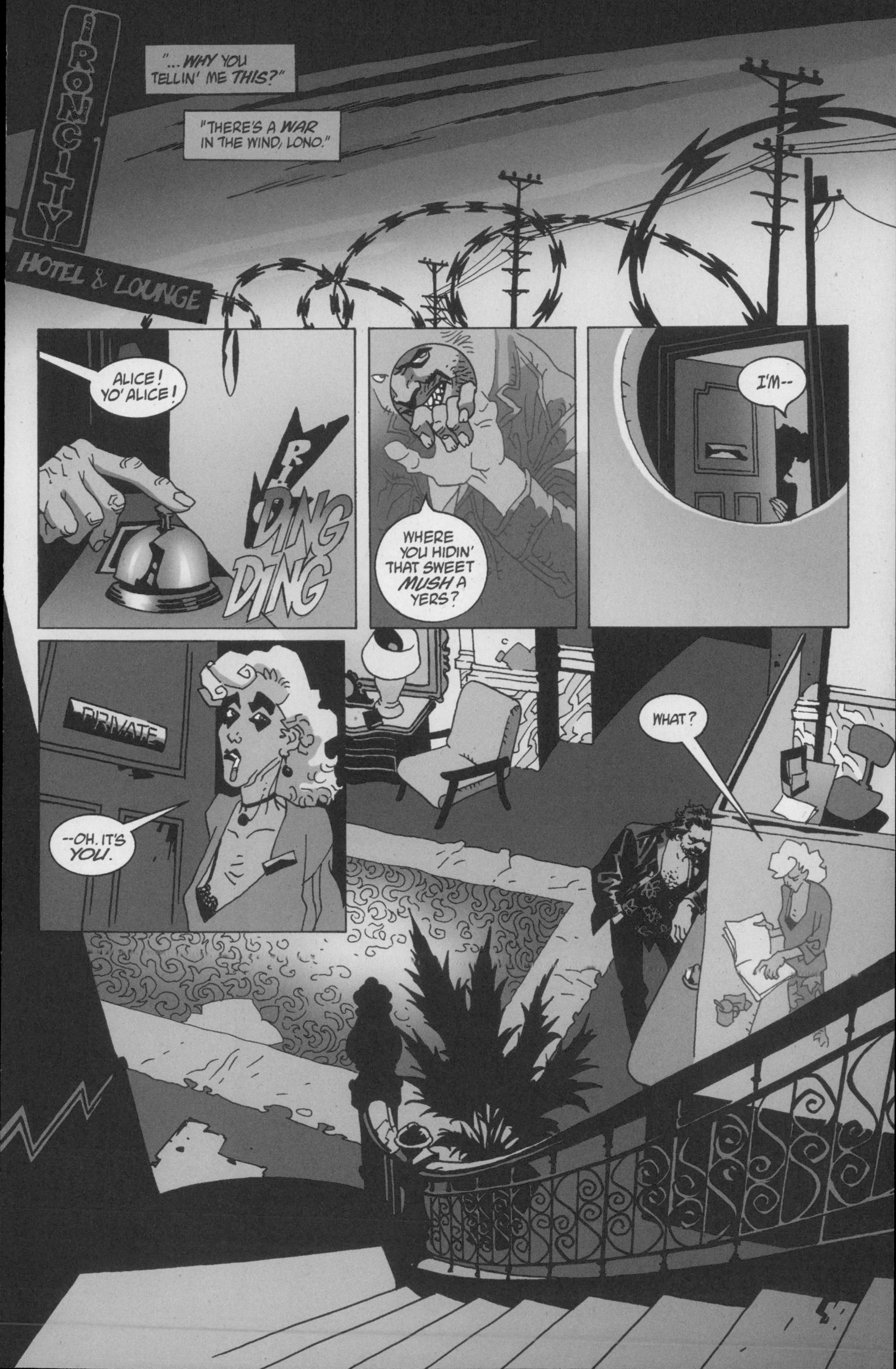

IRONCITY
HOTEL & LOUNGE
"...WHY YOU TELLIN' ME THIS?"
"THERE'S A WAR IN THE WIND, LONO."
ALICE! YO' ALICE!
RING
DING DING
WHERE YOU HIDIN' THAT SWEET MUSH A YERS?
I'M--
PRIVATE
--OH. IT'S YOU.
WHAT?

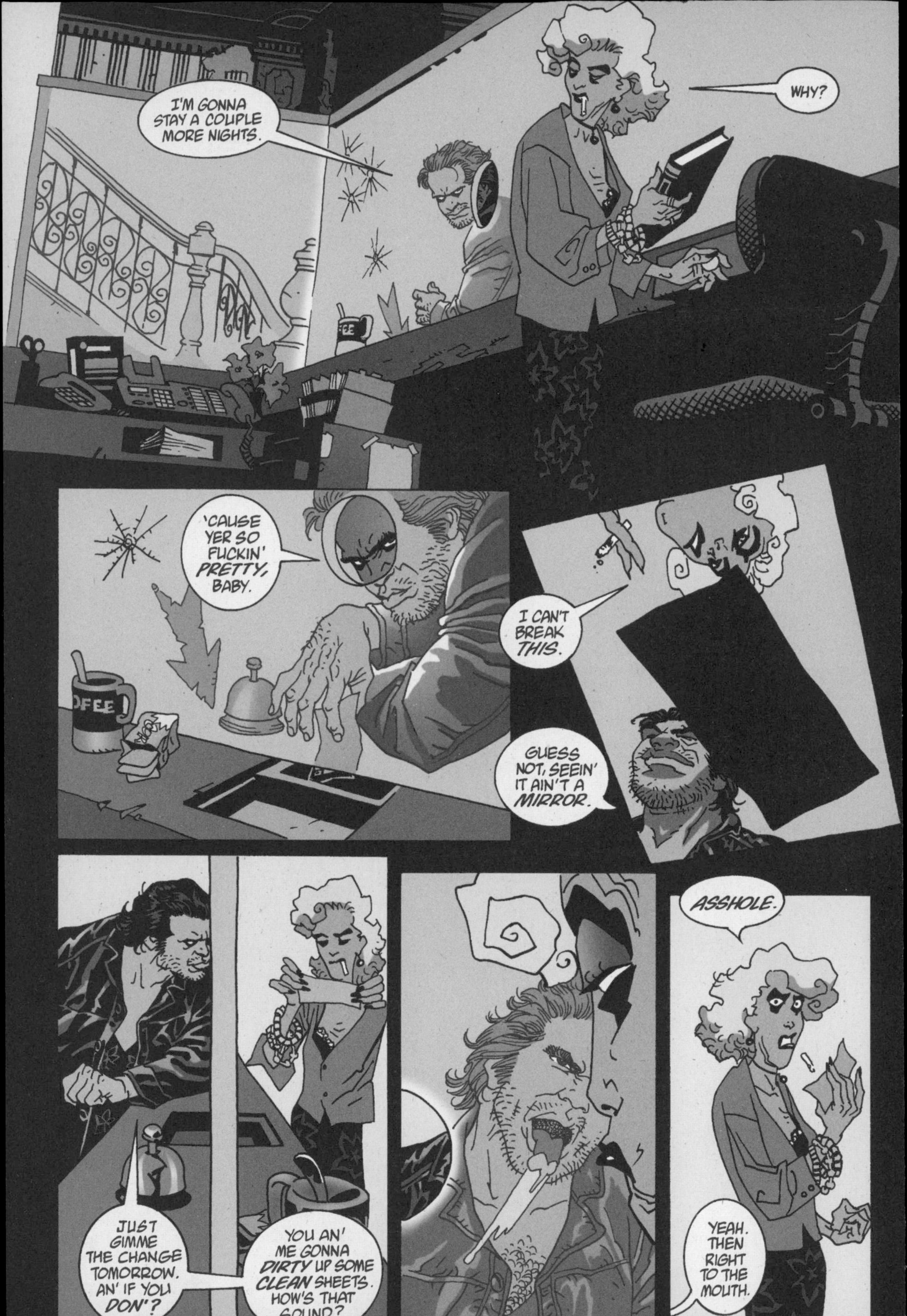
I'M GONNA STAY A COUPLE MORE NIGHTS.
WHY?
'CAUSE YER SO FUCKIN' PRETTY, BABY.
I CAN'T BREAK THIS.
GUESS NOT, SEEIN' IT AIN'T A MIRROR.
JUST GIMME THE CHANGE TOMORROW. AN' IF YOU DON'?
YOU AN' ME GONNA DIRTY UP SOME CLEAN SHEETS. HOW'S THAT SOUND?
ASSHOLE.
YEAH. THEN RIGHT TO THE MOUTH.

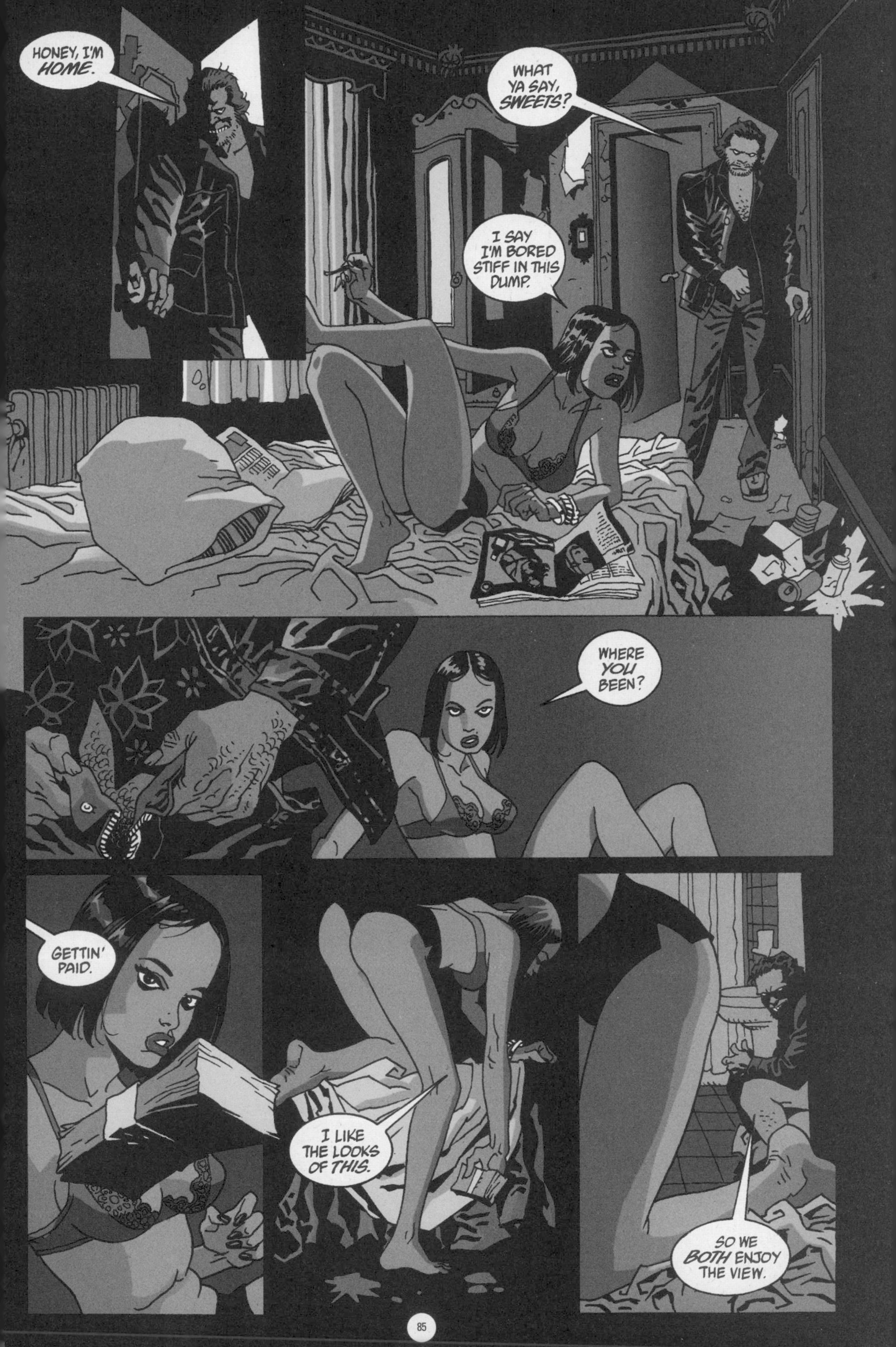
HONEY, I'M HOME.
WHAT YA SAY, SWEETS?
I SAY I'M BORED STIFF IN THIS DUMP.
WHERE YOU BEEN?
GETTIN' PAID.
I LIKE THE LOOKS OF THIS.
SO WE BOTH ENJOY THE VIEW.

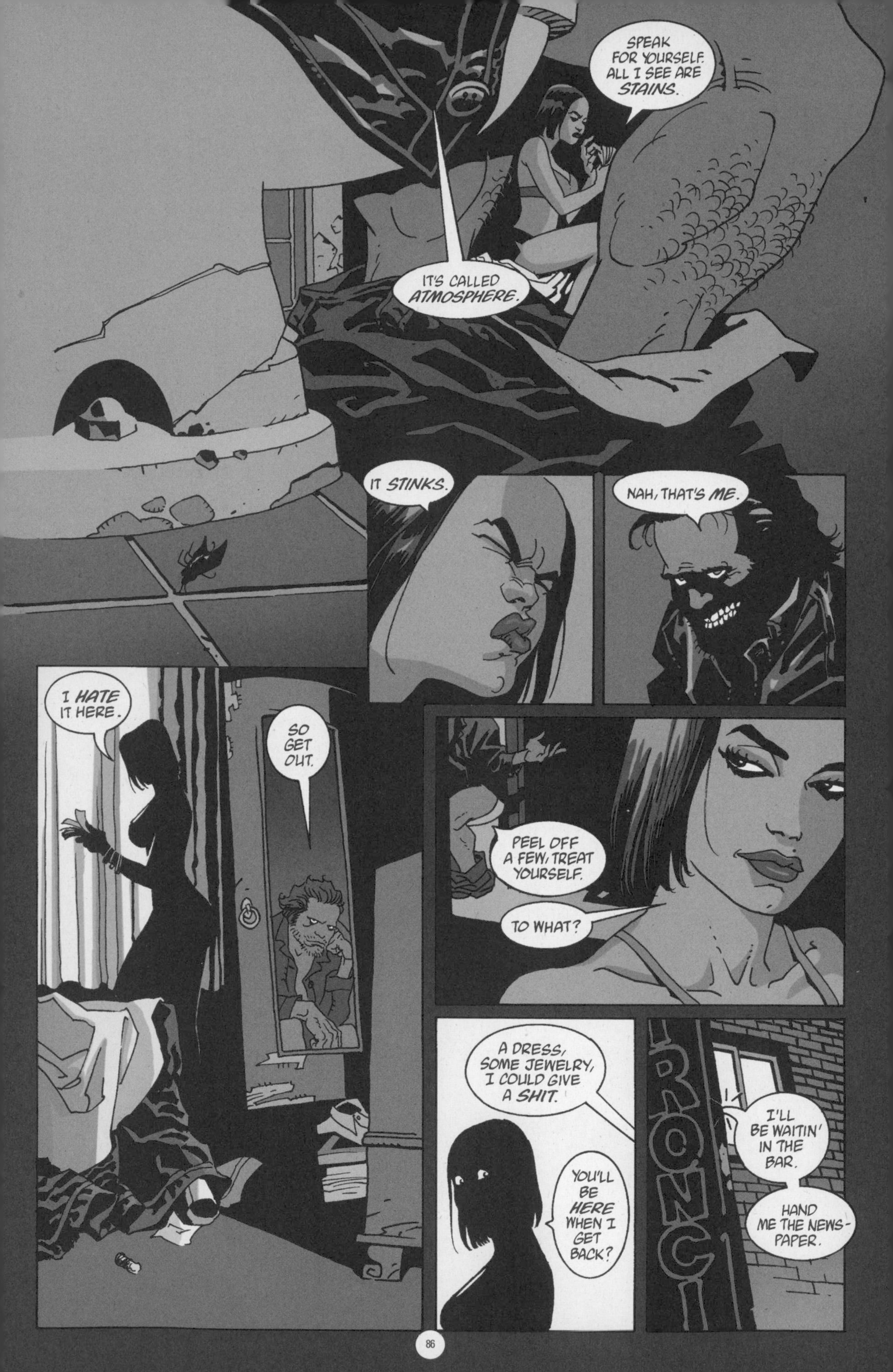
SPEAK FOR YOURSELF. ALL I SEE ARE STAINS.
IT'S CALLED ATMOSPHERE.
IT STINKS.
NAH, THAT'S ME.
I HATE IT HERE.
SO GET OUT.
PEEL OFF A FEW, TREAT YOURSELF.
TO WHAT?
A DRESS, SOME JEWELRY, I COULD GIVE A SHIT.
YOU'LL BE HERE WHEN I GET BACK?
I'LL BE WAITIN' IN THE BAR.
HAND ME THE NEWS-PAPER.
RONC

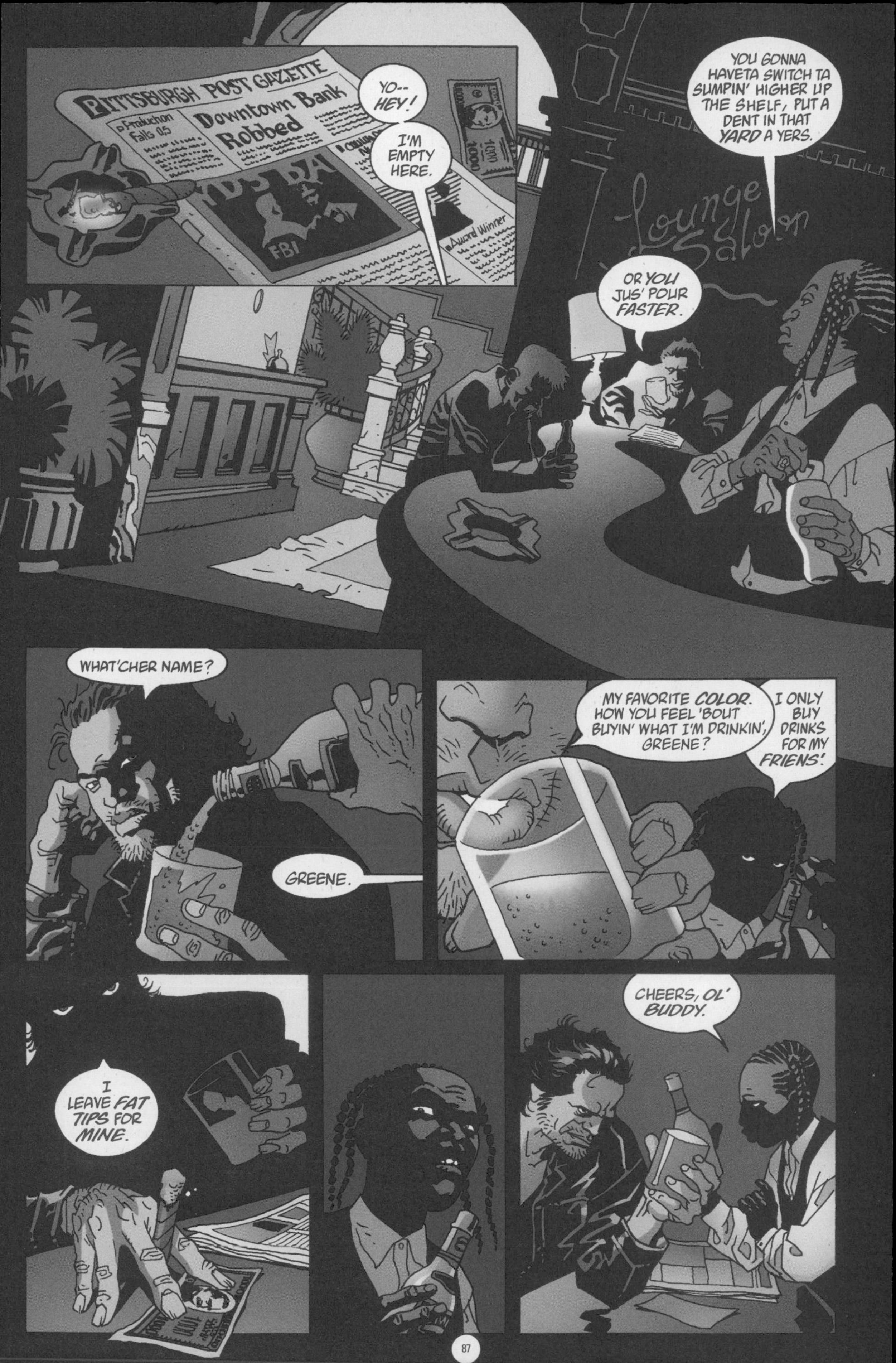
PITTSBURGH POST GAZETTE
Downtown Bank Robbed
FBI
Award Winner
YO-- HEY!
I'M EMPTY HERE.
Lounge Saloon
YOU GONNA HAVETA SWITCH TA SUMPIN' HIGHER UP THE SHELF, PUT A DENT IN THAT YARD A YERS.
OR YOU JUS' POUR FASTER.
WHAT'CHER NAME?
GREENE.
MY FAVORITE COLOR. HOW YOU FEEL 'BOUT BUYIN' WHAT I'M DRINKIN', GREENE?
I ONLY BUY DRINKS FOR MY FRIENS'.
I LEAVE FAT TIPS FOR MINE.
CHEERS, OL' BUDDY.

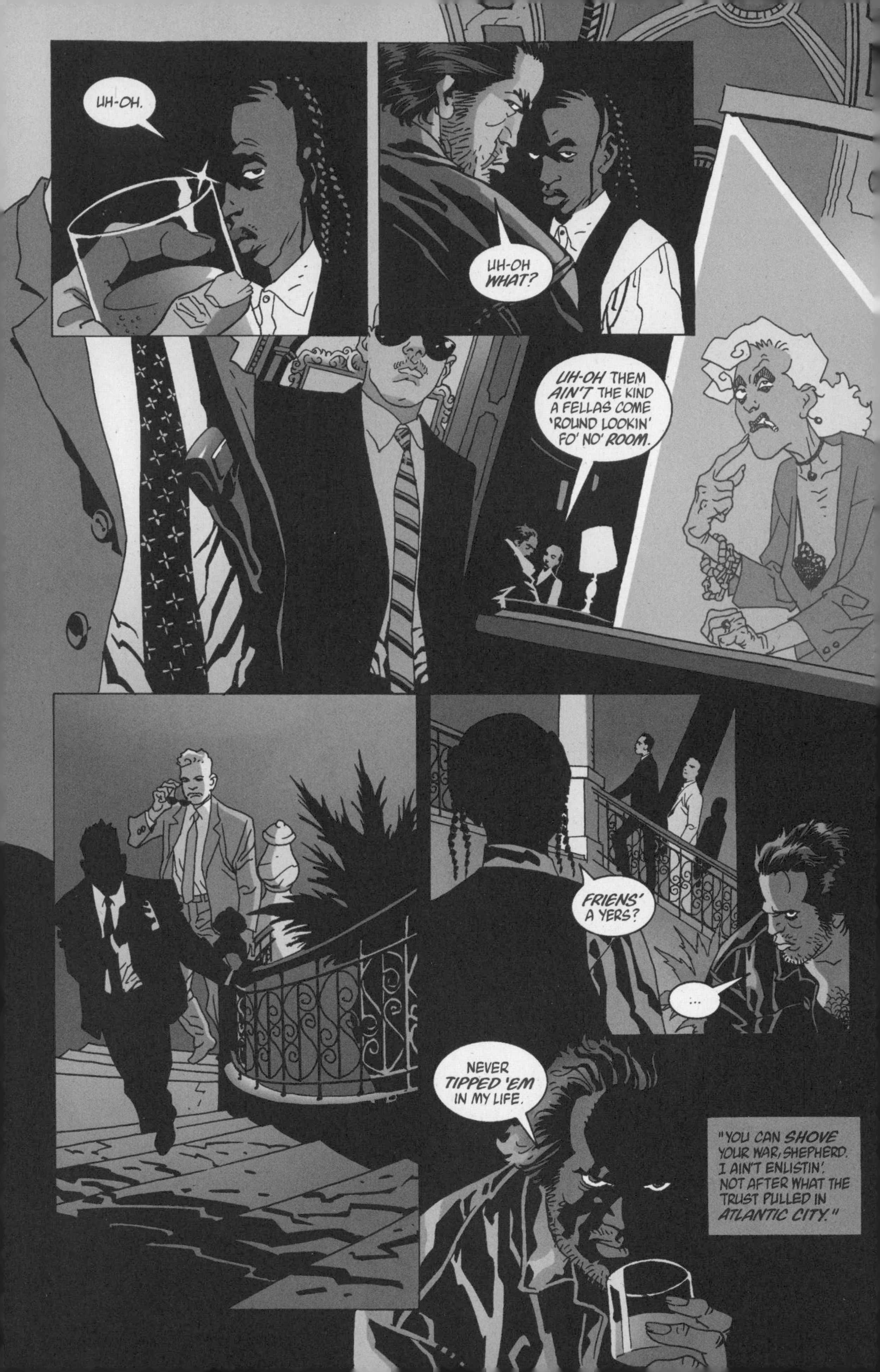
UH-OH.
UH-OH WHAT?
UH-OH THEM AIN'T THE KIND A FELLAS COME 'ROUND LOOKIN' FO' NO' ROOM.
FRIENS' A YERS?
...
NEVER TIPPED 'EM IN MY LIFE.
"YOU CAN SHOVE YOUR WAR, SHEPHERD. I AIN'T ENLISTIN'. NOT AFTER WHAT THE TRUST PULLED IN ATLANTIC CITY."

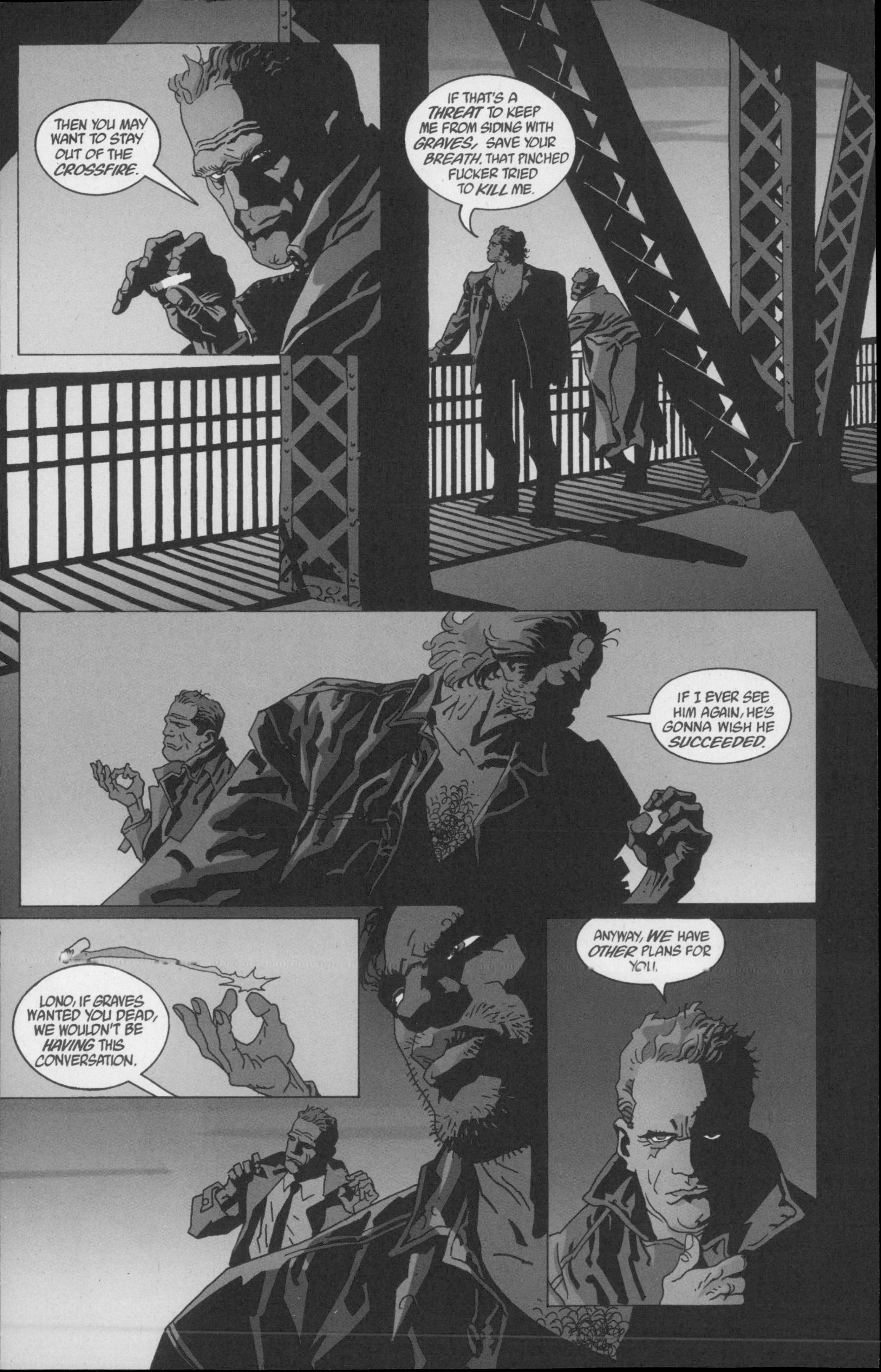
THEN YOU MAY WANT TO STAY OUT OF THE CROSSFIRE.
IF THAT'S A THREAT TO KEEP ME FROM SIDING WITH GRAVES, SAVE YOUR BREATH. THAT PINCHED FUCKER TRIED TO KILL ME.
IF I EVER SEE HIM AGAIN, HE'S GONNA WISH HE SUCCEEDED.
LONO, IF GRAVES WANTED YOU DEAD, WE WOULDN'T BE HAVING THIS CONVERSATION.
ANYWAY, WE HAVE OTHER PLANS FOR YOU.

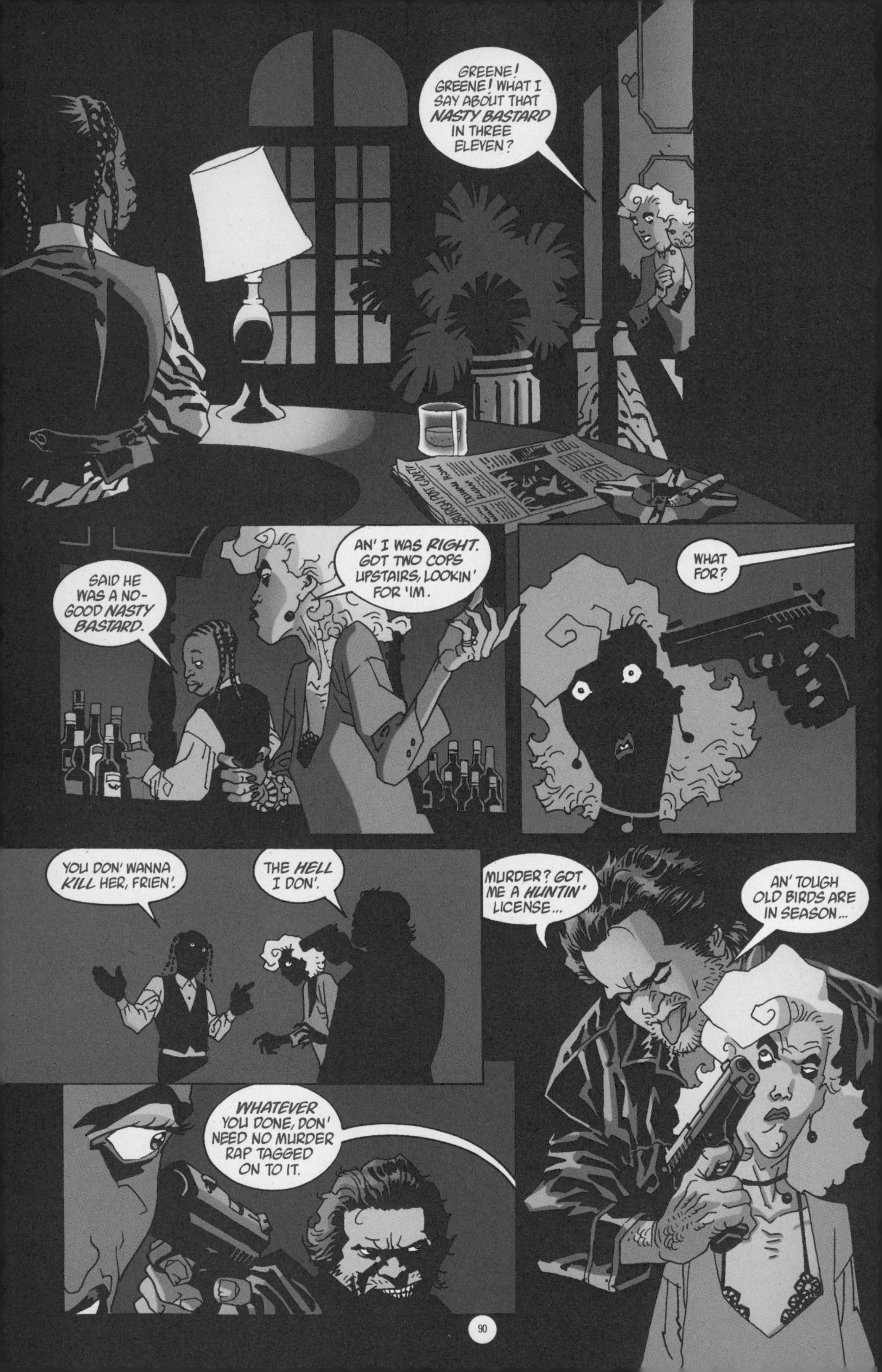
GREENE! GREENE! WHAT I SAY ABOUT THAT NASTY BASTARD IN THREE ELEVEN?
SAID HE WAS A NO-GOOD NASTY BASTARD.
AN' I WAS RIGHT. GOT TWO COPS UPSTAIRS, LOOKIN' FOR 'IM.
WHAT FOR?
YOU DON' WANNA KILL HER, FRIEN'.
THE HELL I DON'.
WHATEVER YOU DONE, DON' NEED NO MURDER RAP TAGGED ON TO IT.
MURDER? GOT ME A HUNTIN' LICENSE...
AN' TOUGH OLD BIRDS ARE IN SEASON...

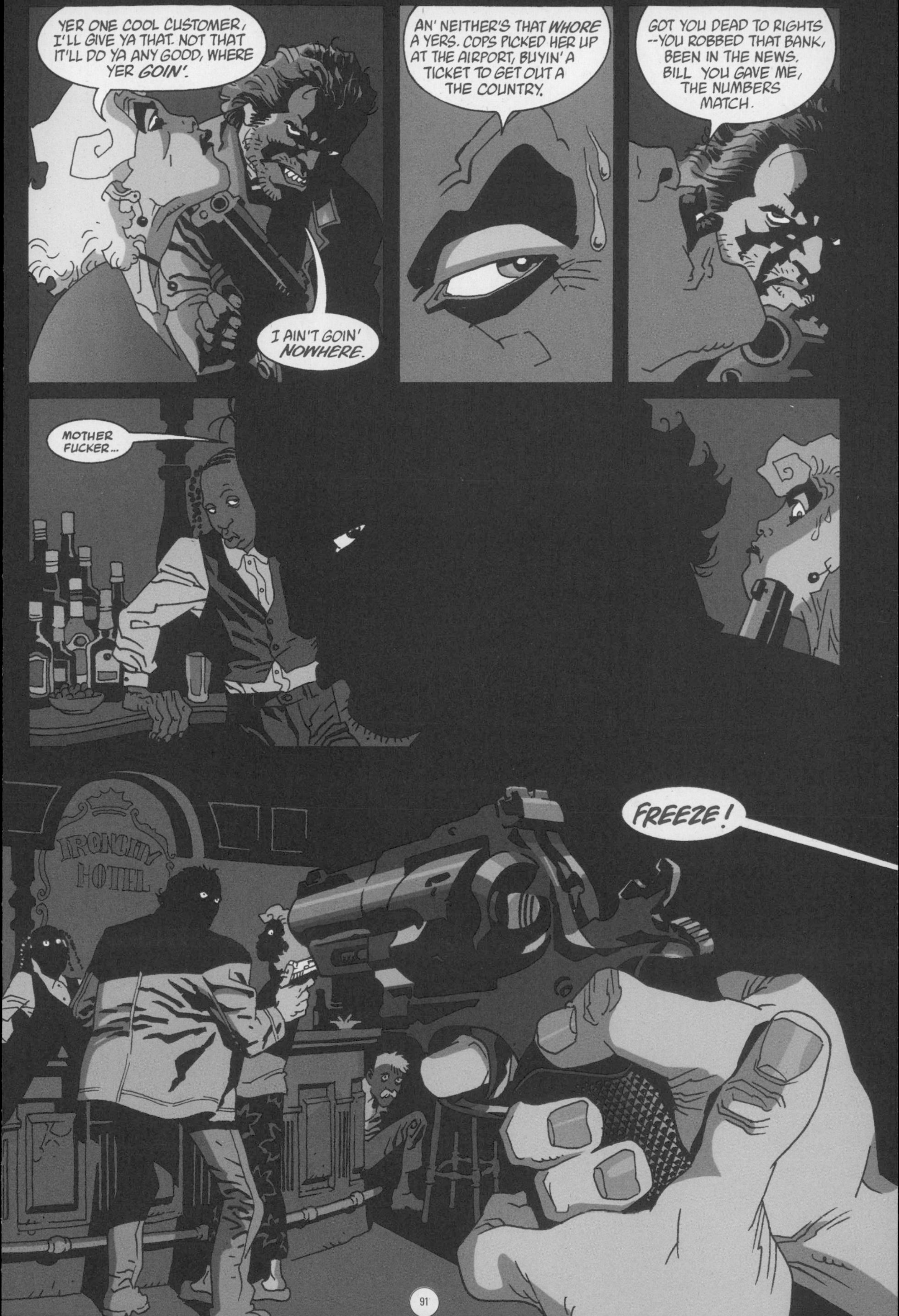

YER ONE COOL CUSTOMER, I'LL GIVE YA THAT. NOT THAT IT'LL DO YA ANY GOOD, WHERE YER GOIN'.
I AIN'T GOIN' NOWHERE.
AN' NEITHER'S THAT WHORE A YERS. COPS PICKED HER UP AT THE AIRPORT, BUYIN' A TICKET TO GET OUT A THE COUNTRY.
GOT YOU DEAD TO RIGHTS --YOU ROBBED THAT BANK, BEEN IN THE NEWS. BILL YOU GAVE ME, THE NUMBERS MATCH.
MOTHER FUCKER...
IRONCITY HOTEL
FREEZE!

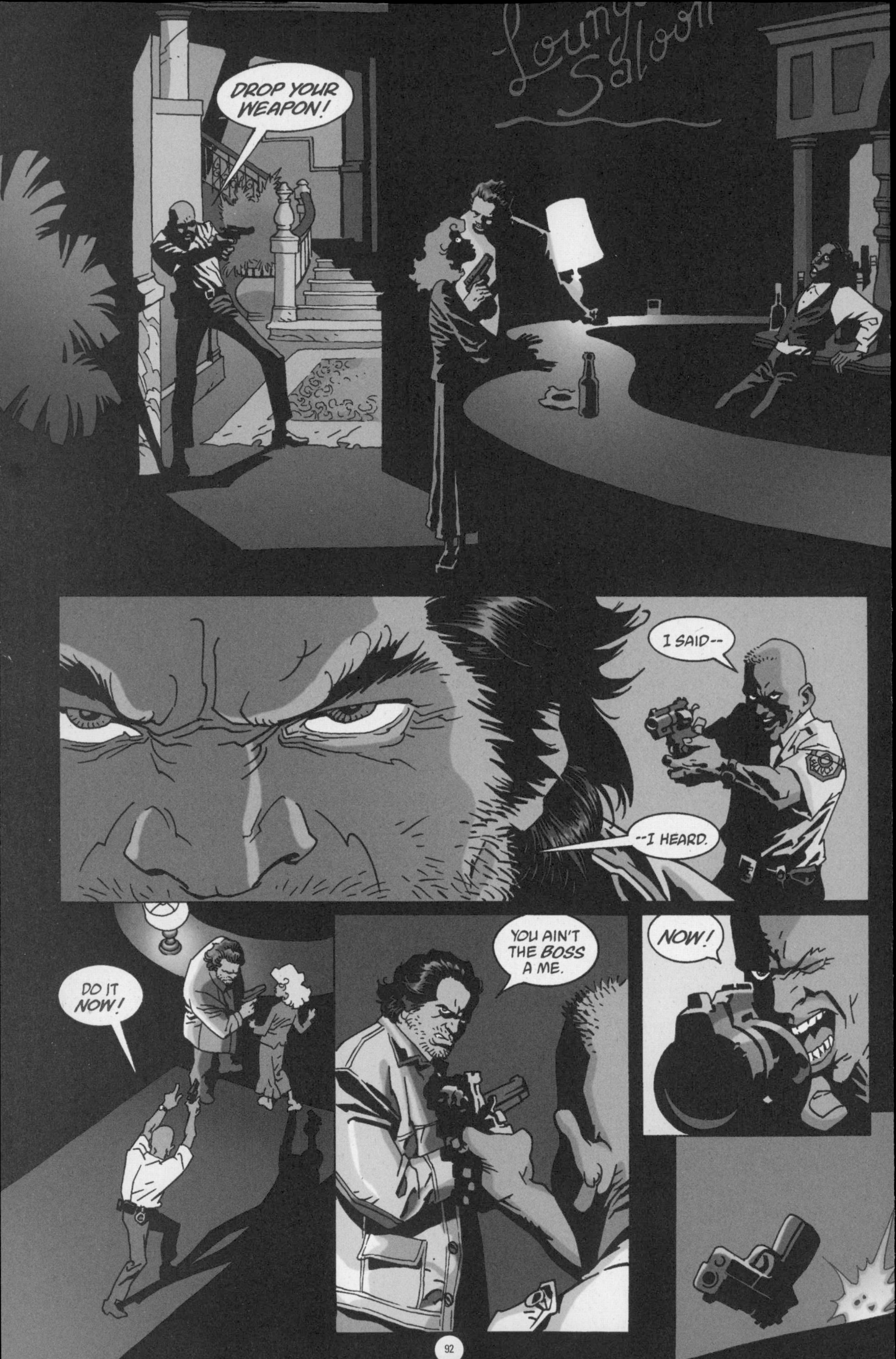
Lounge Saloon
DROP YOUR WEAPON!
I SAID--
--I HEARD.
DO IT NOW!
YOU AIN'T THE BOSS A ME.
NOW!

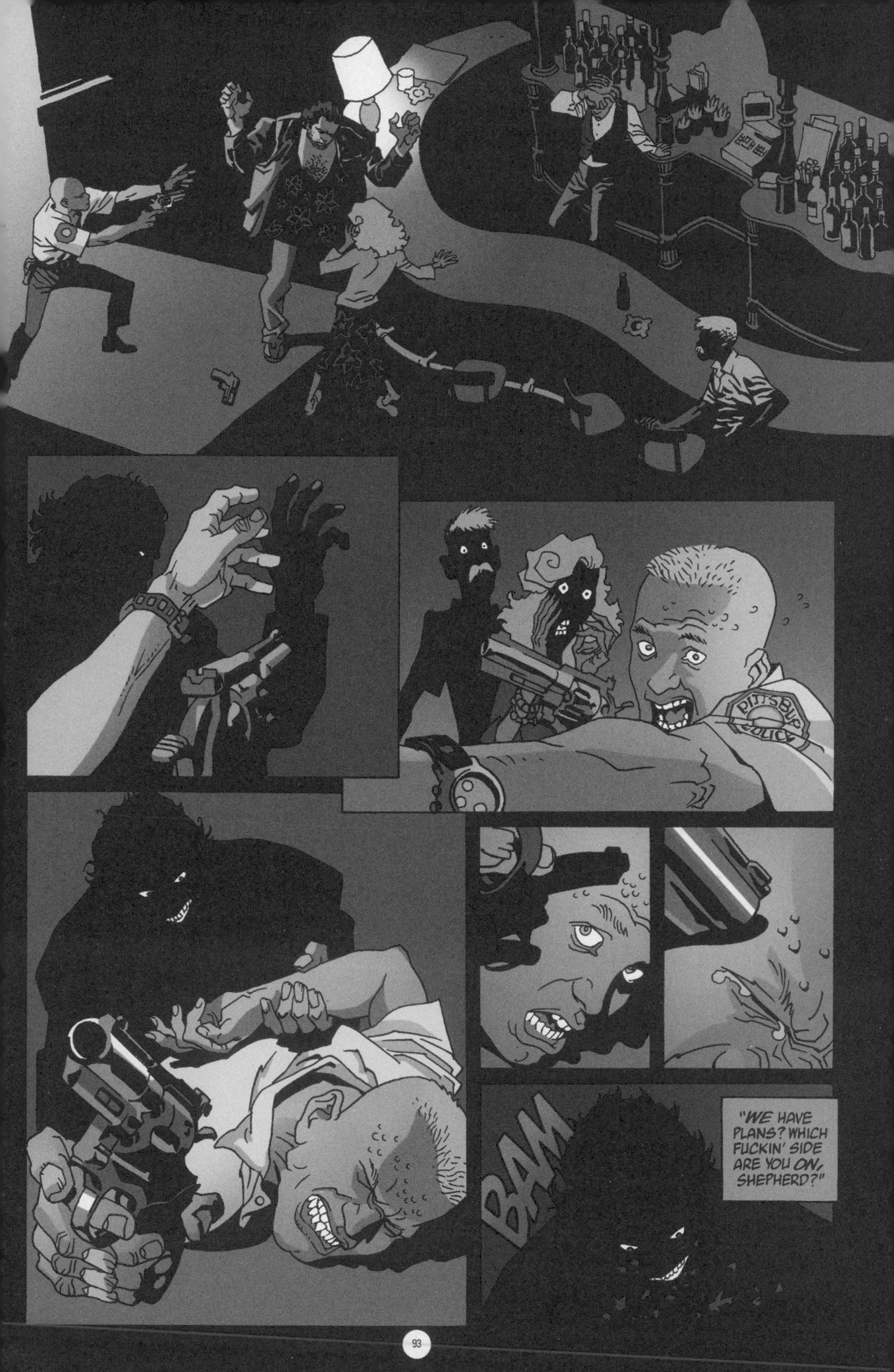
PITTSBURGH POLICE
BAM
"WE HAVE PLANS? WHICH FUCKIN' SIDE ARE YOU ON, SHEPHERD?"

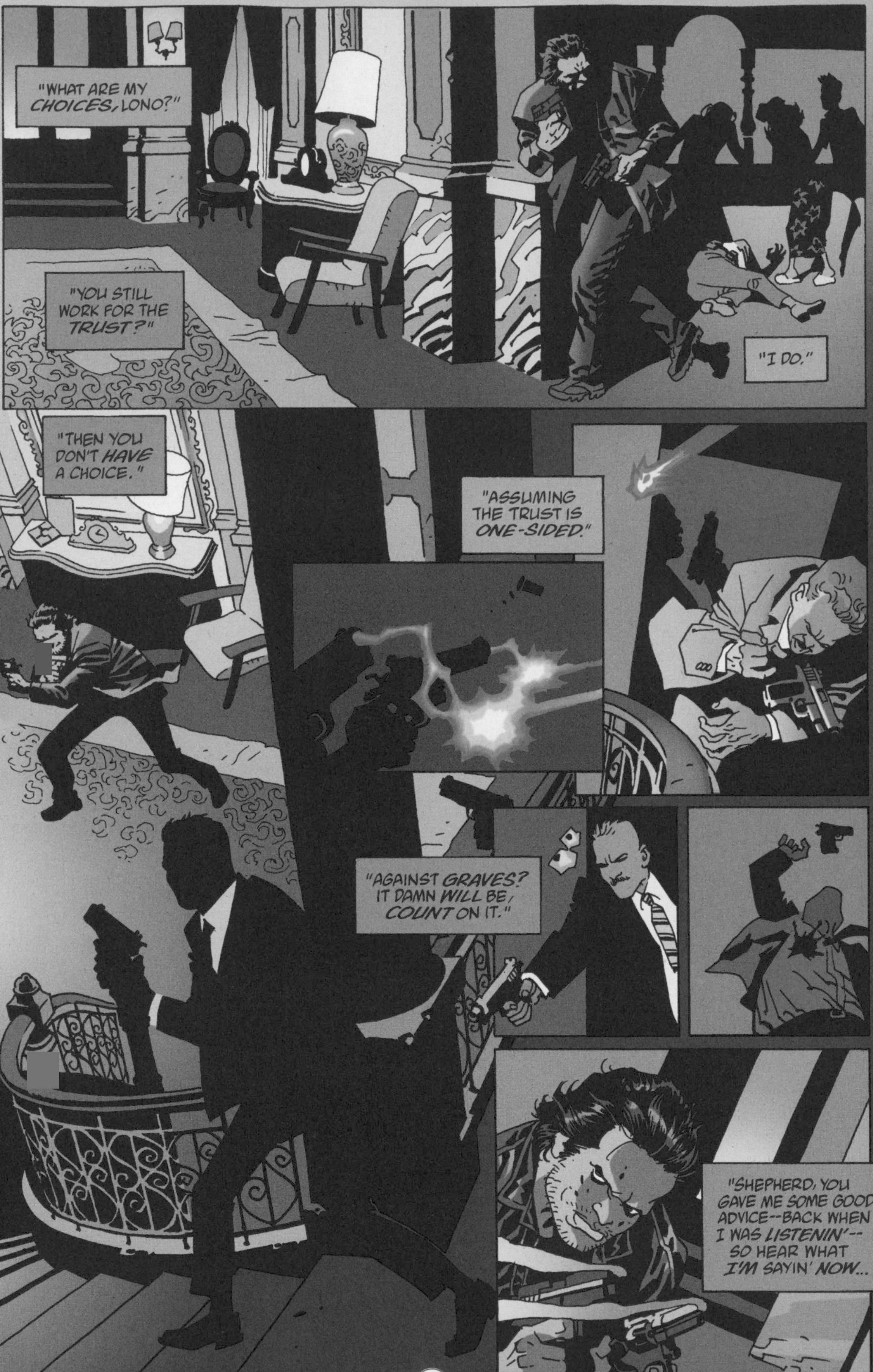
"WHAT ARE MY CHOICES, LONO?"
"YOU STILL WORK FOR THE TRUST?"
"I DO."
"THEN YOU DON'T HAVE A CHOICE."
"ASSUMING THE TRUST IS ONE-SIDED."
"AGAINST GRAVES? IT DAMN WILL BE, COUNT ON IT."
"SHEPHERD, YOU GAVE ME SOME GOOD ADVICE--BACK WHEN I WAS LISTENIN'-- SO HEAR WHAT I'M SAYIN' NOW...

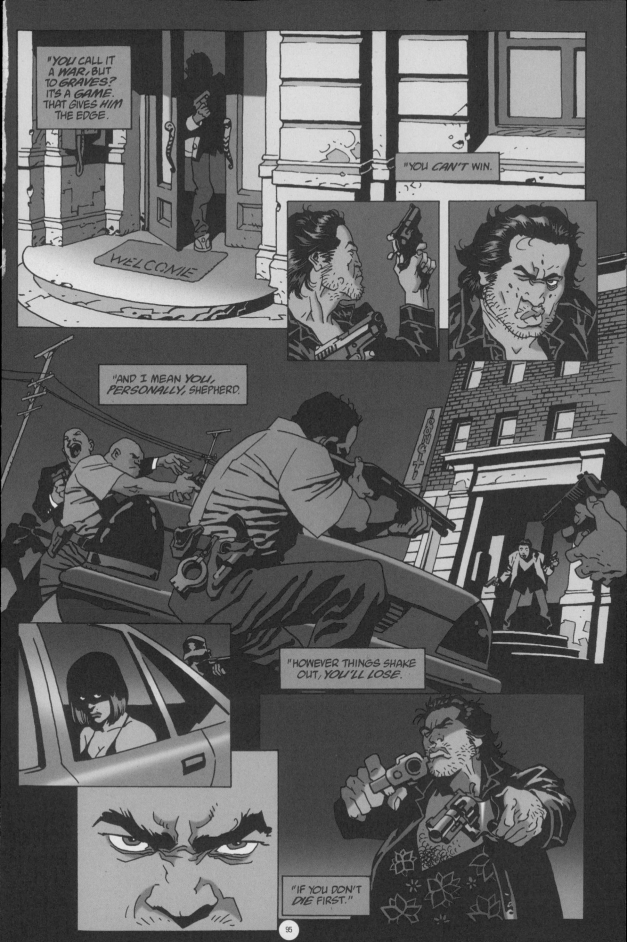

"YOU CALL IT A *WAR*, BUT TO *GRAVES?* IT'S A *GAME*. THAT GIVES *HIM* THE EDGE.

"YOU *CAN'T* WIN.

"AND I MEAN *YOU*, PERSONALLY, SHEPHERD.

"HOWEVER THINGS SHAKE OUT, *YOU'LL LOSE.*

"IF YOU DON'T *DIE* FIRST."

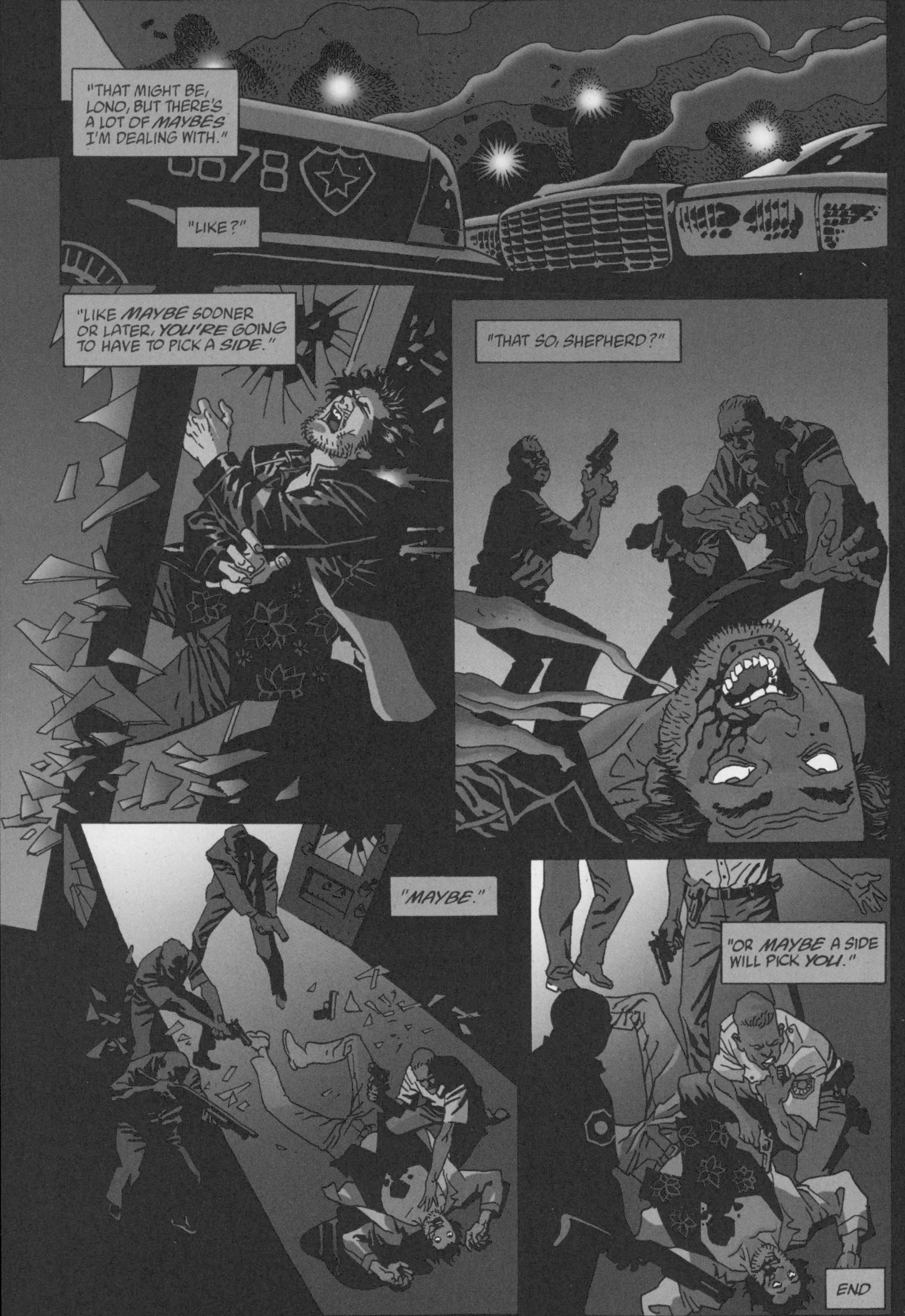
"THAT MIGHT BE, LONO, BUT THERE'S A LOT OF MAYBES I'M DEALING WITH."
"LIKE?"
"LIKE MAYBE SOONER OR LATER, YOU'RE GOING TO HAVE TO PICK A SIDE."
"THAT SO, SHEPHERD?"
"MAYBE."
"OR MAYBE A SIDE WILL PICK YOU."
END

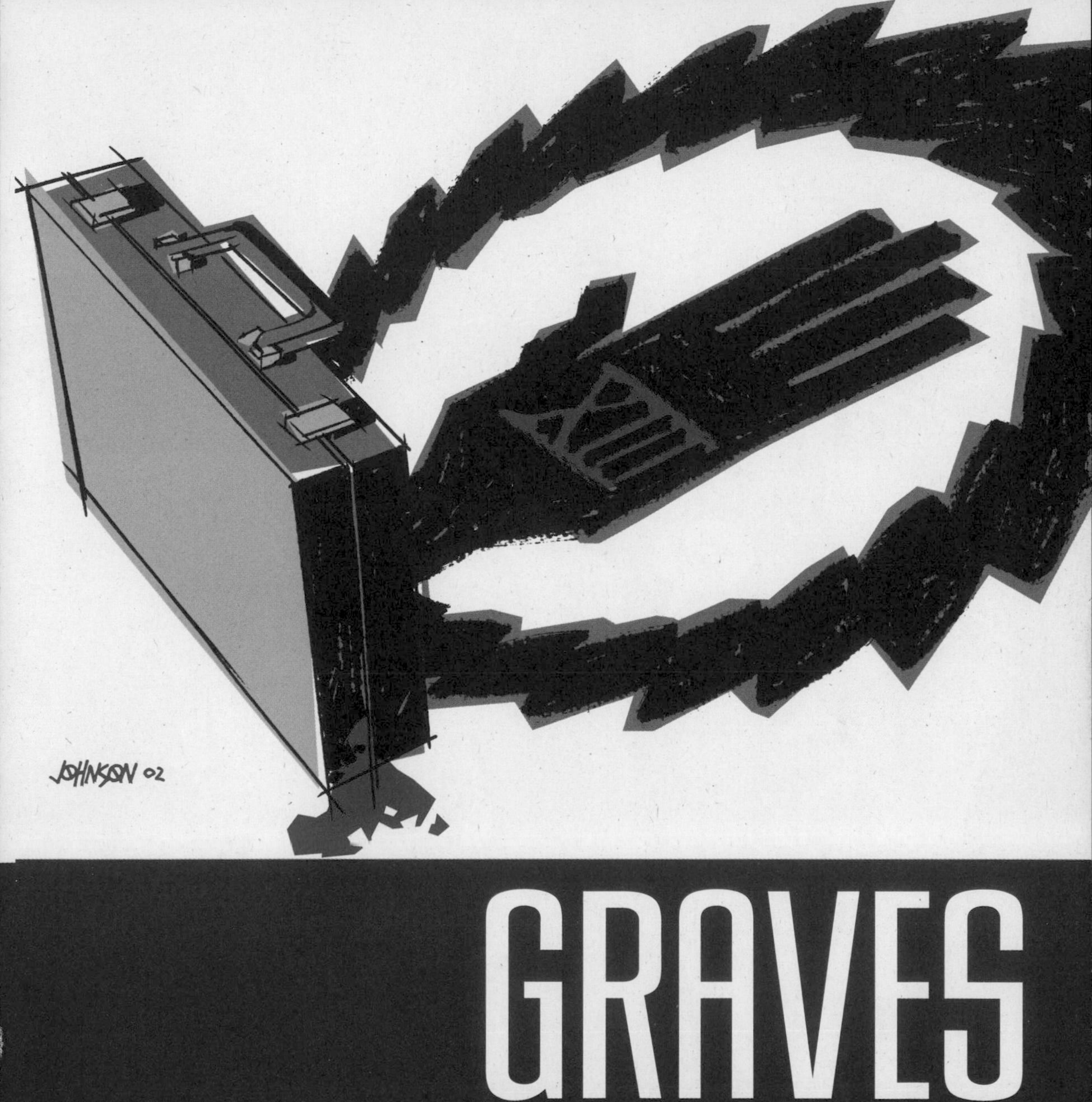
JOHNSON 02

GRAVES

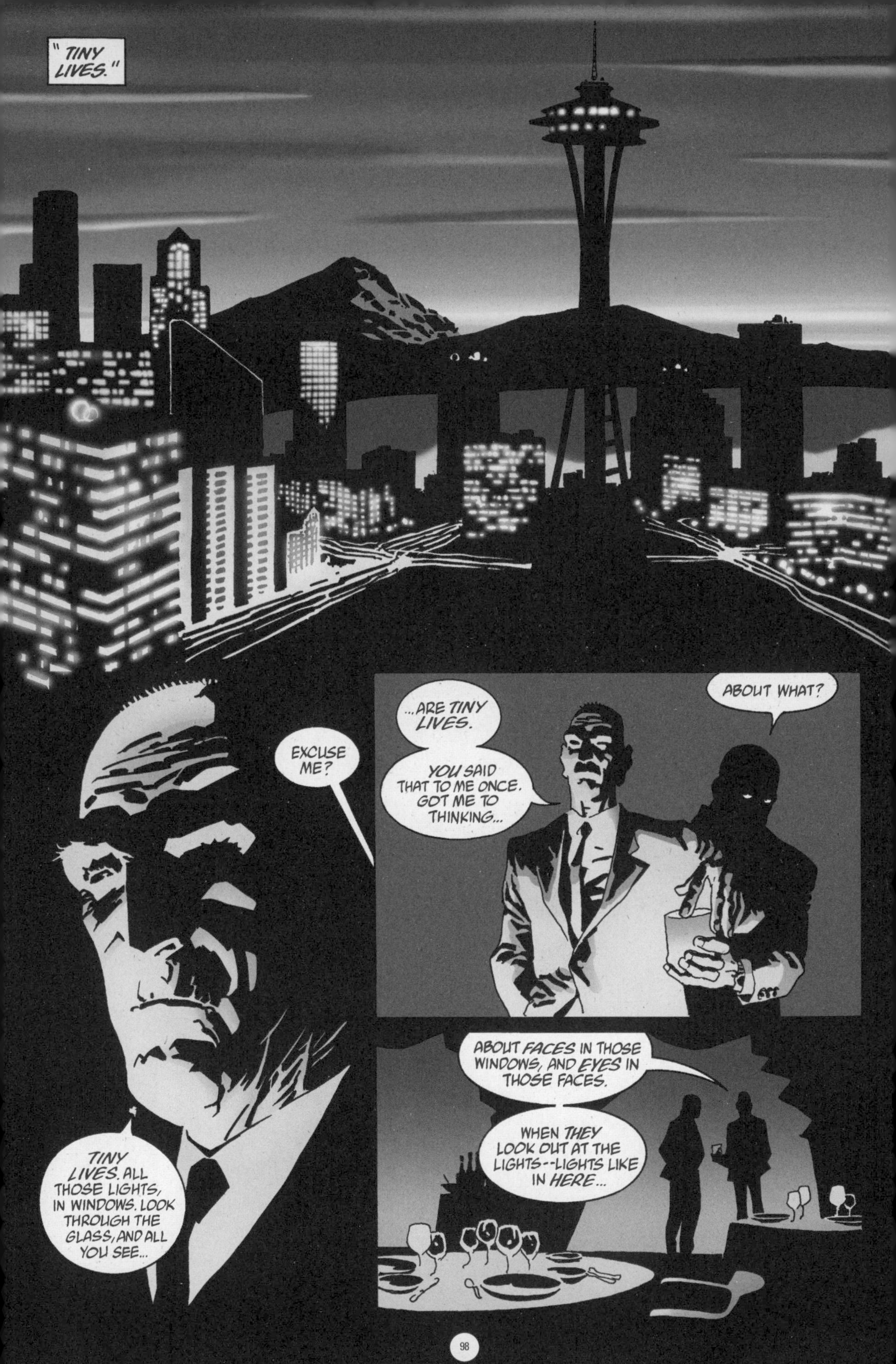
"TINY LIVES."
TINY LIVES. ALL THOSE LIGHTS, IN WINDOWS. LOOK THROUGH THE GLASS, AND ALL YOU SEE...
EXCUSE ME?
...ARE TINY LIVES.
YOU SAID THAT TO ME ONCE. GOT ME TO THINKING...
ABOUT WHAT?
ABOUT FACES IN THOSE WINDOWS, AND EYES IN THOSE FACES.
WHEN THEY LOOK OUT AT THE LIGHTS--LIGHTS LIKE IN HERE...

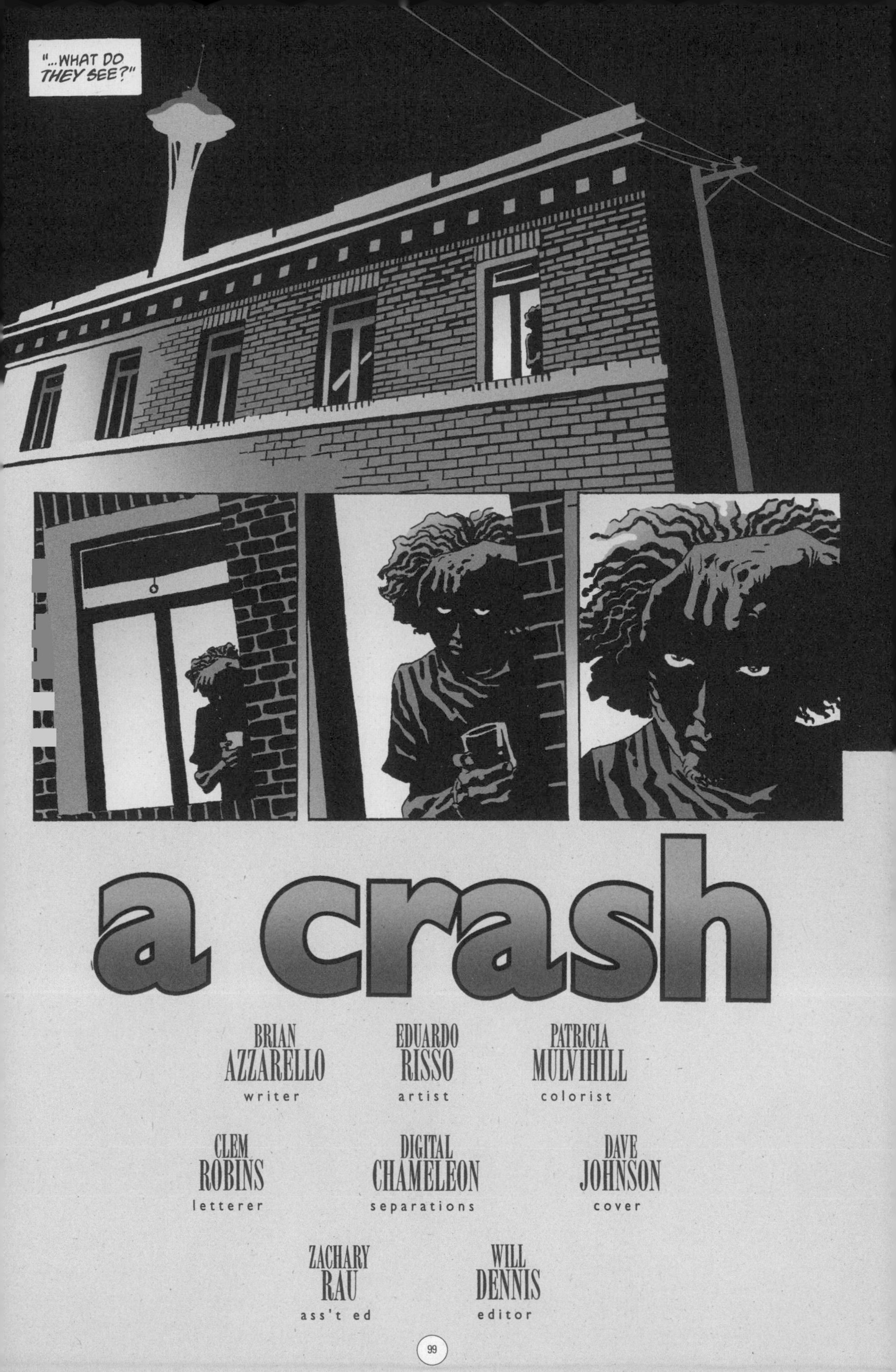
"...WHAT DO THEY SEE?"

a crash

BRIAN AZZARELLO
writer

EDUARDO RISSO
artist

PATRICIA MULVIHILL
colorist

CLEM ROBINS
letterer

DIGITAL CHAMELEON
separations

DAVE JOHNSON
cover

ZACHARY RAU
ass't ed

WILL DENNIS
editor

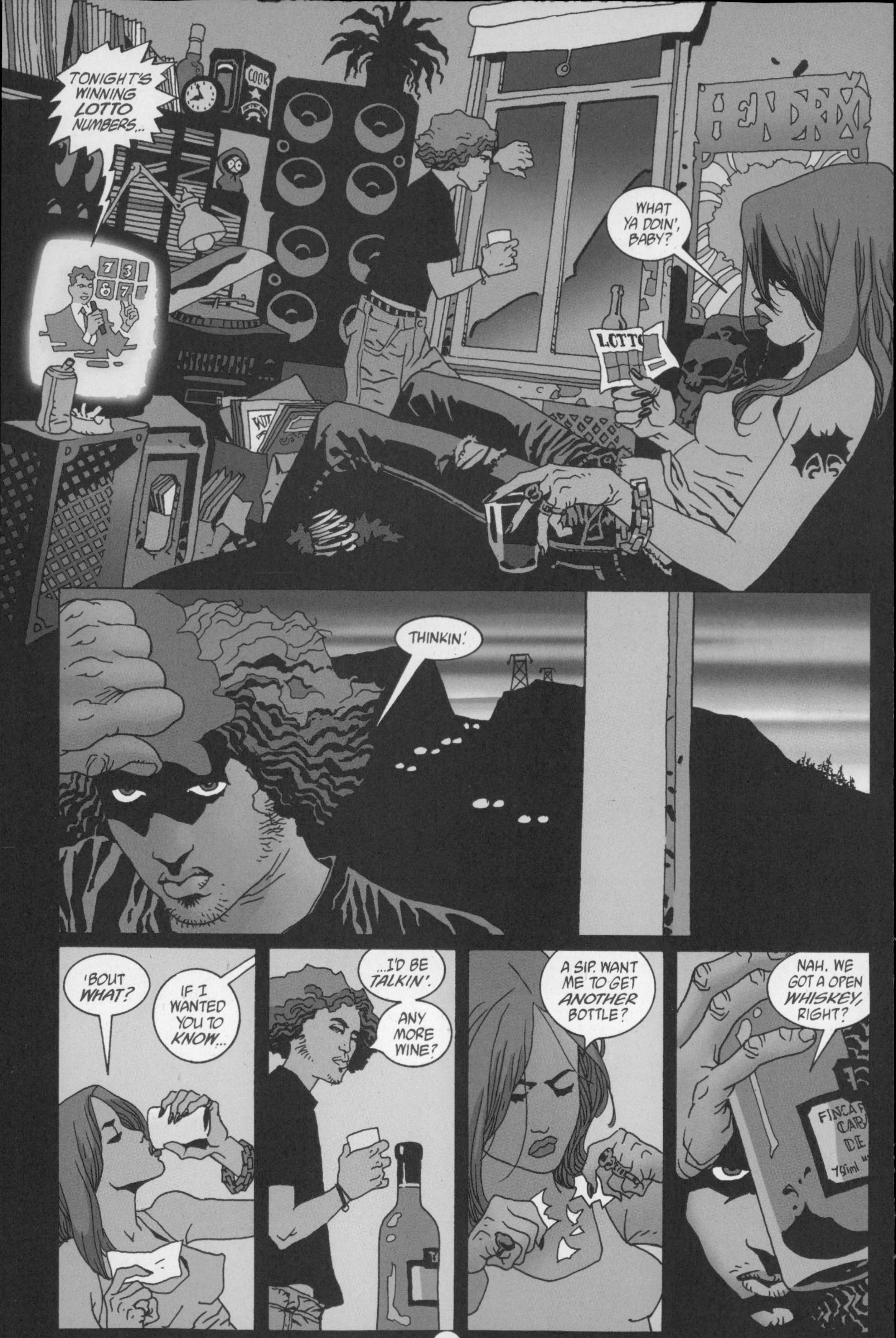

TONIGHT'S WINNING LOTTO NUMBERS...
WHAT YA DOIN', BABY?
LOTTO
THINKIN'.
'BOUT WHAT?
IF I WANTED YOU TO KNOW...
...I'D BE TALKIN'.
ANY MORE WINE?
A SIP. WANT ME TO GET ANOTHER BOTTLE?
NAH. WE GOT A OPEN WHISKEY, RIGHT?

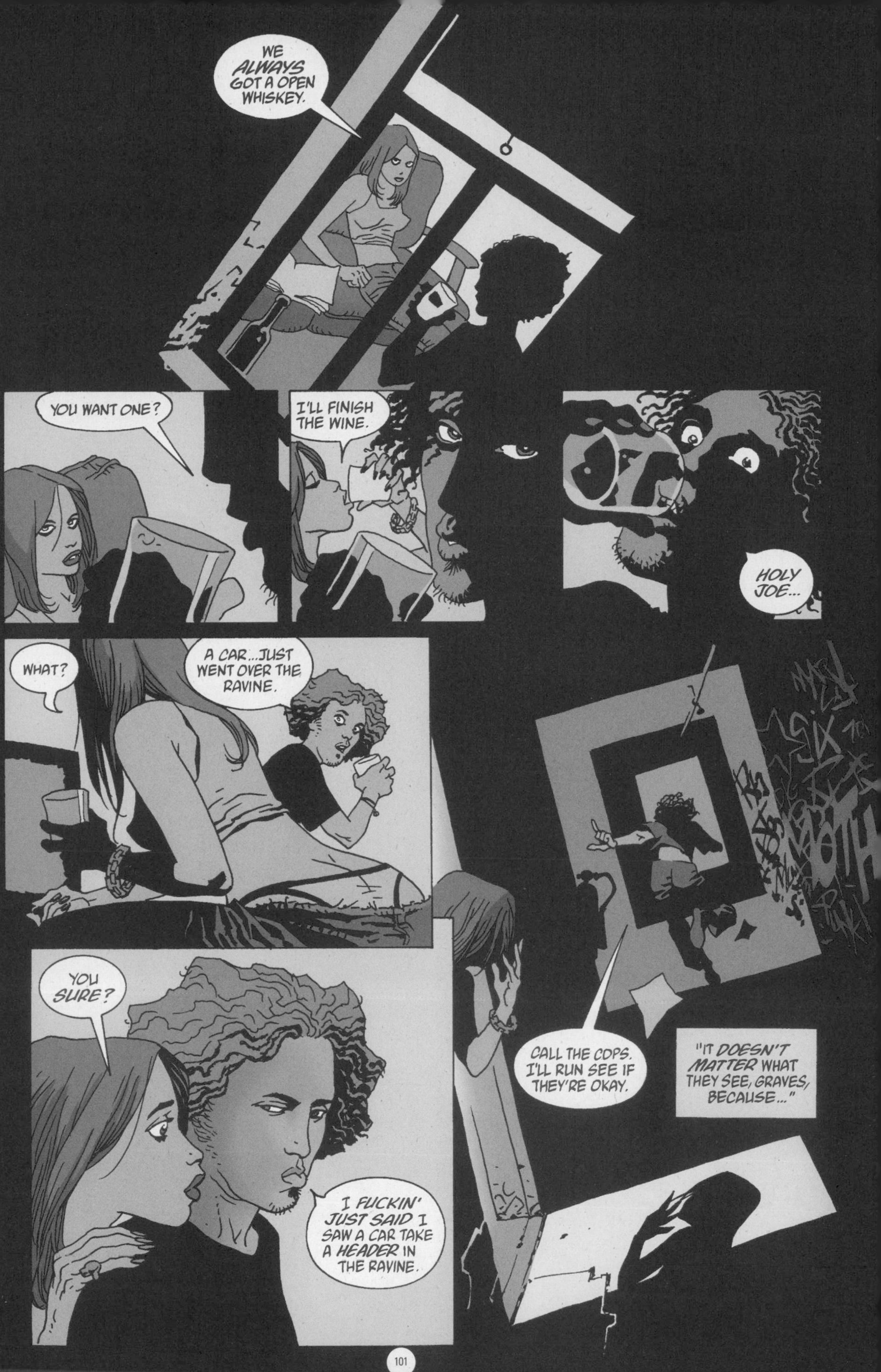
WE ALWAYS GOT A OPEN WHISKEY.
YOU WANT ONE?
I'LL FINISH THE WINE.
HOLY JOE...
WHAT?
A CAR...JUST WENT OVER THE RAVINE.
YOU SURE?
I FUCKIN' JUST SAID I SAW A CAR TAKE A HEADER IN THE RAVINE.
CALL THE COPS. I'LL RUN SEE IF THEY'RE OKAY.
"IT DOESN'T MATTER WHAT THEY SEE, GRAVES, BECAUSE..."

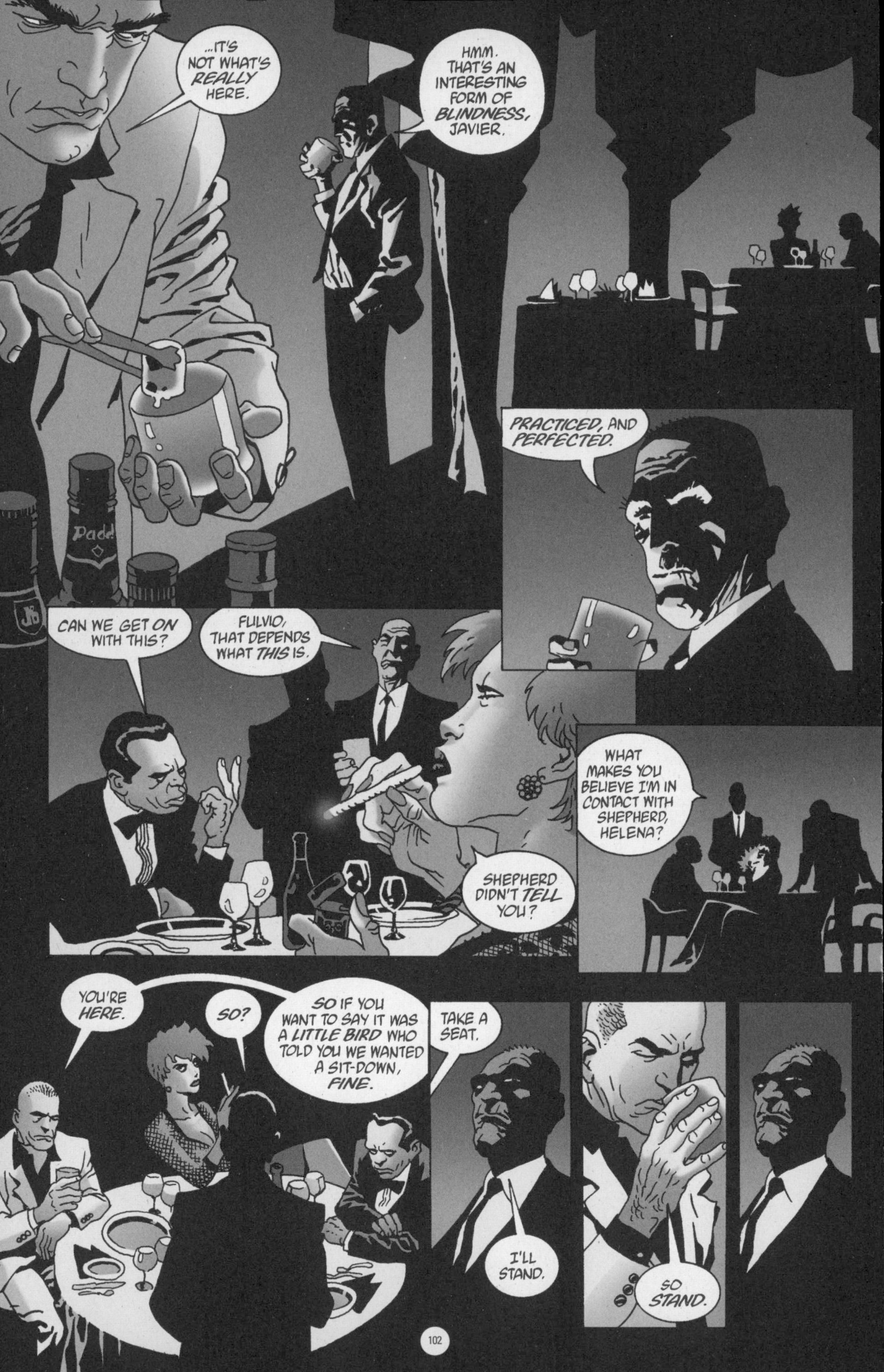
...IT'S NOT WHAT'S REALLY HERE.
HMM. THAT'S AN INTERESTING FORM OF BLINDNESS, JAVIER.
Padd
PRACTICED, AND PERFECTED.
CAN WE GET ON WITH THIS?
FULVIO, THAT DEPENDS WHAT THIS IS.
SHEPHERD DIDN'T TELL YOU?
WHAT MAKES YOU BELIEVE I'M IN CONTACT WITH SHEPHERD, HELENA?
YOU'RE HERE.
SO?
SO IF YOU WANT TO SAY IT WAS A LITTLE BIRD WHO TOLD YOU WE WANTED A SIT-DOWN, FINE.
TAKE A SEAT.
I'LL STAND.
SO STAND.

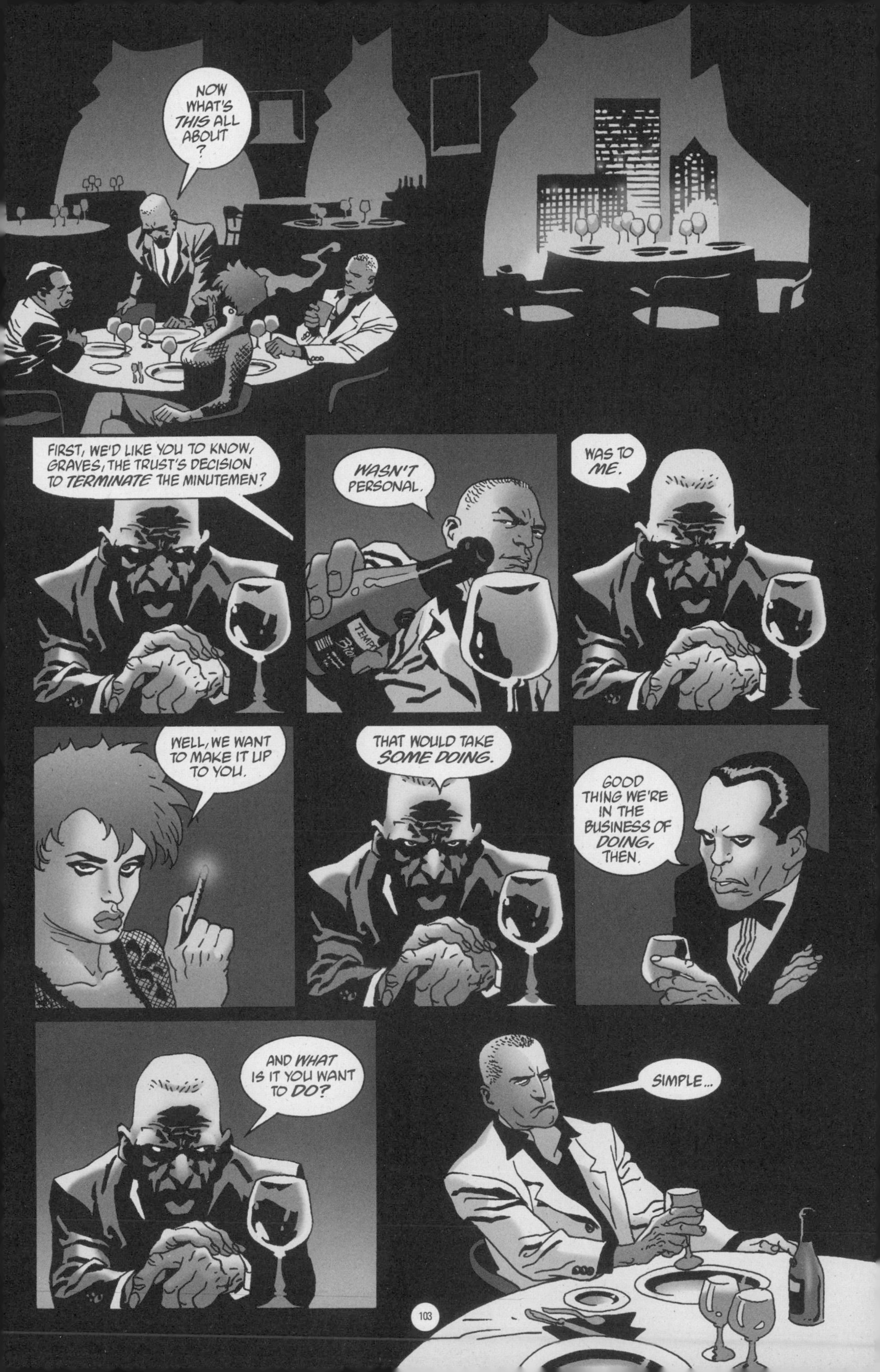
NOW WHAT'S THIS ALL ABOUT?
FIRST, WE'D LIKE YOU TO KNOW, GRAVES, THE TRUST'S DECISION TO TERMINATE THE MINUTEMEN?
WASN'T PERSONAL.
WAS TO ME.
WELL, WE WANT TO MAKE IT UP TO YOU.
THAT WOULD TAKE SOME DOING.
GOOD THING WE'RE IN THE BUSINESS OF DOING, THEN.
AND WHAT IS IT YOU WANT TO DO?
SIMPLE...

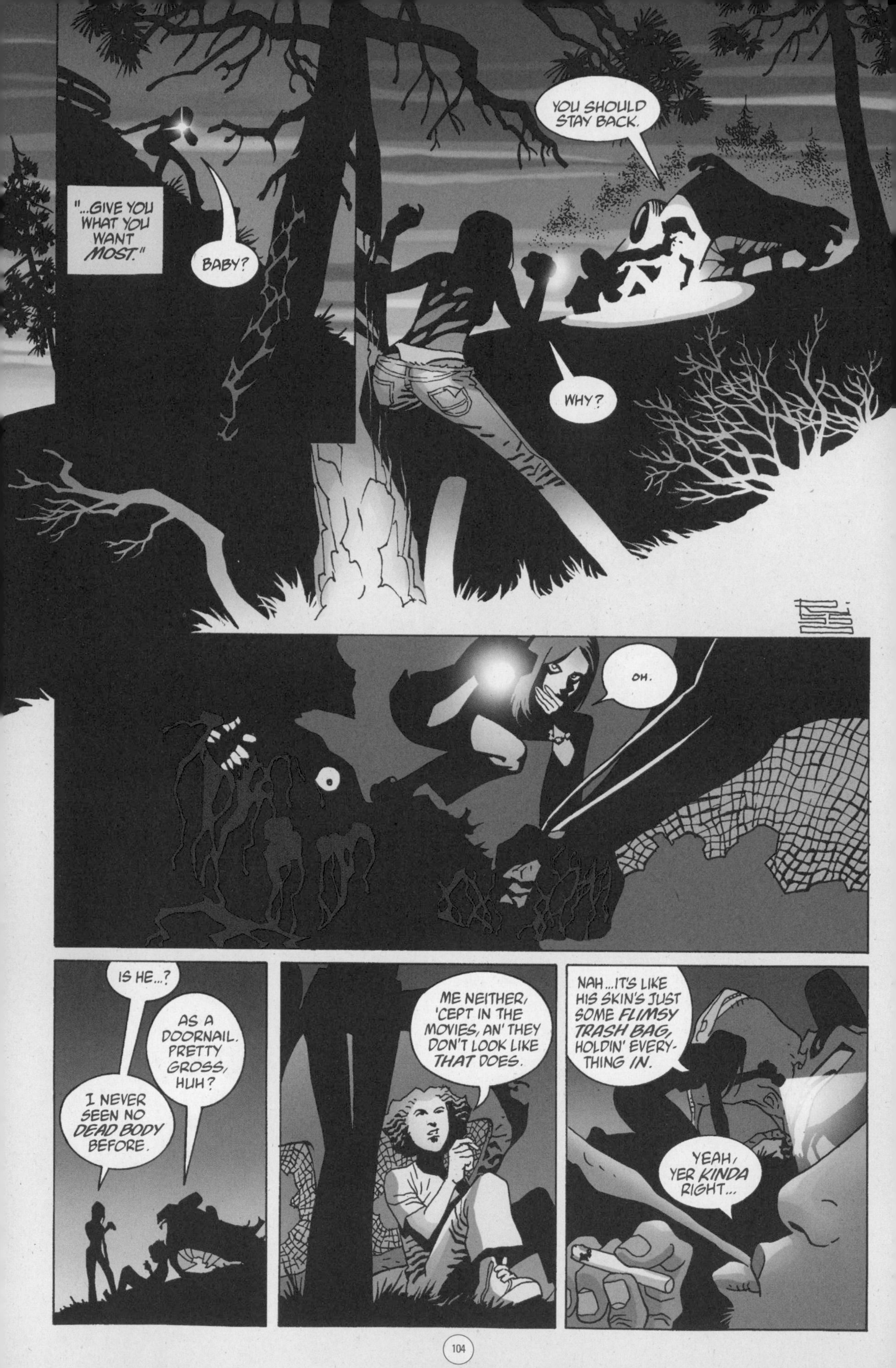
"...GIVE YOU WHAT YOU WANT *MOST.*"
BABY?
YOU SHOULD STAY BACK.
WHY?
OH.
IS HE...?
AS A DOORNAIL. PRETTY GROSS, HUH?
I NEVER SEEN NO *DEAD BODY* BEFORE.
ME NEITHER, 'CEPT IN THE MOVIES, AN' THEY DON'T LOOK LIKE *THAT* DOES.
NAH...IT'S LIKE HIS SKIN'S JUST SOME *FLIMSY TRASH BAG,* HOLDIN' EVERY-THING *IN.*
YEAH, YER *KINDA* RIGHT...

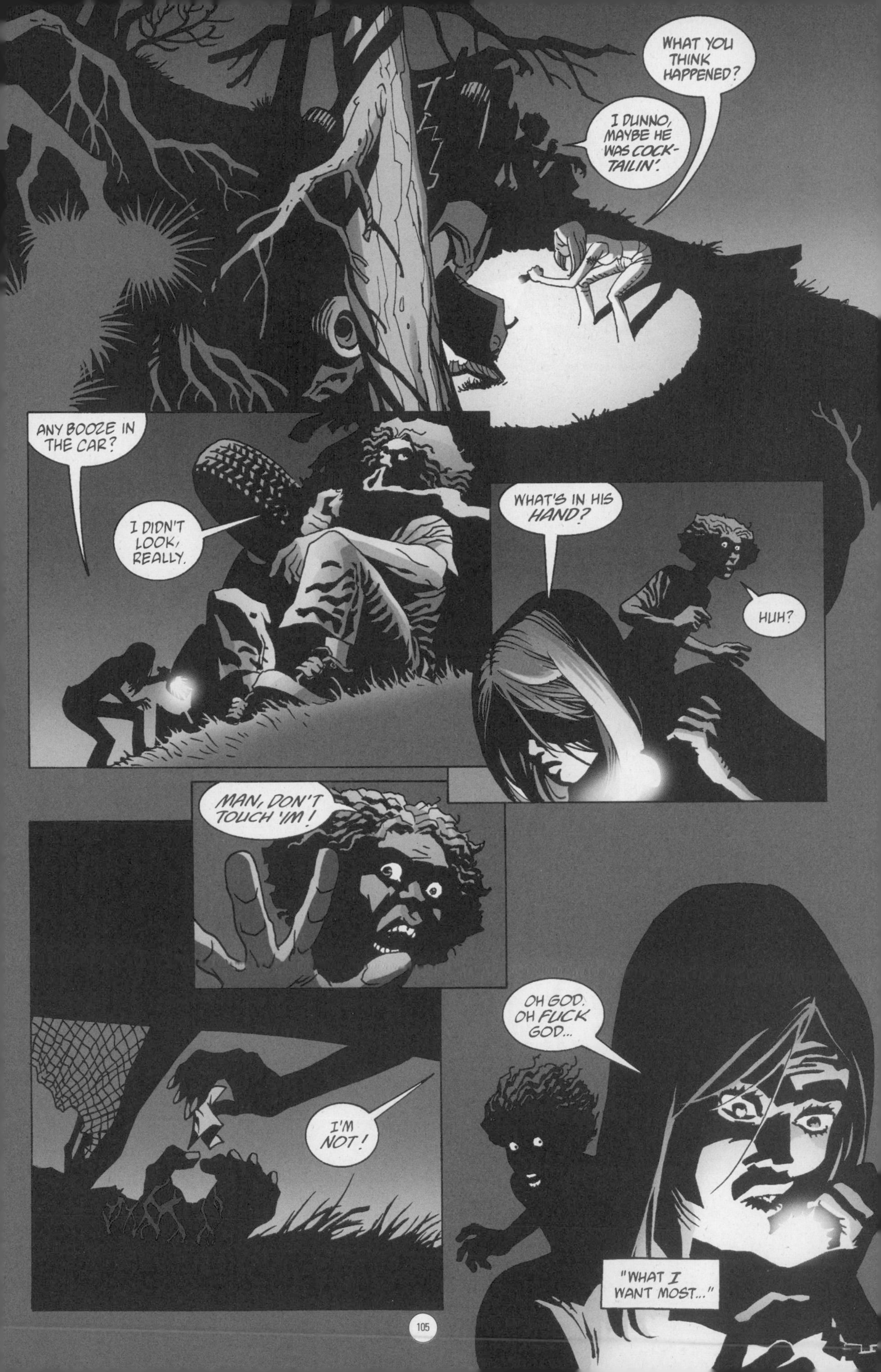
WHAT YOU THINK HAPPENED?
I DUNNO, MAYBE HE WAS COCK-TAILIN'.
ANY BOOZE IN THE CAR?
I DIDN'T LOOK, REALLY.
WHAT'S IN HIS HAND?
HUH?
MAN, DON'T TOUCH 'IM!
I'M NOT!
OH GOD. OH FUCK GOD...
"WHAT I WANT MOST..."

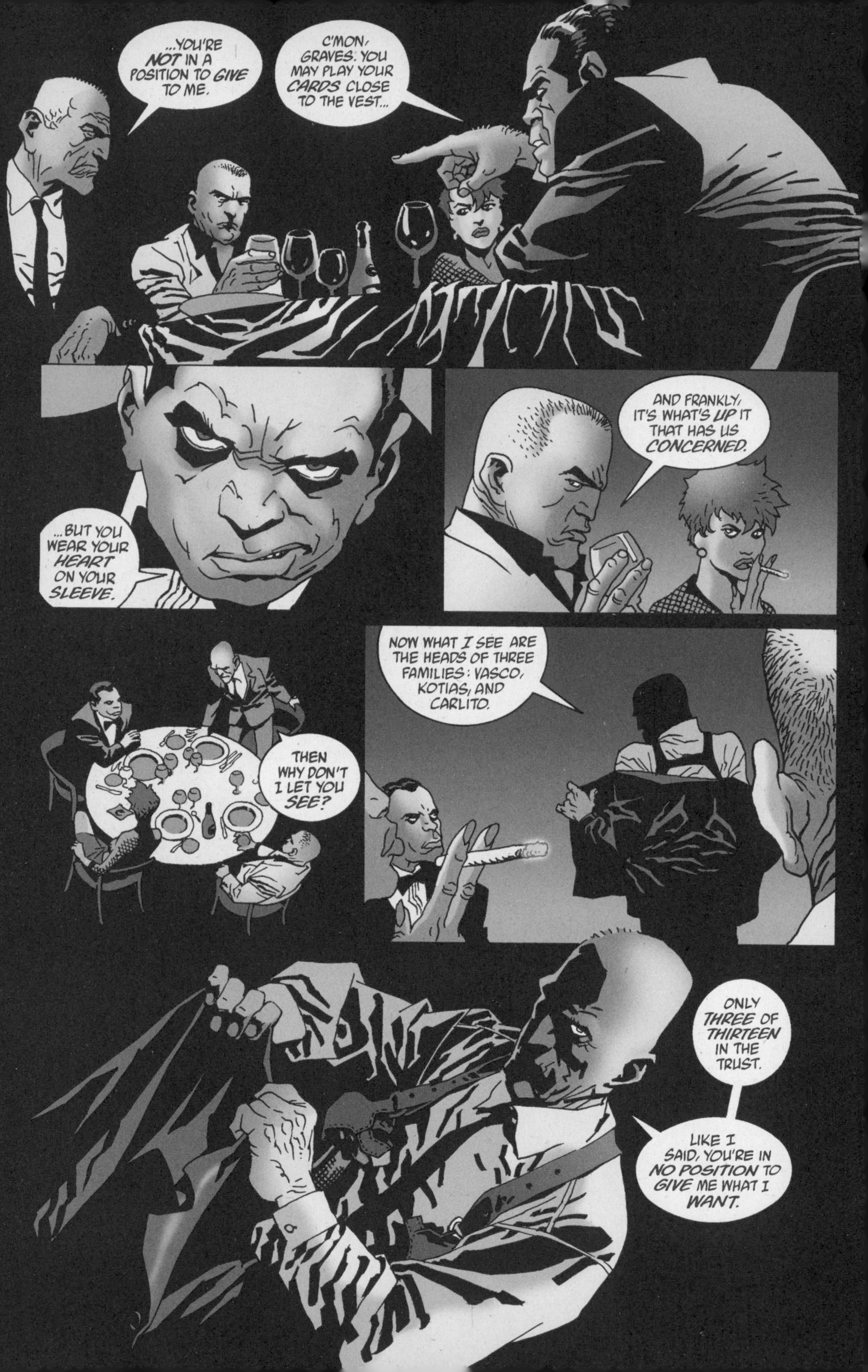

...YOU'RE NOT IN A POSITION TO GIVE TO ME.
C'MON, GRAVES: YOU MAY PLAY YOUR CARDS CLOSE TO THE VEST...
...BUT YOU WEAR YOUR HEART ON YOUR SLEEVE.
AND FRANKLY, IT'S WHAT'S UP IT THAT HAS US CONCERNED.
THEN WHY DON'T I LET YOU SEE?
NOW WHAT I SEE ARE THE HEADS OF THREE FAMILIES: VASCO, KOTIAS, AND CARLITO.
ONLY THREE OF THIRTEEN IN THE TRUST.
LIKE I SAID, YOU'RE IN NO POSITION TO GIVE ME WHAT I WANT.

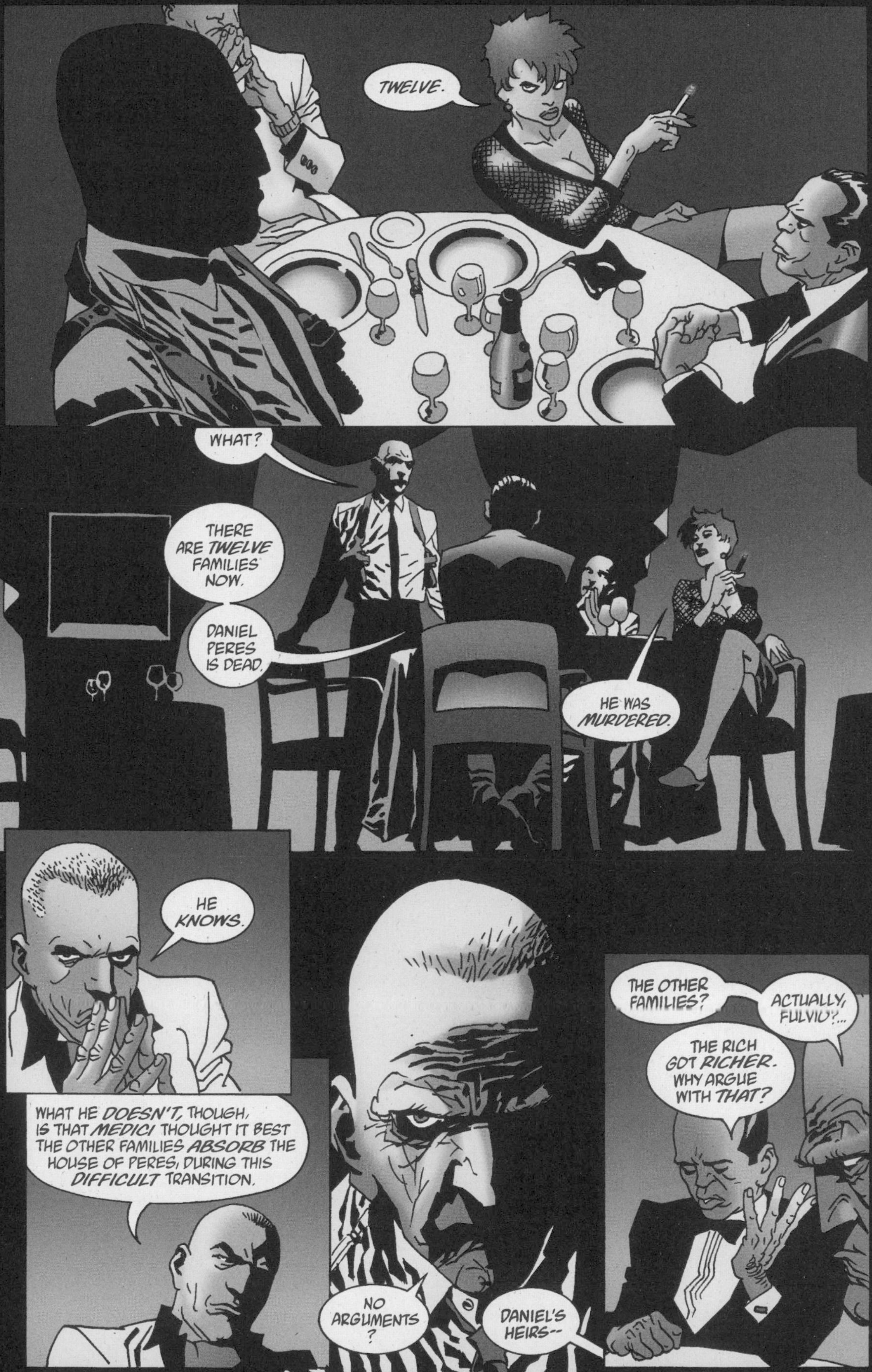
TWELVE.
WHAT?
THERE ARE TWELVE FAMILIES NOW.
DANIEL PERES IS DEAD.
HE WAS MURDERED.
HE KNOWS.
WHAT HE DOESN'T, THOUGH, IS THAT MEDICI THOUGHT IT BEST THE OTHER FAMILIES ABSORB THE HOUSE OF PERES, DURING THIS DIFFICULT TRANSITION.
NO ARGUMENTS ?
DANIEL'S HEIRS--
THE OTHER FAMILIES?
ACTUALLY, FULVIO?...
THE RICH GOT RICHER. WHY ARGUE WITH THAT?

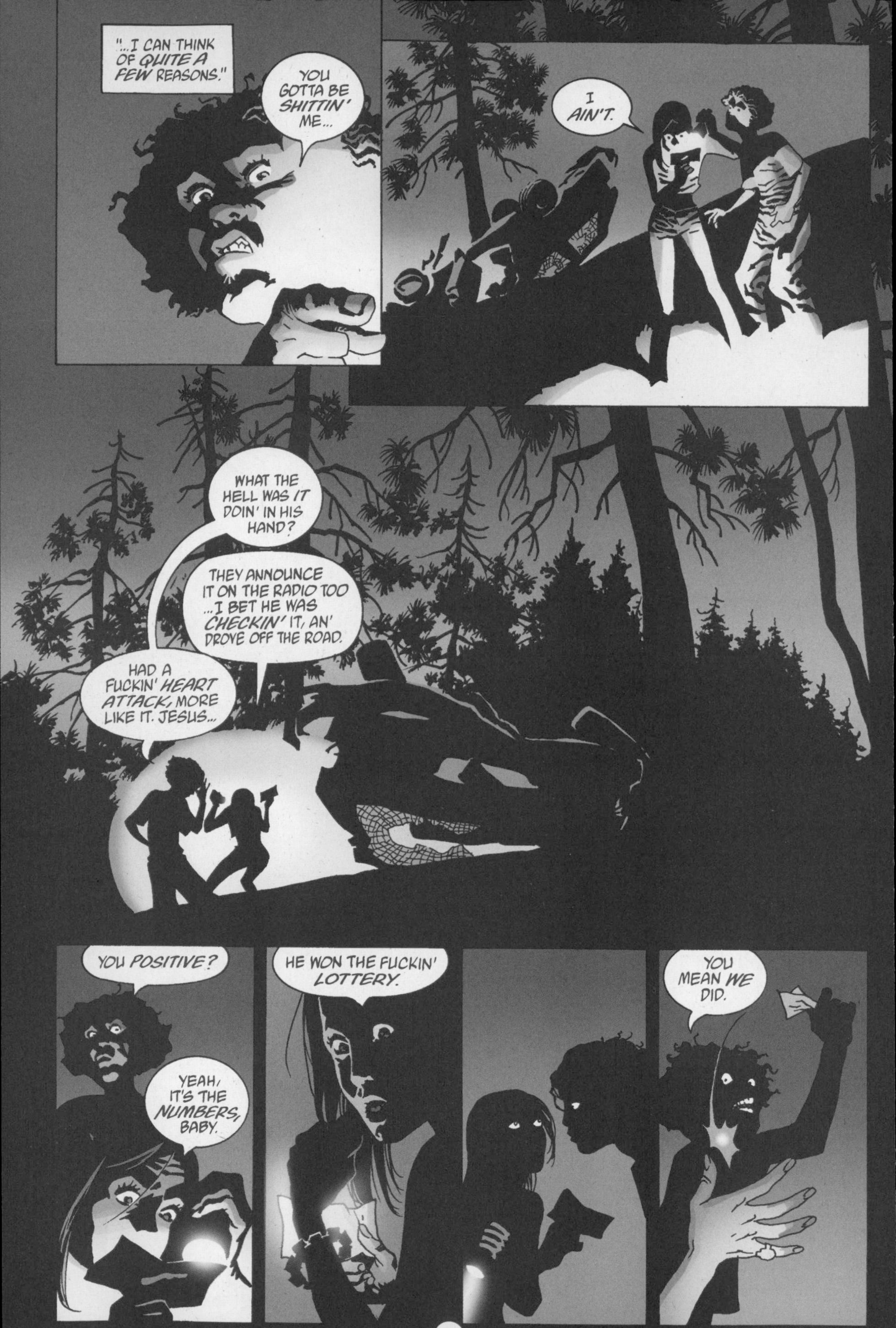
"...I CAN THINK OF QUITE A FEW REASONS."
YOU GOTTA BE SHITTIN' ME...
I AIN'T.
WHAT THE HELL WAS IT DOIN' IN HIS HAND?
THEY ANNOUNCE IT ON THE RADIO TOO ...I BET HE WAS CHECKIN' IT, AN' DROVE OFF THE ROAD.
HAD A FUCKIN' HEART ATTACK, MORE LIKE IT. JESUS...
YOU POSITIVE?
YEAH, IT'S THE NUMBERS, BABY.
HE WON THE FUCKIN' LOTTERY.
YOU MEAN WE DID.

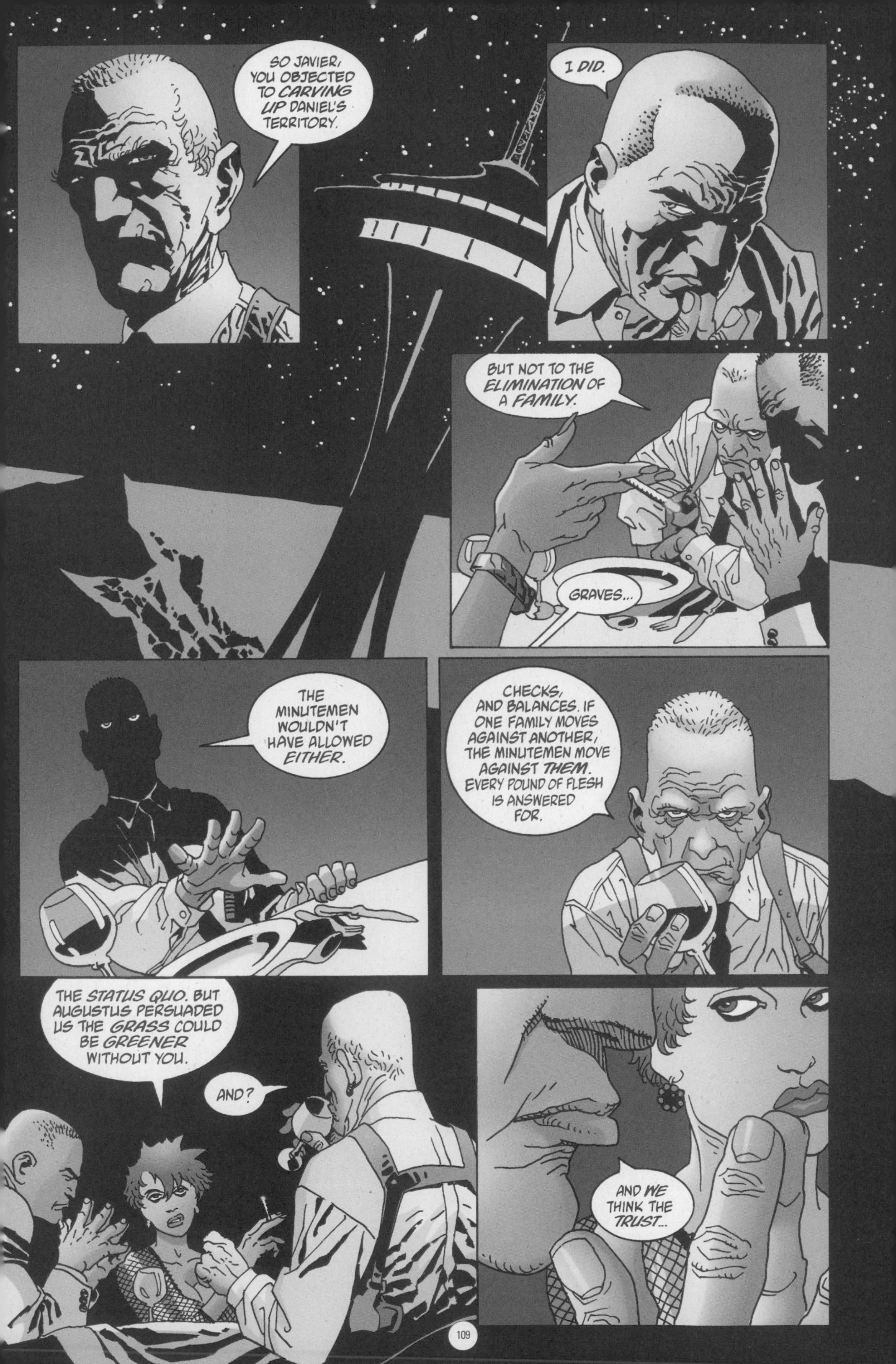
SO JAVIER, YOU OBJECTED TO CARVING UP DANIEL'S TERRITORY.
I DID.
BUT NOT TO THE ELIMINATION OF A FAMILY.
GRAVES...
THE MINUTEMEN WOULDN'T HAVE ALLOWED EITHER.
CHECKS, AND BALANCES. IF ONE FAMILY MOVES AGAINST ANOTHER, THE MINUTEMEN MOVE AGAINST THEM. EVERY POUND OF FLESH IS ANSWERED FOR.
THE STATUS QUO. BUT AUGUSTUS PERSUADED US THE GRASS COULD BE GREENER WITHOUT YOU.
AND?
AND WE THINK THE TRUST...

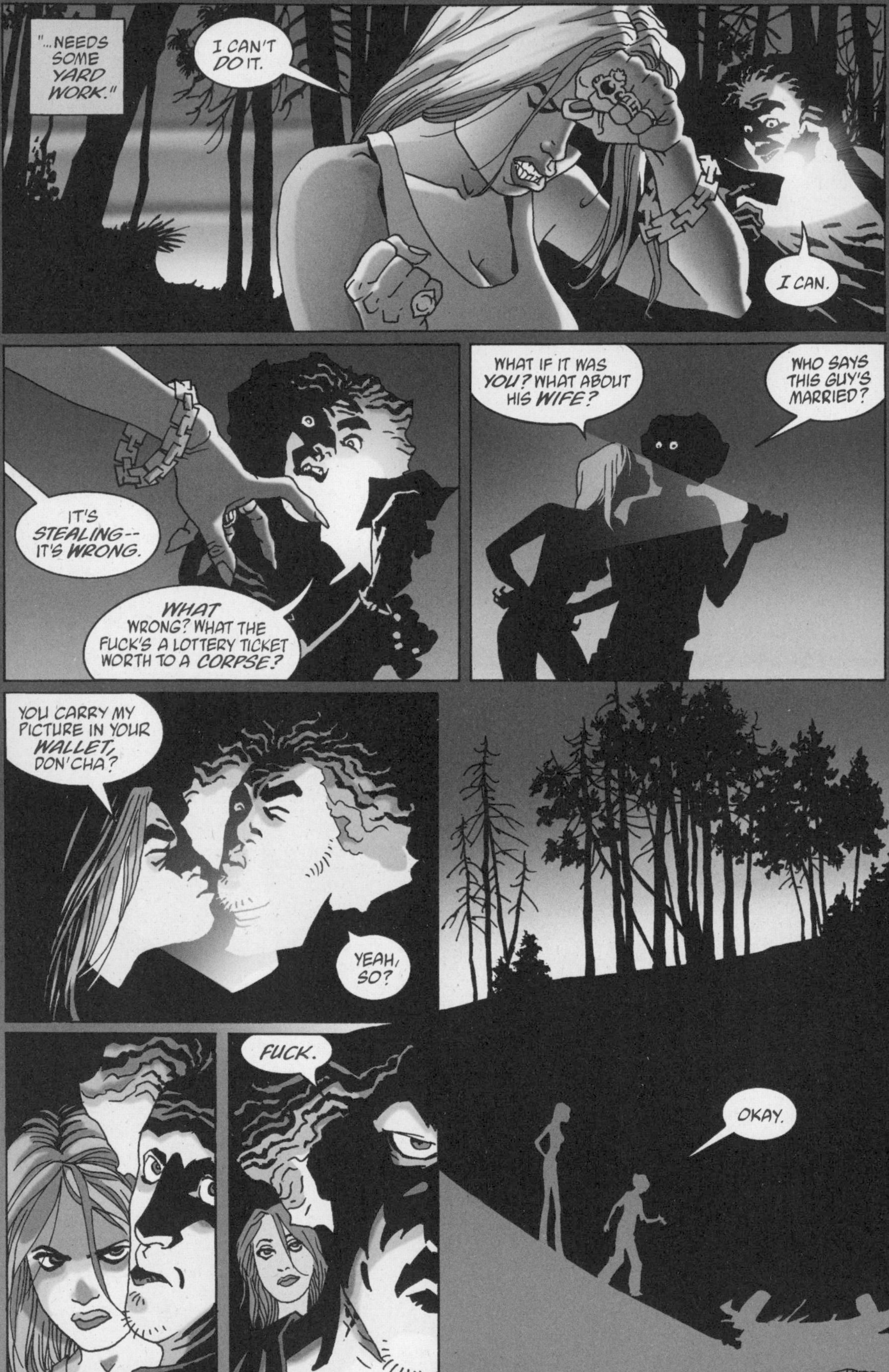
"...NEEDS SOME YARD WORK."
I CAN'T DO IT.
I CAN.
IT'S STEALING-- IT'S WRONG.
WHAT WRONG? WHAT THE FUCK'S A LOTTERY TICKET WORTH TO A CORPSE?
WHAT IF IT WAS YOU? WHAT ABOUT HIS WIFE?
WHO SAYS THIS GUY'S MARRIED?
YOU CARRY MY PICTURE IN YOUR WALLET, DON'CHA?
YEAH, SO?
FUCK.
OKAY.

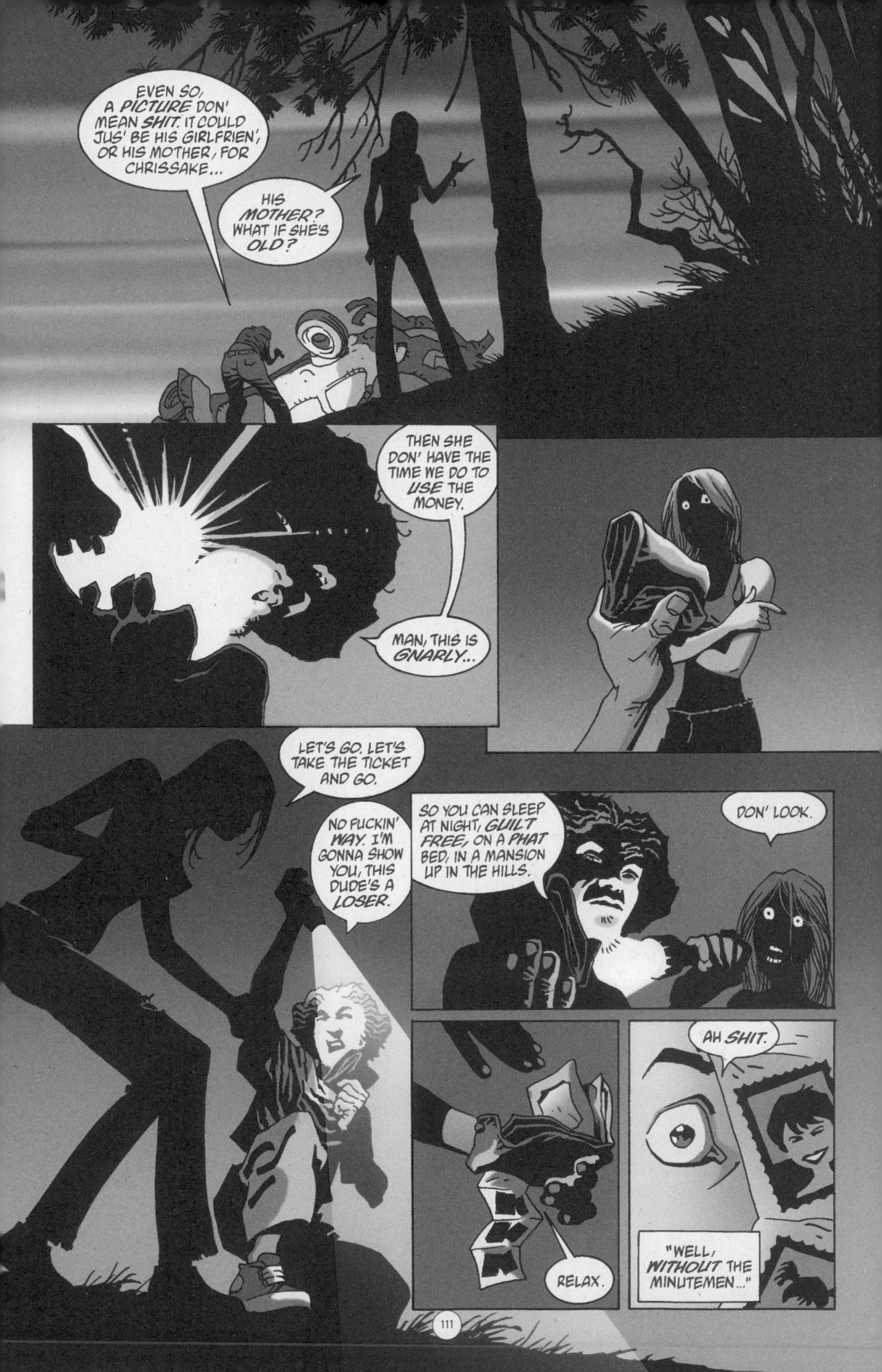
EVEN SO, A PICTURE DON' MEAN SHIT. IT COULD JUS' BE HIS GIRLFRIEN', OR HIS MOTHER, FOR CHRISSAKE...
HIS MOTHER? WHAT IF SHE'S OLD?
THEN SHE DON' HAVE THE TIME WE DO TO USE THE MONEY.
MAN, THIS IS GNARLY...
LET'S GO. LET'S TAKE THE TICKET AND GO.
NO FUCKIN' WAY. I'M GONNA SHOW YOU, THIS DUDE'S A LOSER.
SO YOU CAN SLEEP AT NIGHT, GUILT FREE, ON A PHAT BED, IN A MANSION UP IN THE HILLS.
DON' LOOK.
AH SHIT.
RELAX.
"WELL, WITHOUT THE MINUTEMEN..."

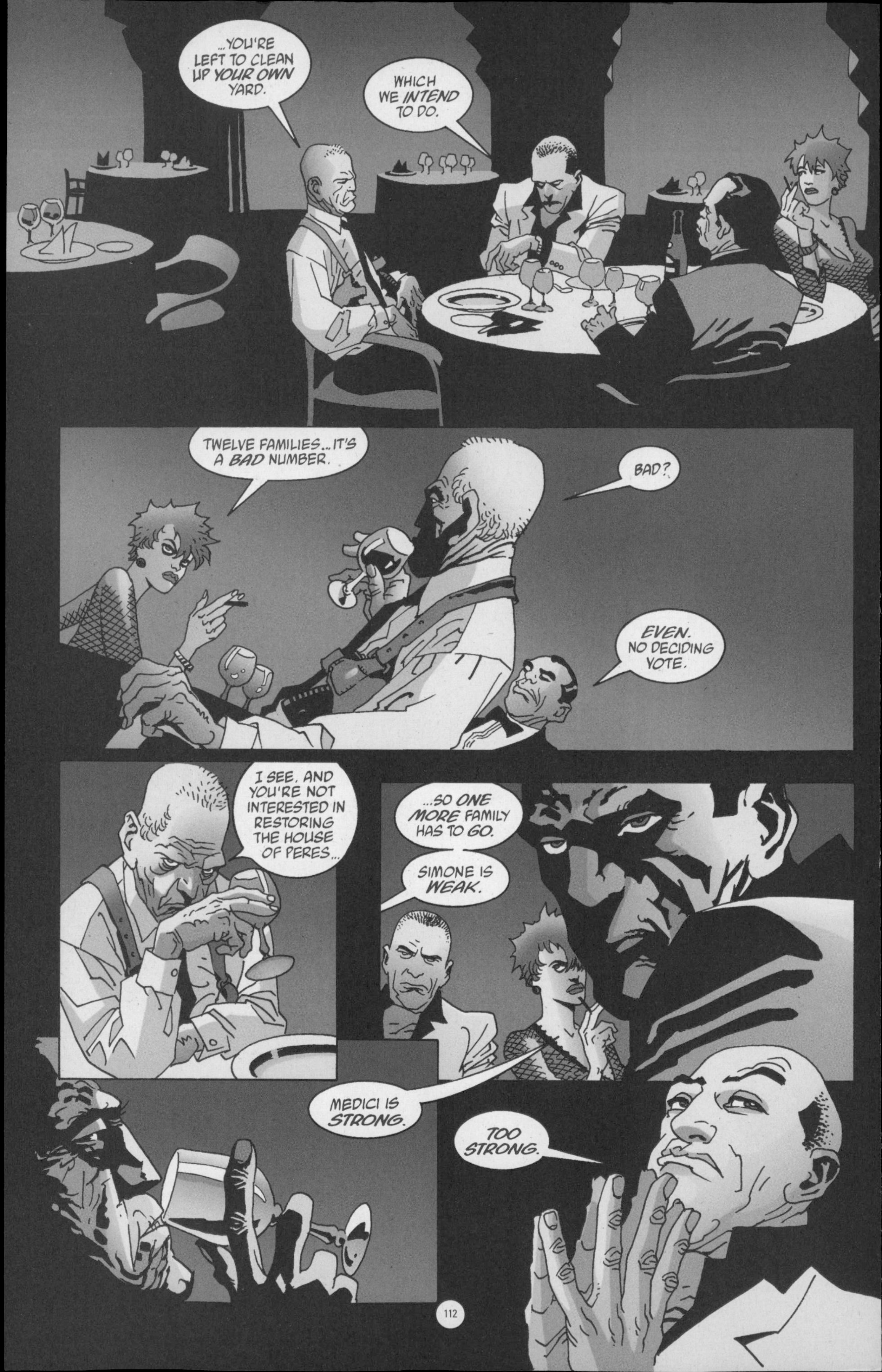
...YOU'RE LEFT TO CLEAN UP YOUR OWN YARD.
WHICH WE INTEND TO DO.
TWELVE FAMILIES... IT'S A BAD NUMBER.
BAD?
EVEN. NO DECIDING VOTE.
I SEE. AND YOU'RE NOT INTERESTED IN RESTORING THE HOUSE OF PERES...
...SO ONE MORE FAMILY HAS TO GO.
SIMONE IS WEAK.
MEDICI IS STRONG.
TOO STRONG.

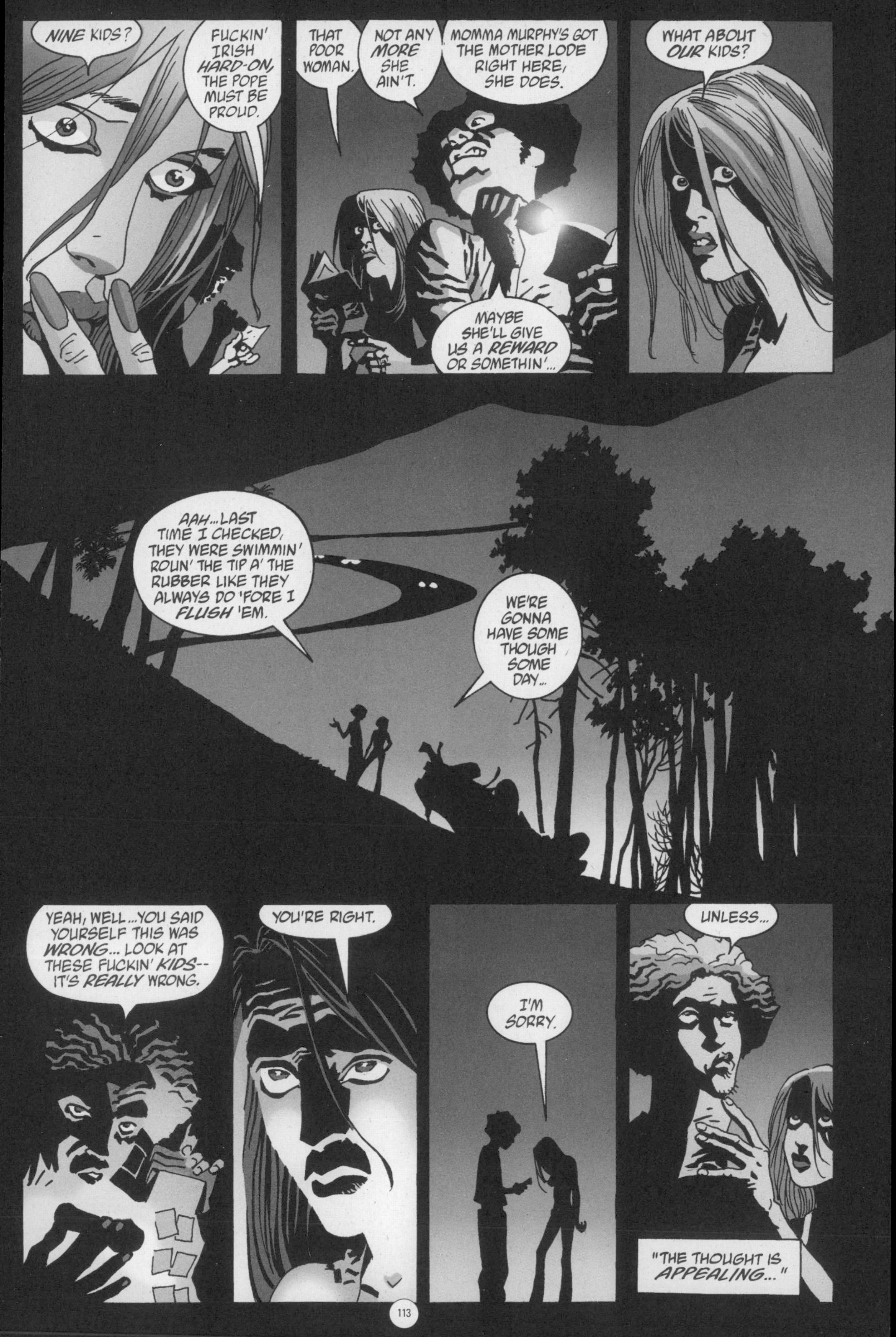
NINE KIDS?
FUCKIN' IRISH HARD-ON, THE POPE MUST BE PROUD.
THAT POOR WOMAN.
NOT ANY MORE SHE AIN'T.
MOMMA MURPHY'S GOT THE MOTHER LODE RIGHT HERE, SHE DOES.
MAYBE SHE'LL GIVE US A REWARD OR SOMETHIN'...
WHAT ABOUT OUR KIDS?
AAH...LAST TIME I CHECKED, THEY WERE SWIMMIN' ROUN' THE TIP A' THE RUBBER LIKE THEY ALWAYS DO 'FORE I FLUSH 'EM.
WE'RE GONNA HAVE SOME THOUGH SOME DAY...
YEAH, WELL...YOU SAID YOURSELF THIS WAS WRONG... LOOK AT THESE FUCKIN' KIDS-- IT'S REALLY WRONG.
YOU'RE RIGHT.
I'M SORRY.
UNLESS...
"THE THOUGHT IS APPEALING..."

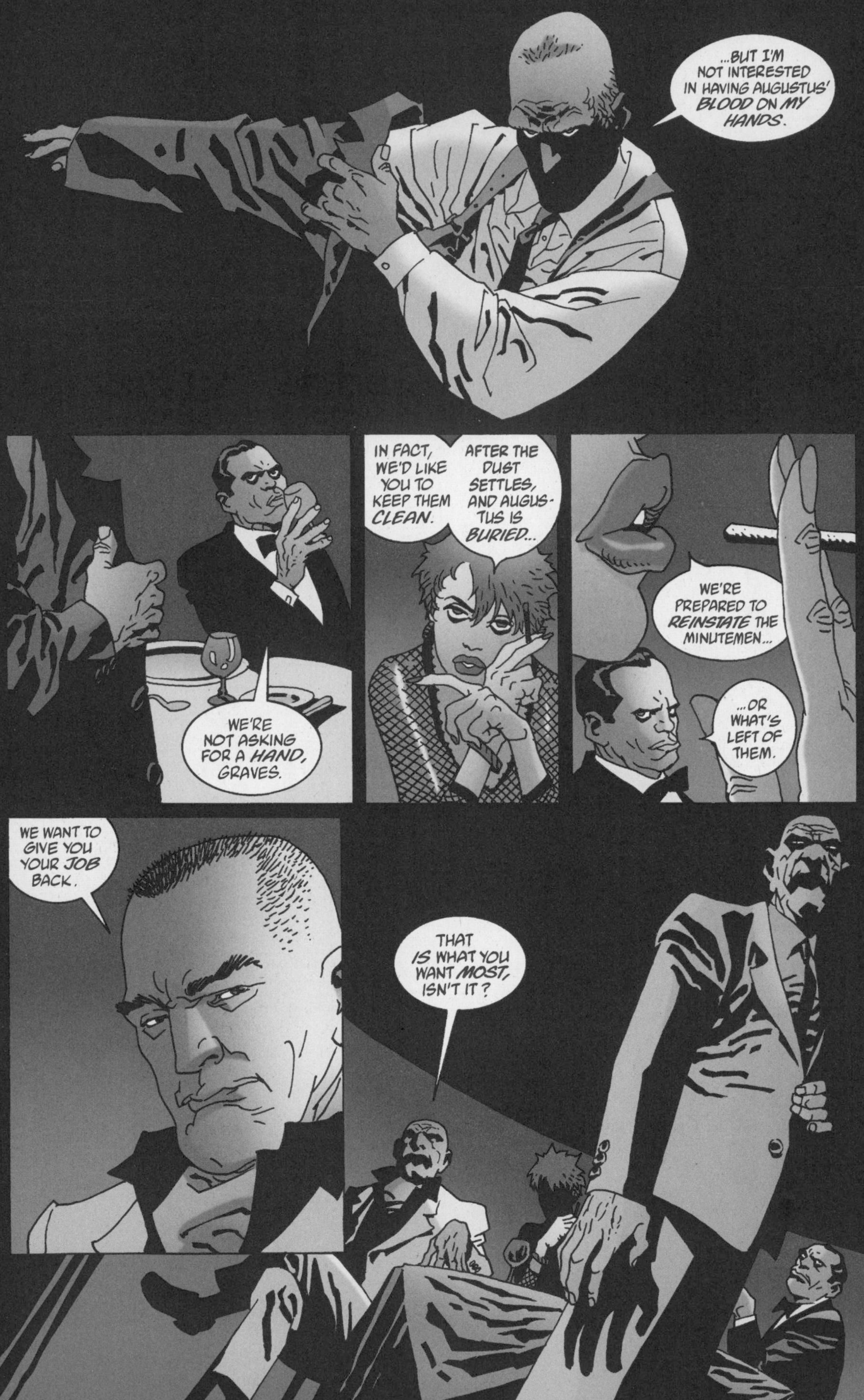
...BUT I'M NOT INTERESTED IN HAVING AUGUSTUS' BLOOD ON MY HANDS.
WE'RE NOT ASKING FOR A HAND, GRAVES.
IN FACT, WE'D LIKE YOU TO KEEP THEM CLEAN.
AFTER THE DUST SETTLES, AND AUGUSTUS IS BURIED...
WE'RE PREPARED TO REINSTATE THE MINUTEMEN...
...OR WHAT'S LEFT OF THEM.
WE WANT TO GIVE YOU YOUR JOB BACK.
THAT IS WHAT YOU WANT MOST, ISN'T IT?

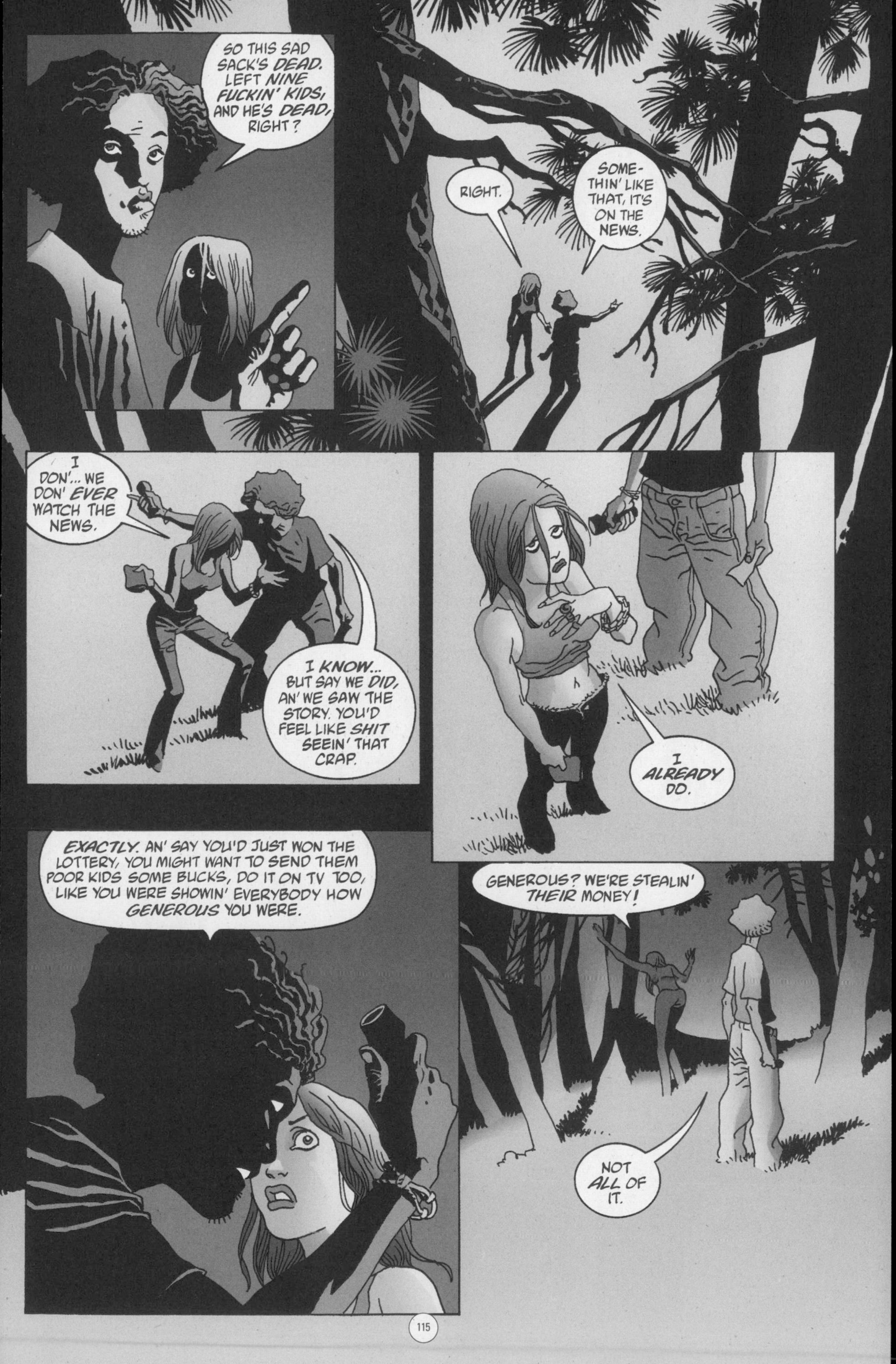

SO THIS SAD SACK'S DEAD. LEFT NINE FUCKIN' KIDS, AND HE'S DEAD, RIGHT?
RIGHT.
SOME-THIN' LIKE THAT, IT'S ON THE NEWS.
I DON'... WE DON' EVER WATCH THE NEWS.
I KNOW... BUT SAY WE DID, AN' WE SAW THE STORY. YOU'D FEEL LIKE SHIT SEEIN' THAT CRAP.
I ALREADY DO.
EXACTLY. AN' SAY YOU'D JUST WON THE LOTTERY, YOU MIGHT WANT TO SEND THEM POOR KIDS SOME BUCKS, DO IT ON TV TOO, LIKE YOU WERE SHOWIN' EVERYBODY HOW GENEROUS YOU WERE.
GENEROUS? WE'RE STEALIN' THEIR MONEY!
NOT ALL OF IT.

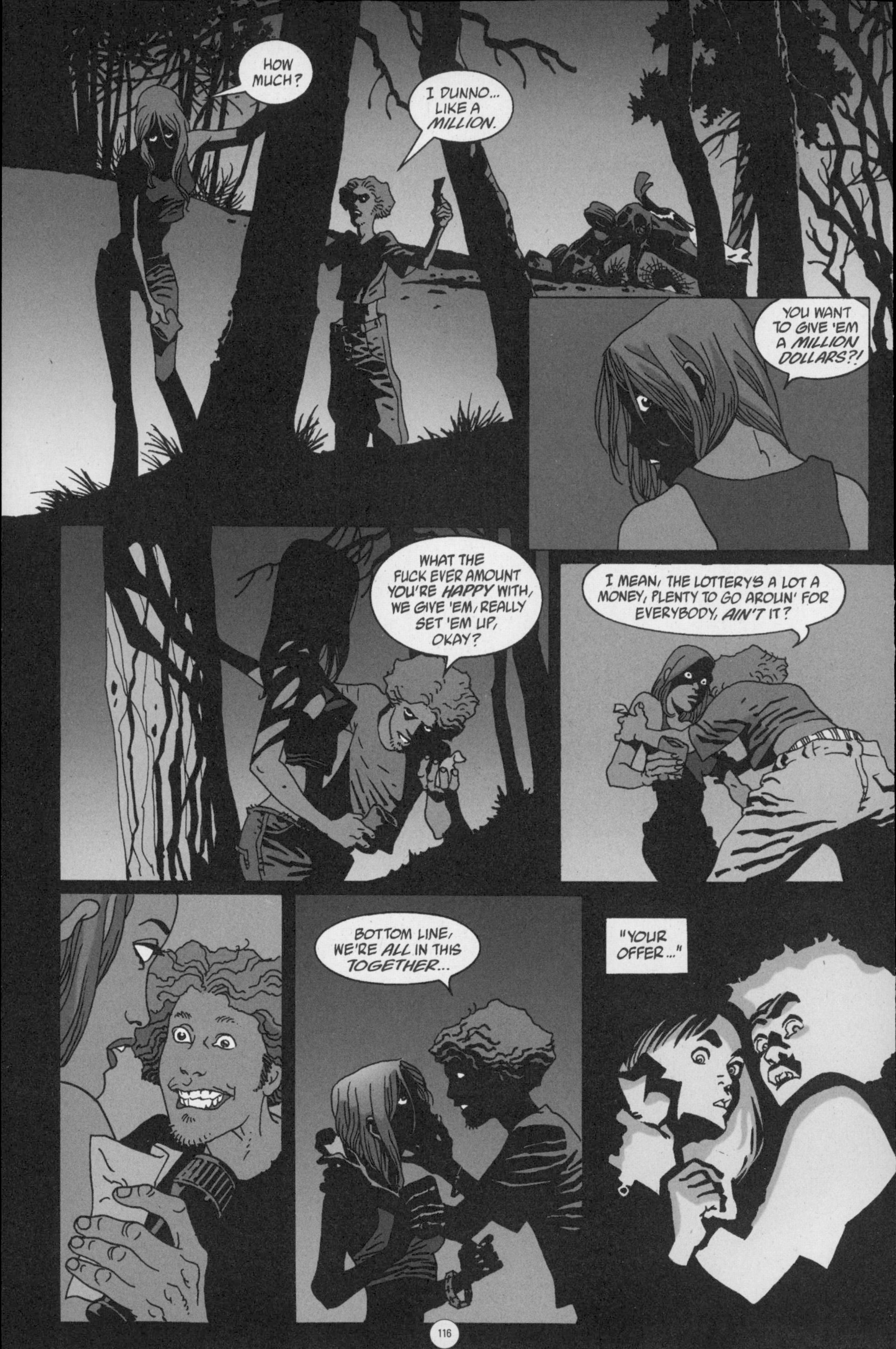
HOW MUCH?
I DUNNO... LIKE A *MILLION.*
YOU WANT TO GIVE 'EM A *MILLION DOLLARS?!*
WHAT THE FUCK EVER AMOUNT YOU'RE *HAPPY* WITH, WE GIVE 'EM, REALLY SET 'EM UP, OKAY?
I MEAN, THE LOTTERY'S A LOT A MONEY, PLENTY TO GO AROUN' FOR EVERYBODY, *AIN'T* IT?
BOTTOM LINE, WE'RE *ALL* IN THIS *TOGETHER...*
"YOUR OFFER..."

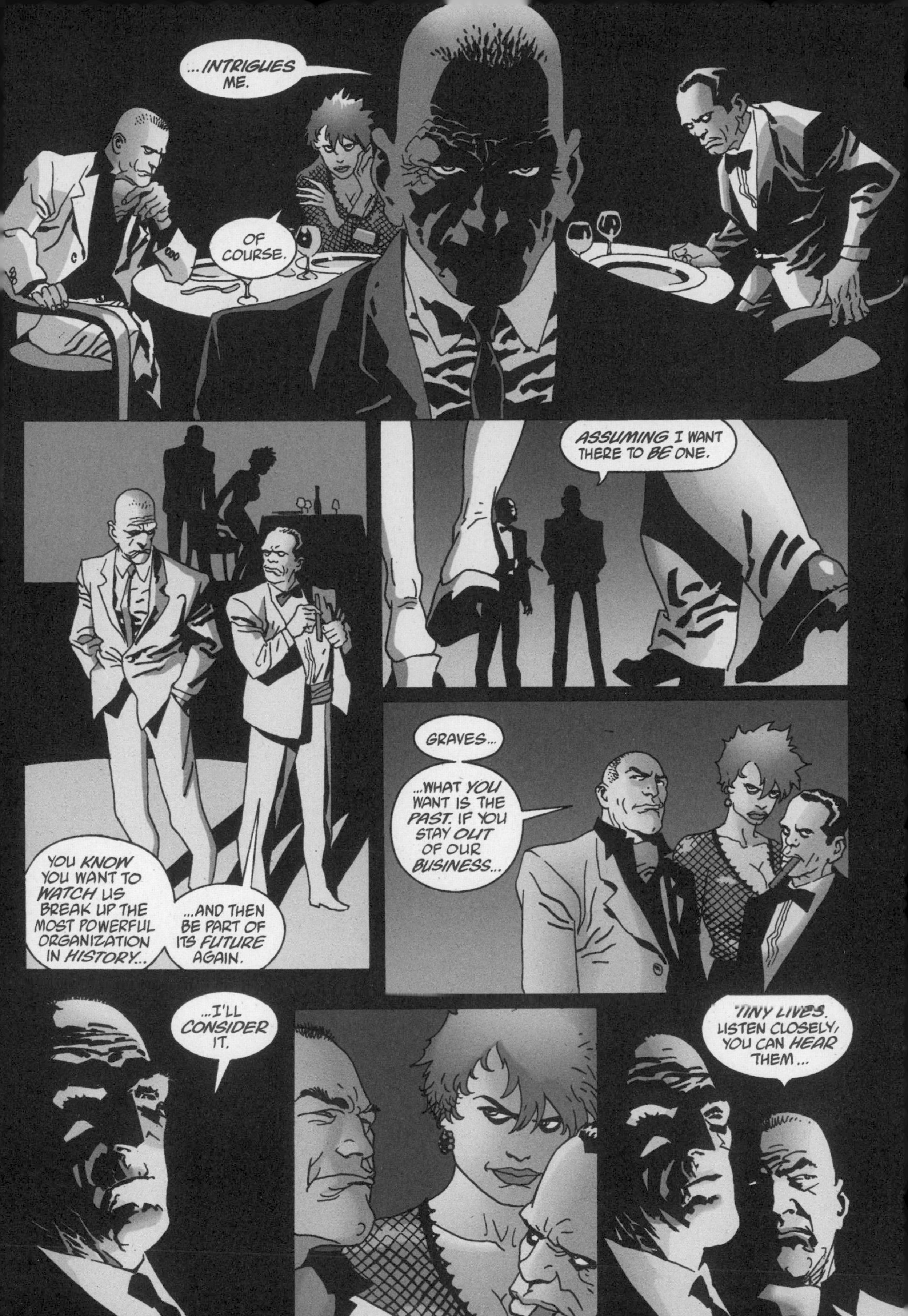
...INTRIGUES ME.
OF COURSE.
ASSUMING I WANT THERE TO BE ONE.
YOU KNOW YOU WANT TO WATCH US BREAK UP THE MOST POWERFUL ORGANIZATION IN HISTORY...
...AND THEN BE PART OF ITS FUTURE AGAIN.
GRAVES...
...WHAT YOU WANT IS THE PAST. IF YOU STAY OUT OF OUR BUSINESS...
...I'LL CONSIDER IT.
TINY LIVES. LISTEN CLOSELY, YOU CAN HEAR THEM...

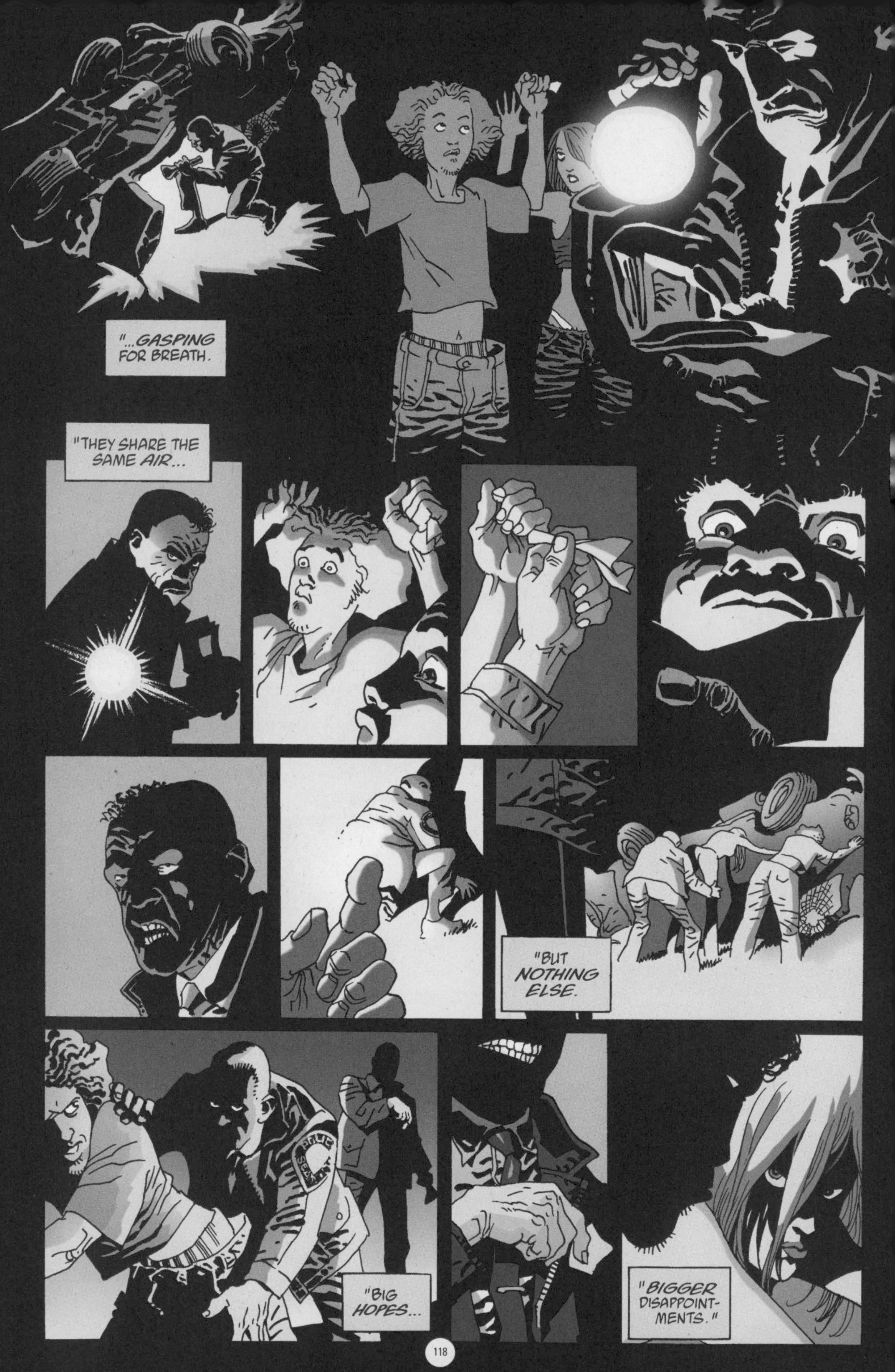
"...GASPING FOR BREATH.
"THEY SHARE THE SAME AIR...
"BUT NOTHING ELSE.
"BIG HOPES...
"BIGGER DISAPPOINT-MENTS."

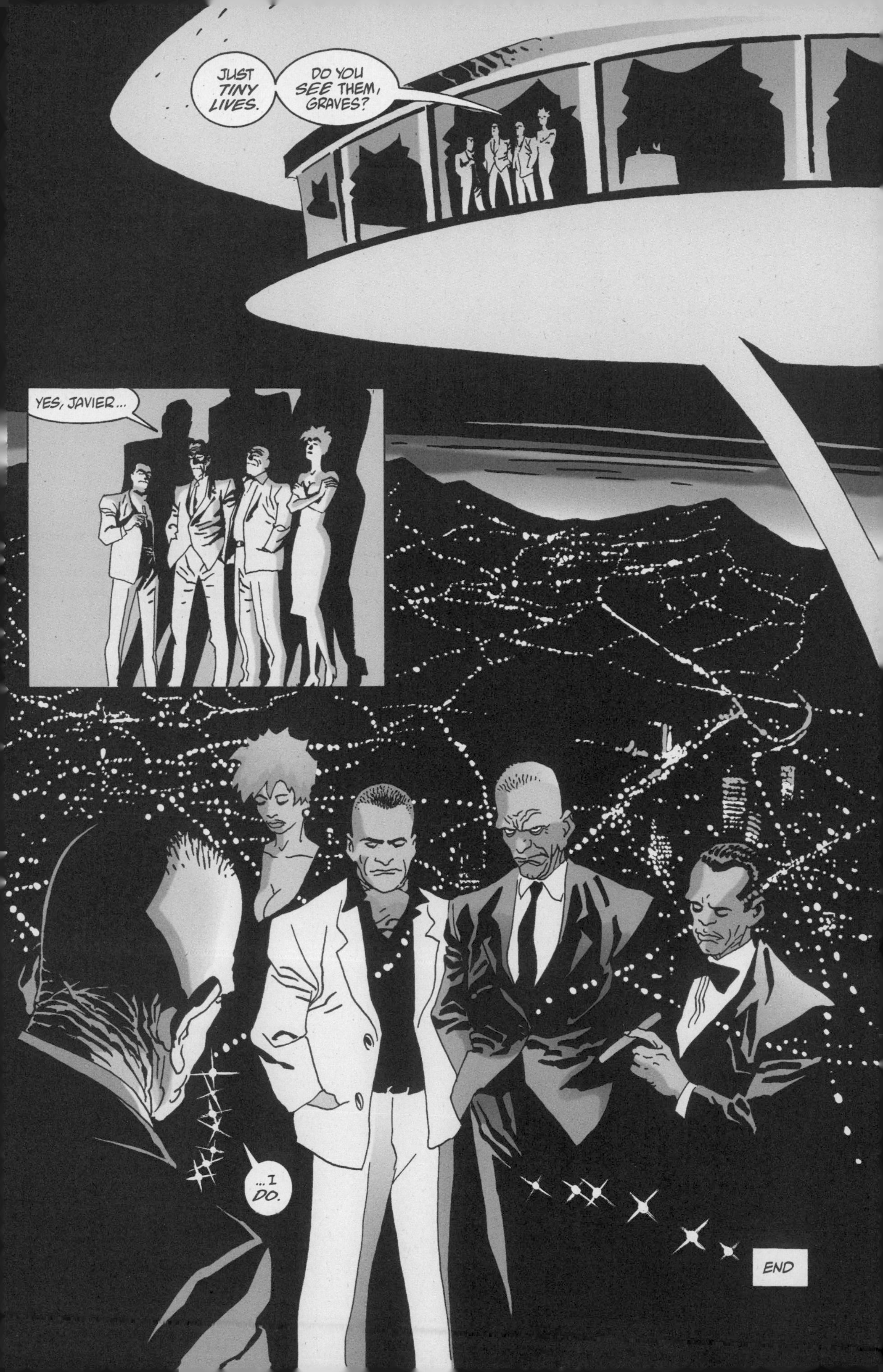
JUST TINY LIVES.
DO YOU SEE THEM, GRAVES?
YES, JAVIER...
...I DO.
END

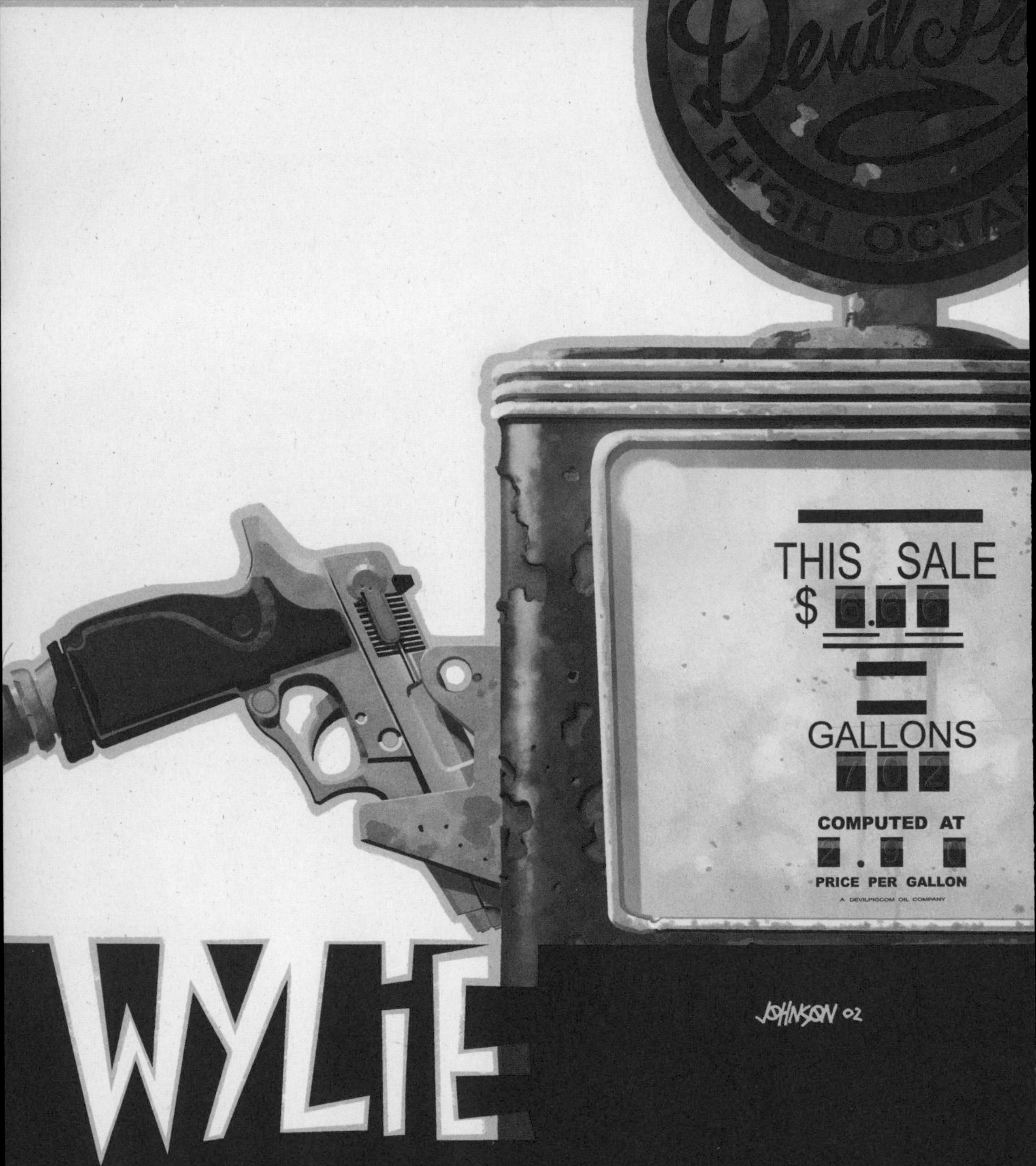

HIGH OCTA
THIS SALE
$ 6.66
GALLONS
7 0 2
COMPUTED AT
2 . 6 0
PRICE PER GALLON
A DEVILPIGCOM OIL COMPANY
WYLIE
JOHNSON 02

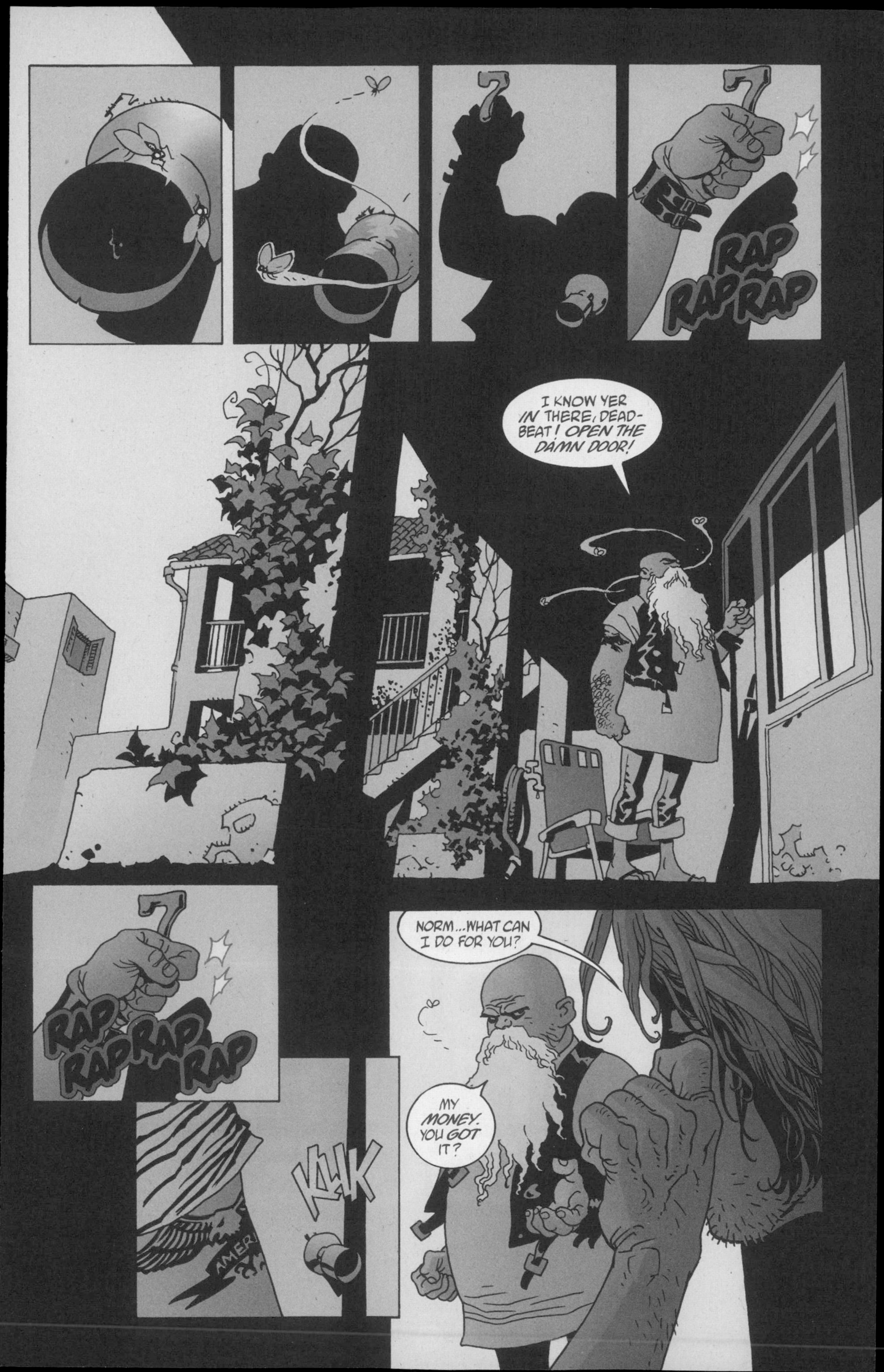
RAP
RAP RAP
I KNOW YER IN THERE, DEAD-BEAT! OPEN THE DAMN DOOR!
RAP RAP RAP RAP
KLIK
NORM...WHAT CAN I DO FOR YOU?
MY MONEY. YOU GOT IT?

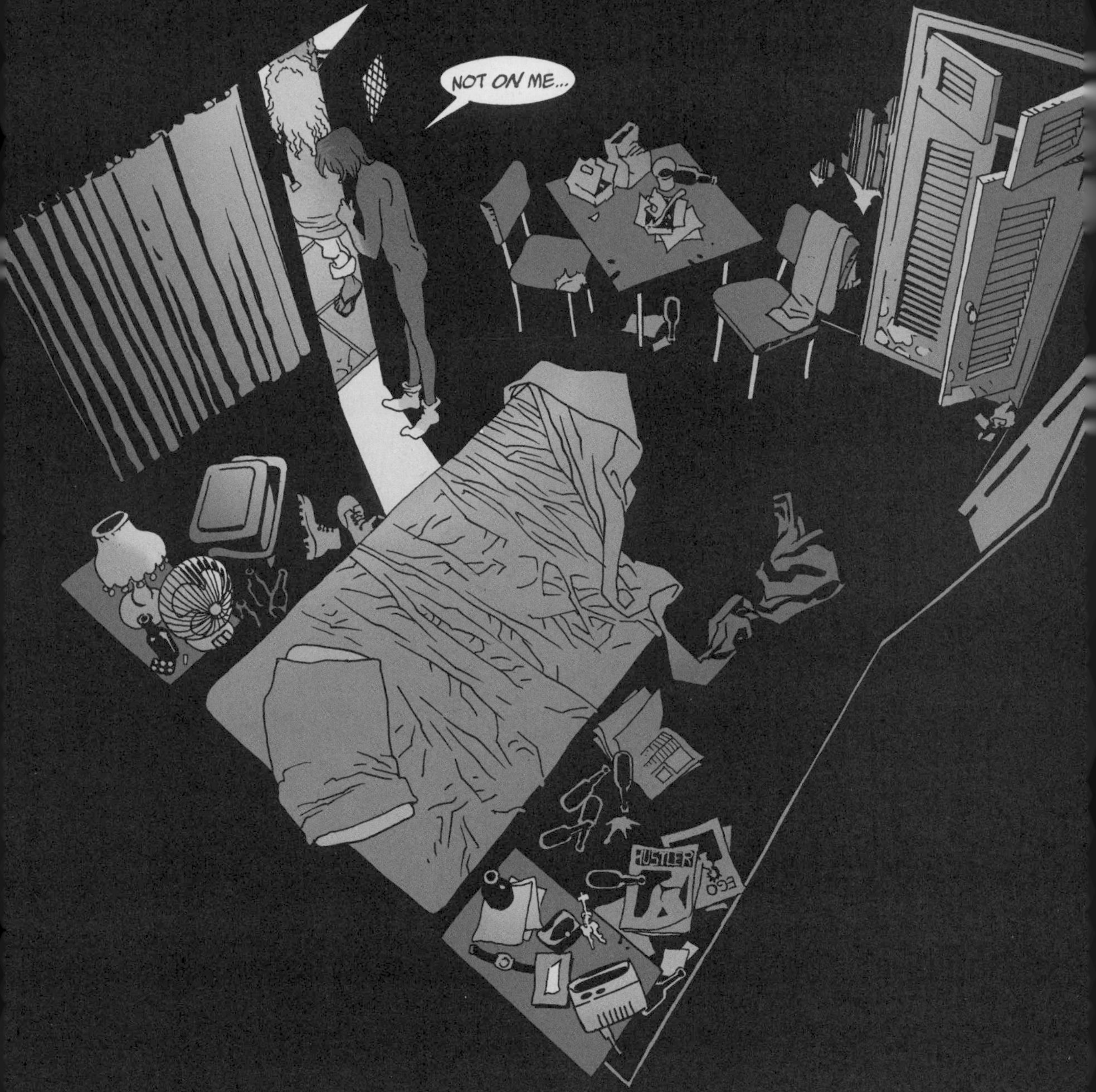
NOT ON ME...
HUSTLER
EGO

POINT OFF THE EDGE

BRIAN AZZARELLO WRITER
EDUARDO RISSO ARTIST
PATRICIA MULVIHILL COLORIST
CLEM ROBINS LETTERER
ZYLONOL SEPARATIONS
DAVE JOHNSON COVER
ZACHARY RAU ASS'T ED
WILL DENNIS EDITOR

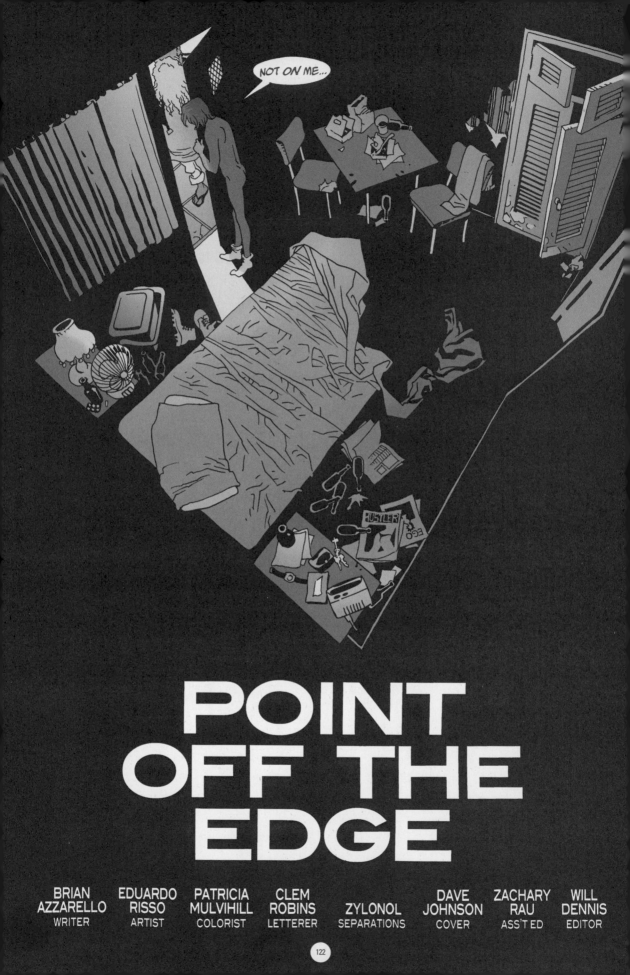

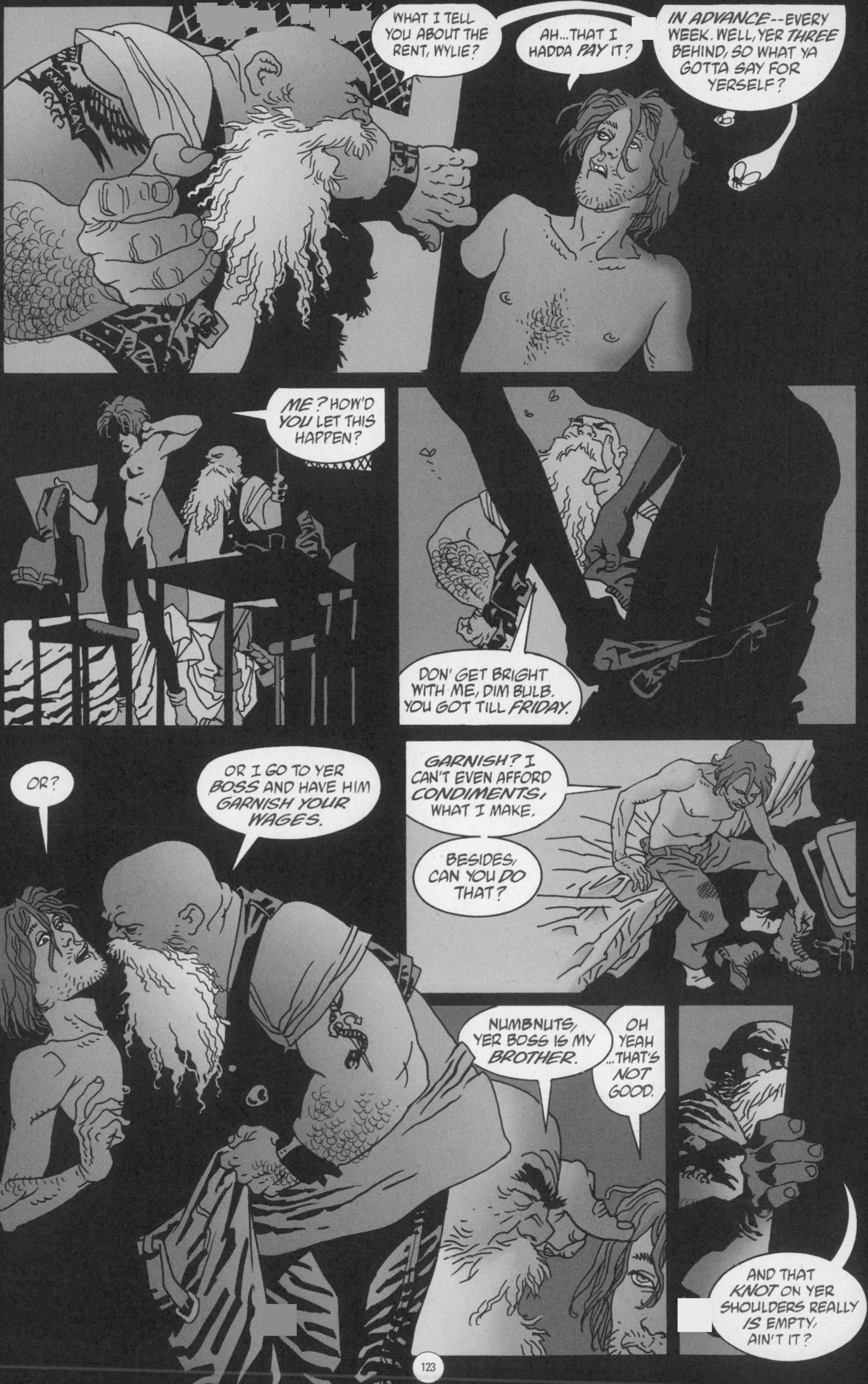

WHAT I TELL YOU ABOUT THE RENT, WYLIE?
AH...THAT I HADDA PAY IT?
IN ADVANCE--EVERY WEEK. WELL, YER THREE BEHIND, SO WHAT YA GOTTA SAY FOR YERSELF?
ME? HOW'D YOU LET THIS HAPPEN?
DON' GET BRIGHT WITH ME, DIM BULB. YOU GOT TILL FRIDAY.
OR?
OR I GO TO YER BOSS AND HAVE HIM GARNISH YOUR WAGES.
GARNISH? I CAN'T EVEN AFFORD CONDIMENTS, WHAT I MAKE.
BESIDES, CAN YOU DO THAT?
NUMBNUTS, YER BOSS IS MY BROTHER.
OH YEAH ...THAT'S NOT GOOD.
AND THAT KNOT ON YER SHOULDERS REALLY IS EMPTY, AIN'T IT?

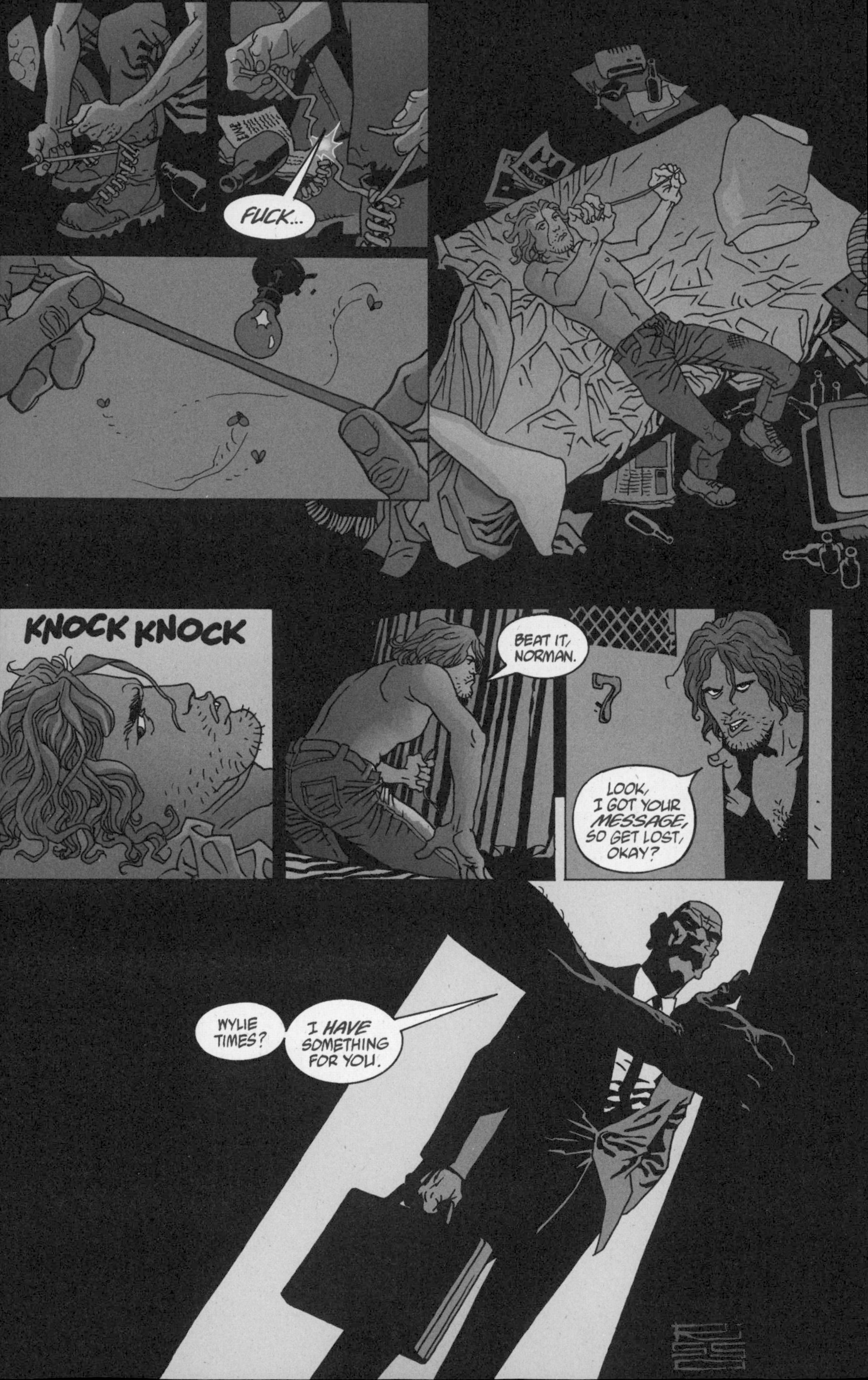
FUCK...
KNOCK KNOCK
BEAT IT, NORMAN.
LOOK, I GOT YOUR MESSAGE, SO GET LOST, OKAY?
WYLIE TIMES?
I HAVE SOMETHING FOR YOU.

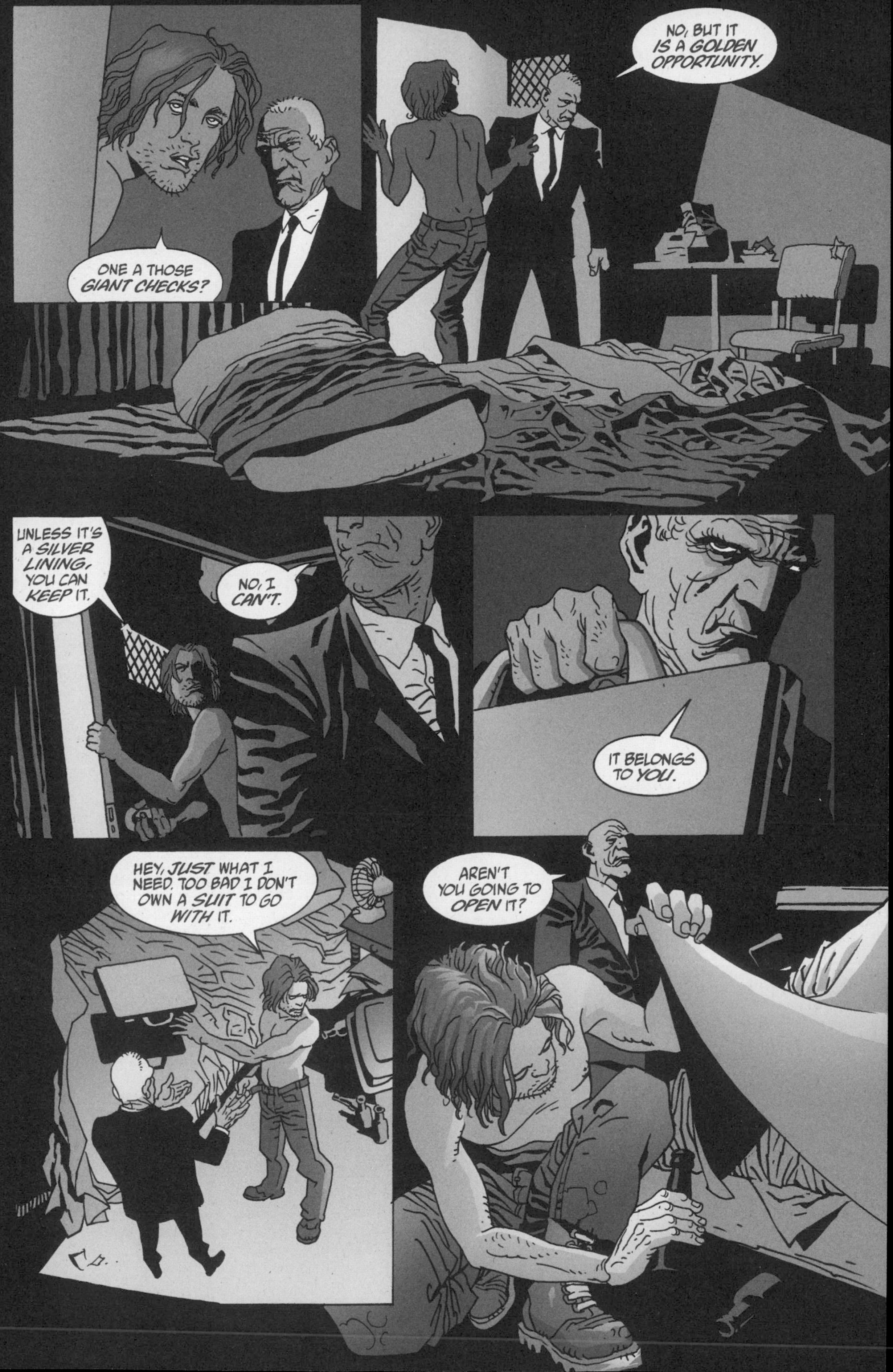
ONE A THOSE GIANT CHECKS?
NO, BUT IT IS A GOLDEN OPPORTUNITY.
UNLESS IT'S A SILVER LINING, YOU CAN KEEP IT.
NO, I CAN'T.
IT BELONGS TO YOU.
HEY, JUST WHAT I NEED. TOO BAD I DON'T OWN A SUIT TO GO WITH IT.
AREN'T YOU GOING TO OPEN IT?

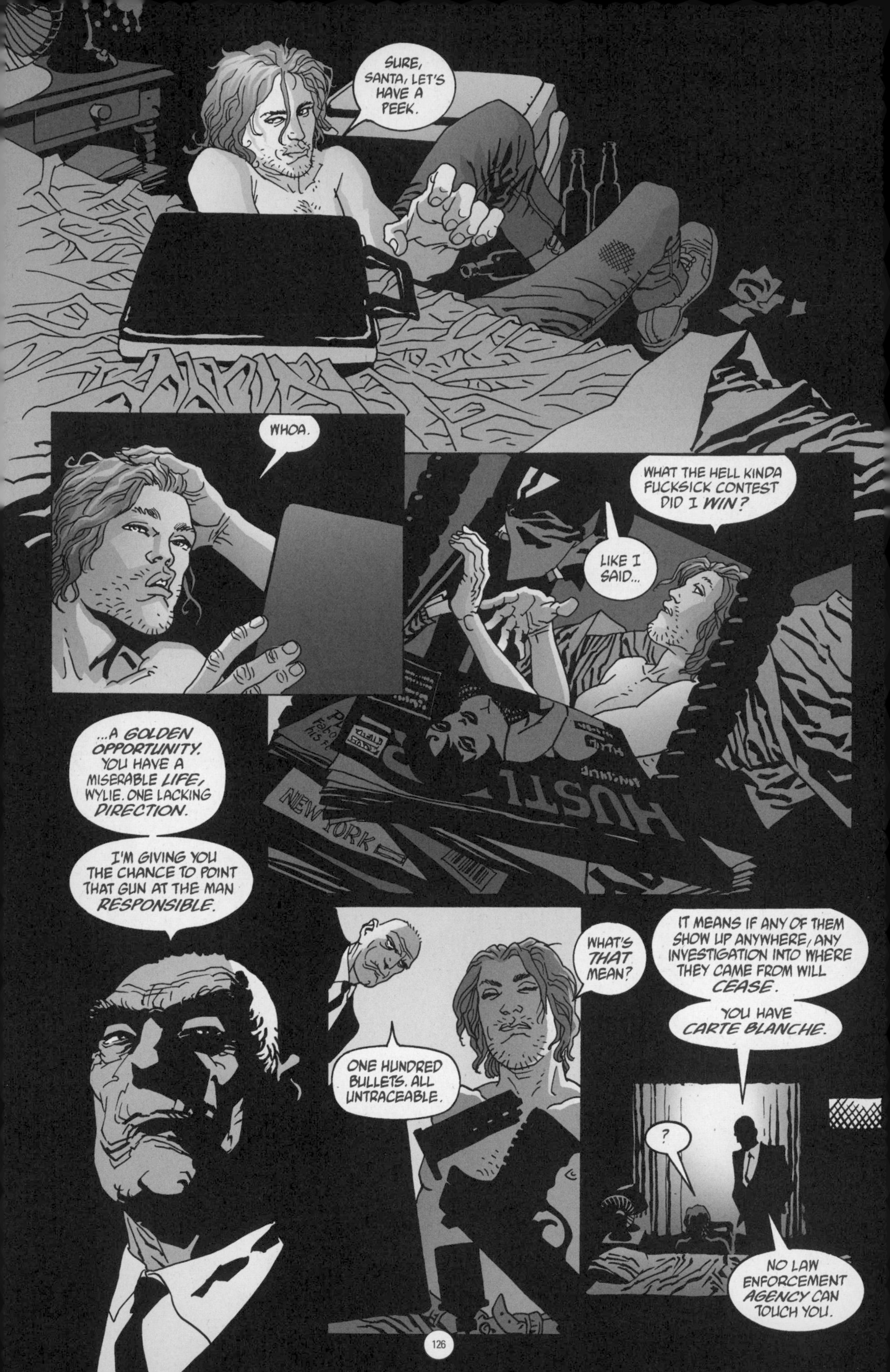
SURE, SANTA, LET'S HAVE A PEEK.
WHOA.
WHAT THE HELL KINDA FUCKSICK CONTEST DID I WIN?
LIKE I SAID...
...A GOLDEN OPPORTUNITY. YOU HAVE A MISERABLE LIFE, WYLIE. ONE LACKING DIRECTION.
I'M GIVING YOU THE CHANCE TO POINT THAT GUN AT THE MAN RESPONSIBLE.
NEW YORK
HUSTL
ONE HUNDRED BULLETS. ALL UNTRACEABLE.
WHAT'S THAT MEAN?
IT MEANS IF ANY OF THEM SHOW UP ANYWHERE, ANY INVESTIGATION INTO WHERE THEY CAME FROM WILL CEASE.
YOU HAVE CARTE BLANCHE.
?
NO LAW ENFORCEMENT AGENCY CAN TOUCH YOU.

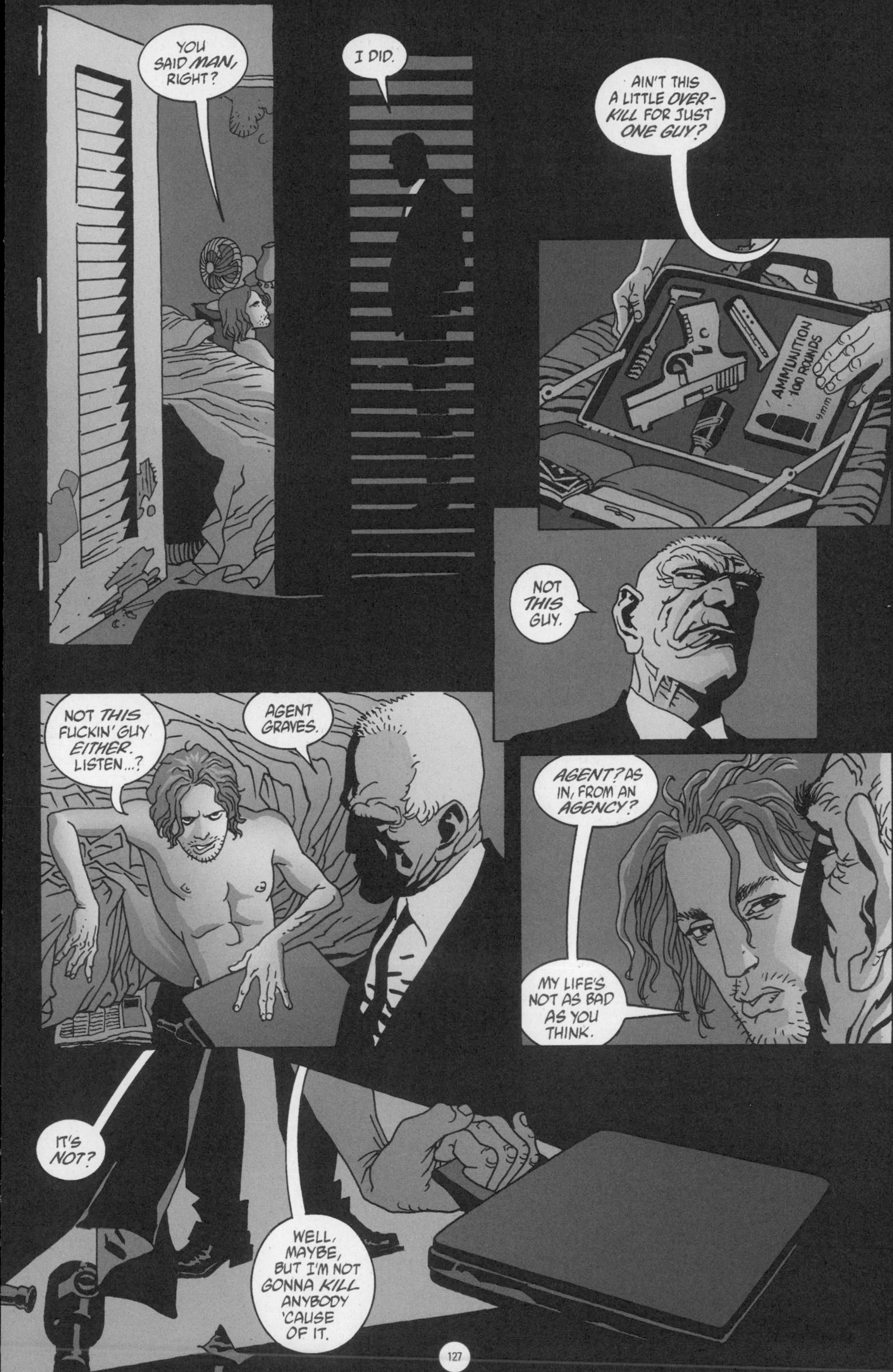

YOU SAID MAN, RIGHT?
I DID.
AIN'T THIS A LITTLE OVER-KILL FOR JUST ONE GUY?
AMMUNITION 100 ROUNDS
9mm
NOT THIS GUY.
NOT THIS FUCKIN' GUY EITHER. LISTEN...?
AGENT GRAVES.
AGENT? AS IN, FROM AN AGENCY?
MY LIFE'S NOT AS BAD AS YOU THINK.
IT'S NOT?
WELL, MAYBE, BUT I'M NOT GONNA KILL ANYBODY 'CAUSE OF IT.

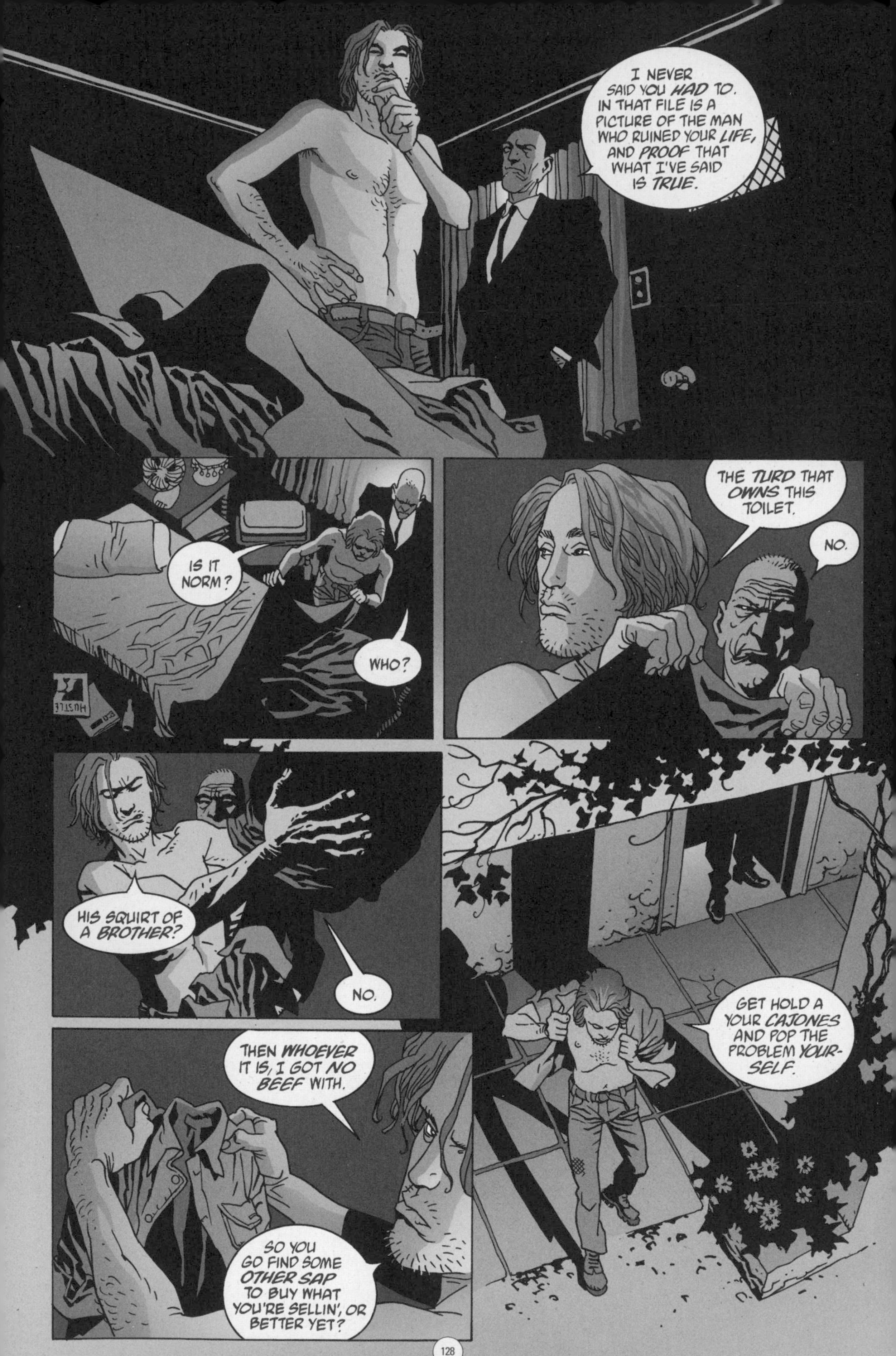

I NEVER SAID YOU *HAD* TO. IN THAT FILE IS A PICTURE OF THE MAN WHO RUINED YOUR *LIFE*, AND *PROOF* THAT WHAT I'VE SAID IS *TRUE*.
IS IT NORM?
WHO?
THE *TURD* THAT *OWNS* THIS TOILET.
NO.
HIS SQUIRT OF A *BROTHER*?
NO.
THEN *WHOEVER* IT IS, I GOT *NO BEEF* WITH.
SO YOU GO FIND SOME *OTHER SAP* TO BUY WHAT YOU'RE SELLIN', OR BETTER YET?
GET HOLD A YOUR *CAJONES* AND POP THE PROBLEM *YOURSELF*.

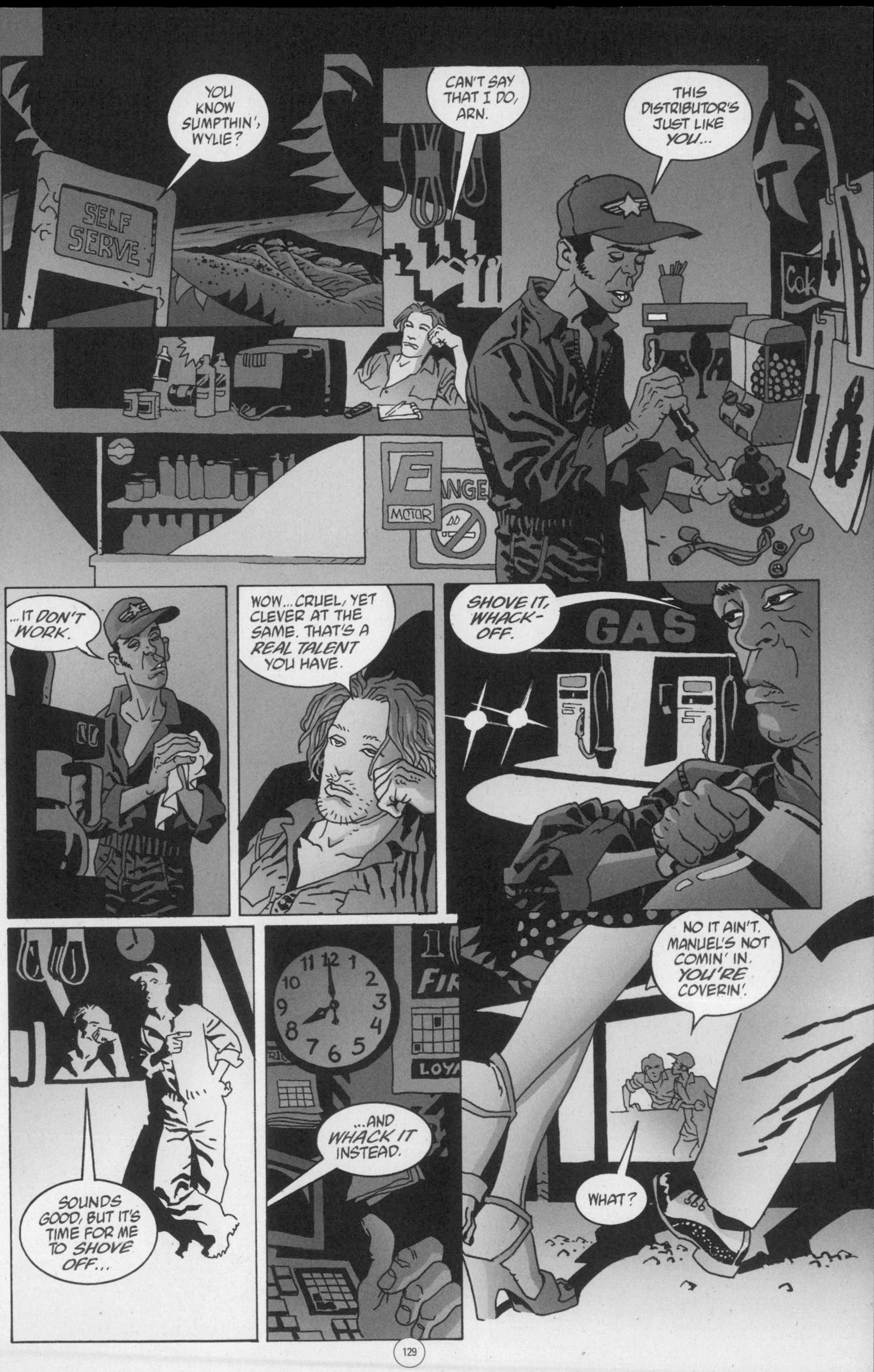
YOU KNOW SUMPTHIN', WYLIE?
CAN'T SAY THAT I DO, ARN.
THIS DISTRIBUTOR'S JUST LIKE YOU...
SELF SERVE
MOTOR
...IT DON'T WORK.
WOW...CRUEL, YET CLEVER AT THE SAME. THAT'S A REAL TALENT YOU HAVE.
SHOVE IT, WHACK-OFF.
GAS
SOUNDS GOOD, BUT IT'S TIME FOR ME TO SHOVE OFF...
...AND WHACK IT INSTEAD.
NO IT AIN'T. MANUEL'S NOT COMIN' IN. YOU'RE COVERIN'.
WHAT?

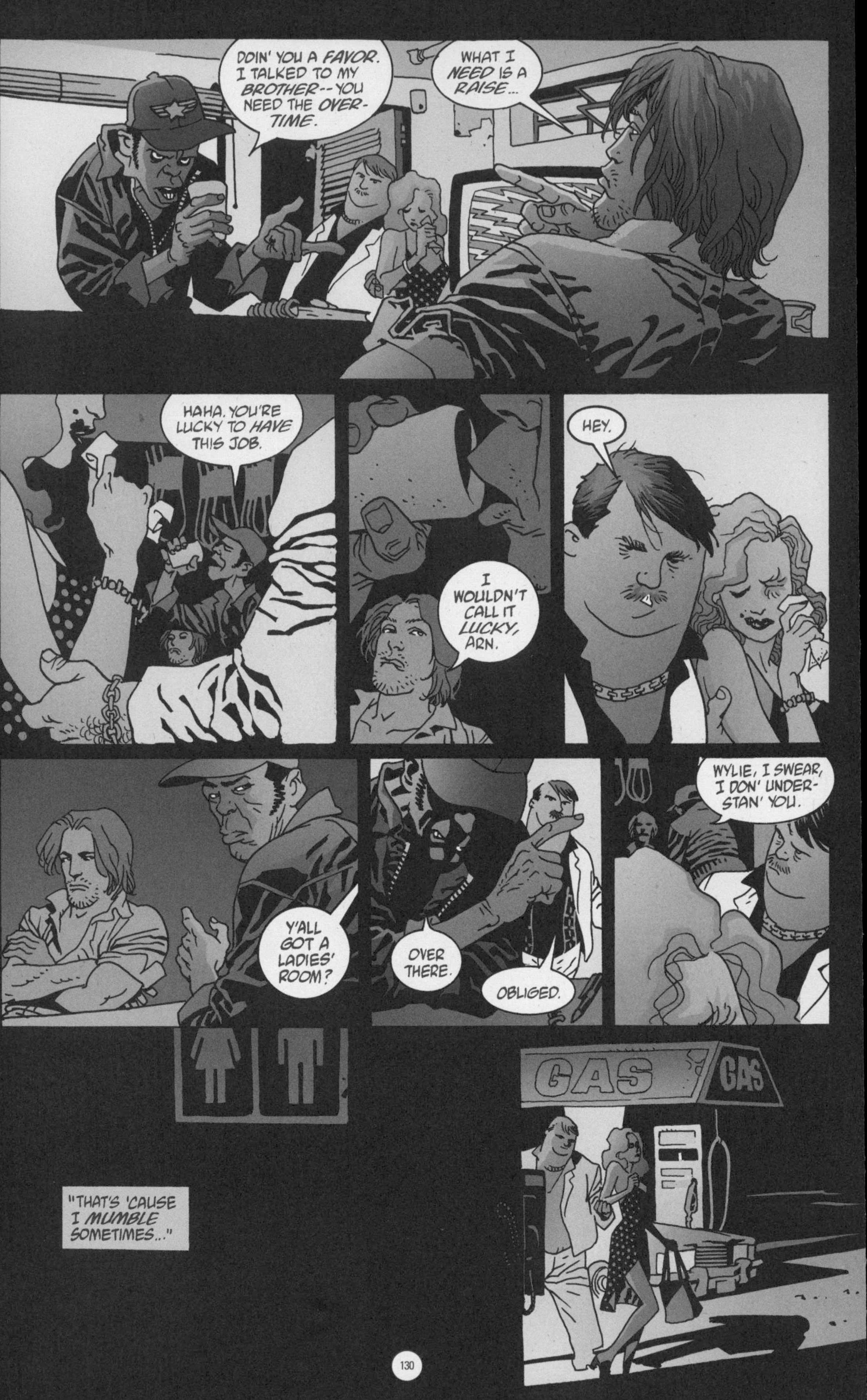
DOIN' YOU A FAVOR. I TALKED TO MY BROTHER-- YOU NEED THE OVER-TIME.
WHAT I NEED IS A RAISE...
HAHA. YOU'RE LUCKY TO HAVE THIS JOB.
I WOULDN'T CALL IT LUCKY, ARN.
HEY.
Y'ALL GOT A LADIES' ROOM?
OVER THERE.
OBLIGED.
WYLIE, I SWEAR, I DON' UNDER-STAN' YOU.
GAS
GAS
"THAT'S 'CAUSE I MUMBLE SOMETIMES..."

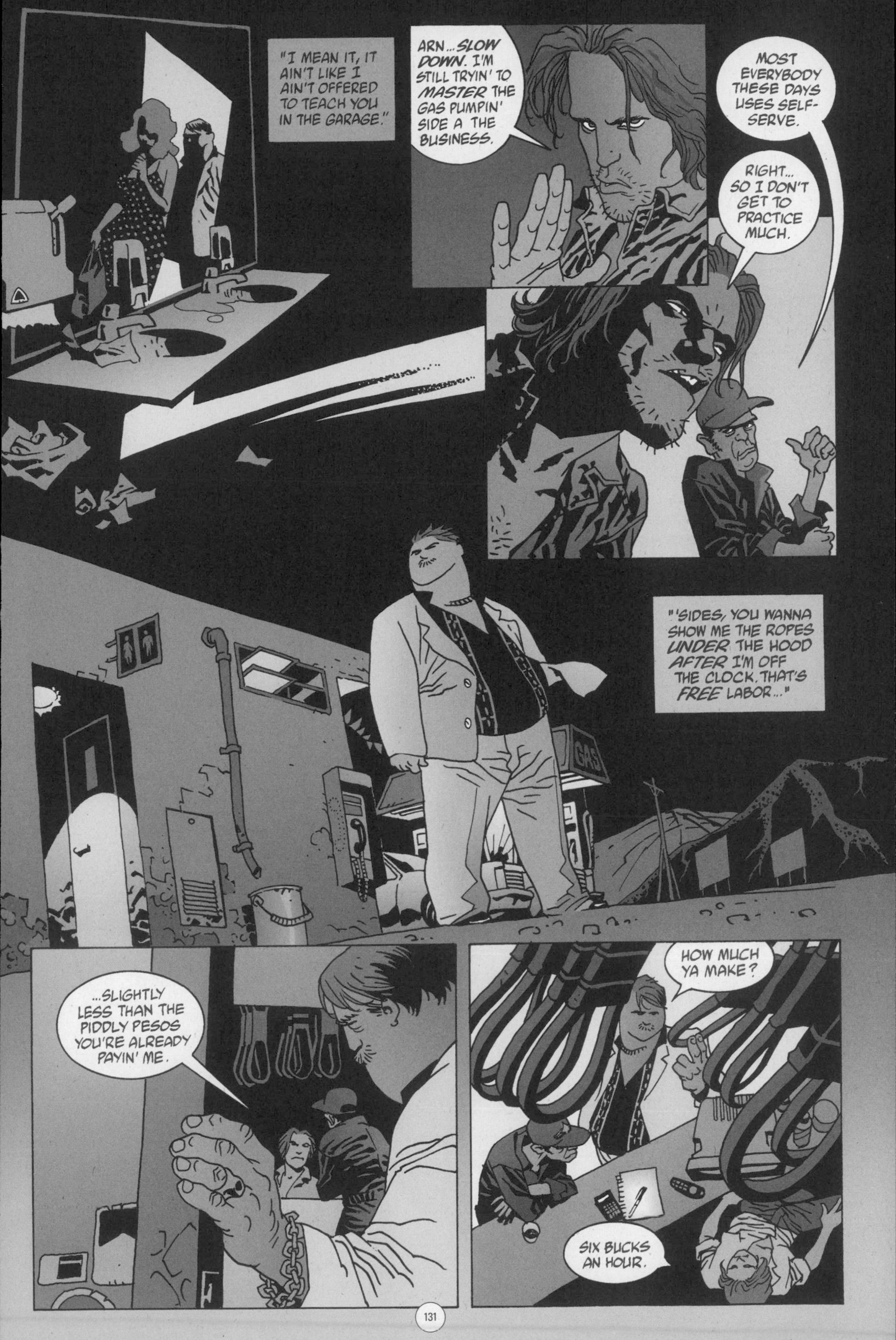
"I MEAN IT, IT AIN'T LIKE I AIN'T OFFERED TO TEACH YOU IN THE GARAGE."
ARN... SLOW DOWN. I'M STILL TRYIN' TO MASTER THE GAS PUMPIN' SIDE A THE BUSINESS.
MOST EVERYBODY THESE DAYS USES SELF-SERVE.
RIGHT... SO I DON'T GET TO PRACTICE MUCH.
"'SIDES, YOU WANNA SHOW ME THE ROPES UNDER THE HOOD AFTER I'M OFF THE CLOCK, THAT'S FREE LABOR..."
GAS
...SLIGHTLY LESS THAN THE PIDDLY PESOS YOU'RE ALREADY PAYIN' ME.
HOW MUCH YA MAKE?
SIX BUCKS AN HOUR.

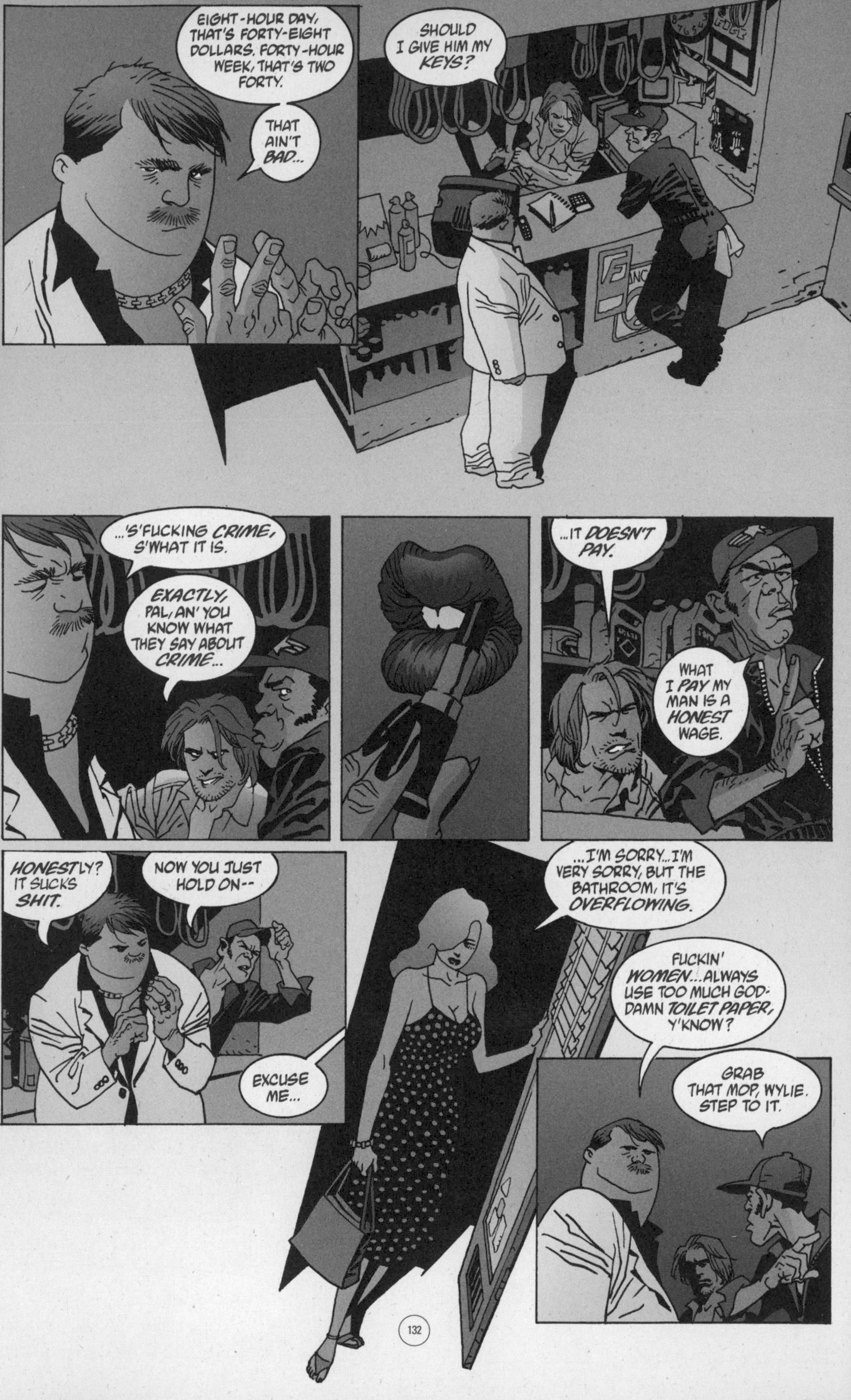
EIGHT-HOUR DAY, THAT'S FORTY-EIGHT DOLLARS. FORTY-HOUR WEEK, THAT'S TWO FORTY.
THAT AIN'T BAD...
SHOULD I GIVE HIM MY KEYS?
...'S'FUCKING CRIME, S'WHAT IT IS.
EXACTLY, PAL, AN' YOU KNOW WHAT THEY SAY ABOUT CRIME...
...IT DOESN'T PAY.
WHAT I PAY MY MAN IS A HONEST WAGE.
HONESTLY? IT SUCKS SHIT.
NOW YOU JUST HOLD ON--
EXCUSE ME...
...I'M SORRY...I'M VERY SORRY, BUT THE BATHROOM, IT'S OVERFLOWING.
FUCKIN' WOMEN...ALWAYS USE TOO MUCH GOD-DAMN TOILET PAPER, Y'KNOW?
GRAB THAT MOP, WYLIE. STEP TO IT.

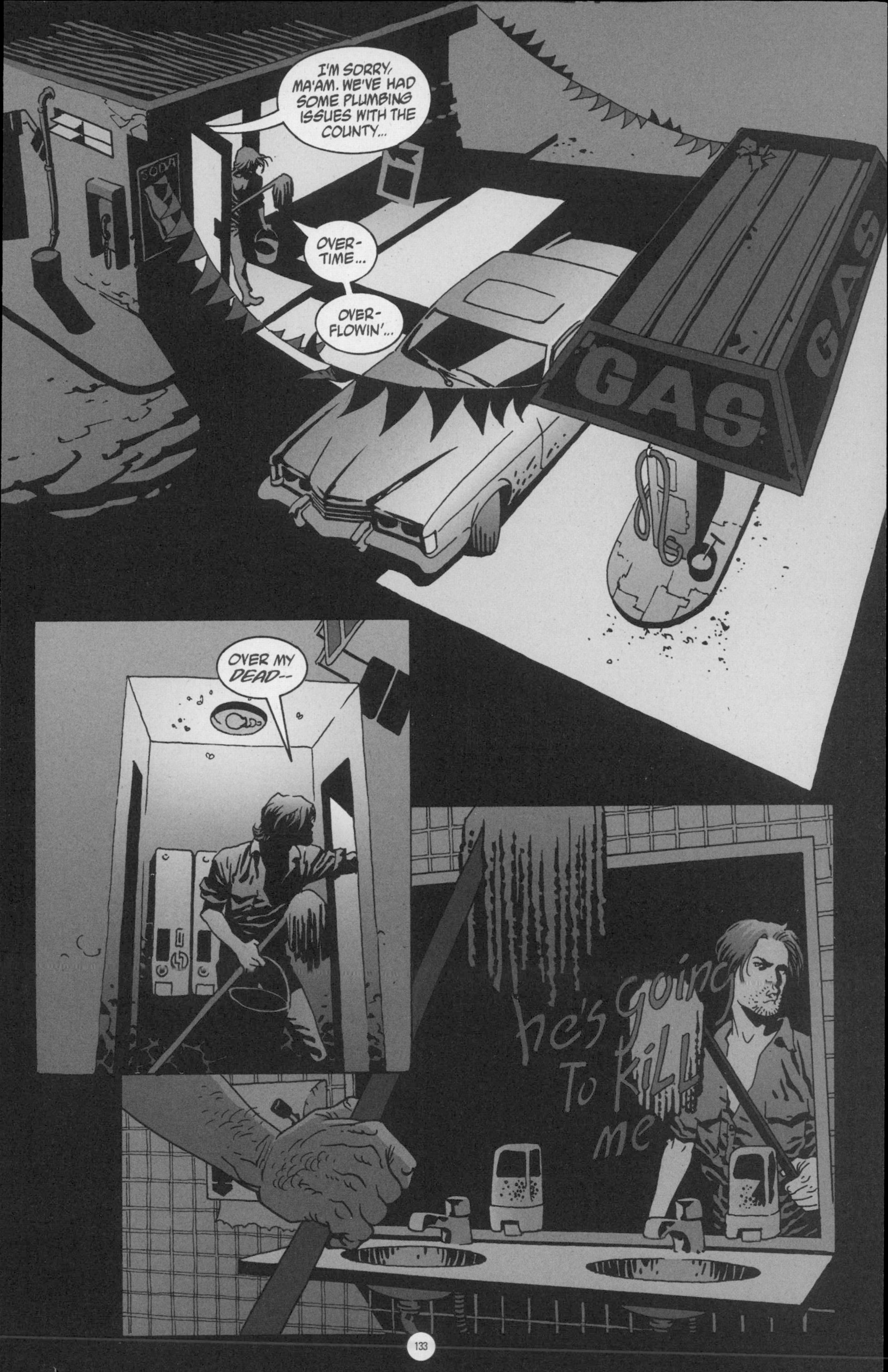
I'M SORRY, MA'AM. WE'VE HAD SOME PLUMBING ISSUES WITH THE COUNTY...
SODA
OVER-TIME...
OVER-FLOWIN'...
GAS
GAS
OVER MY DEAD--
he's going To kiLL me

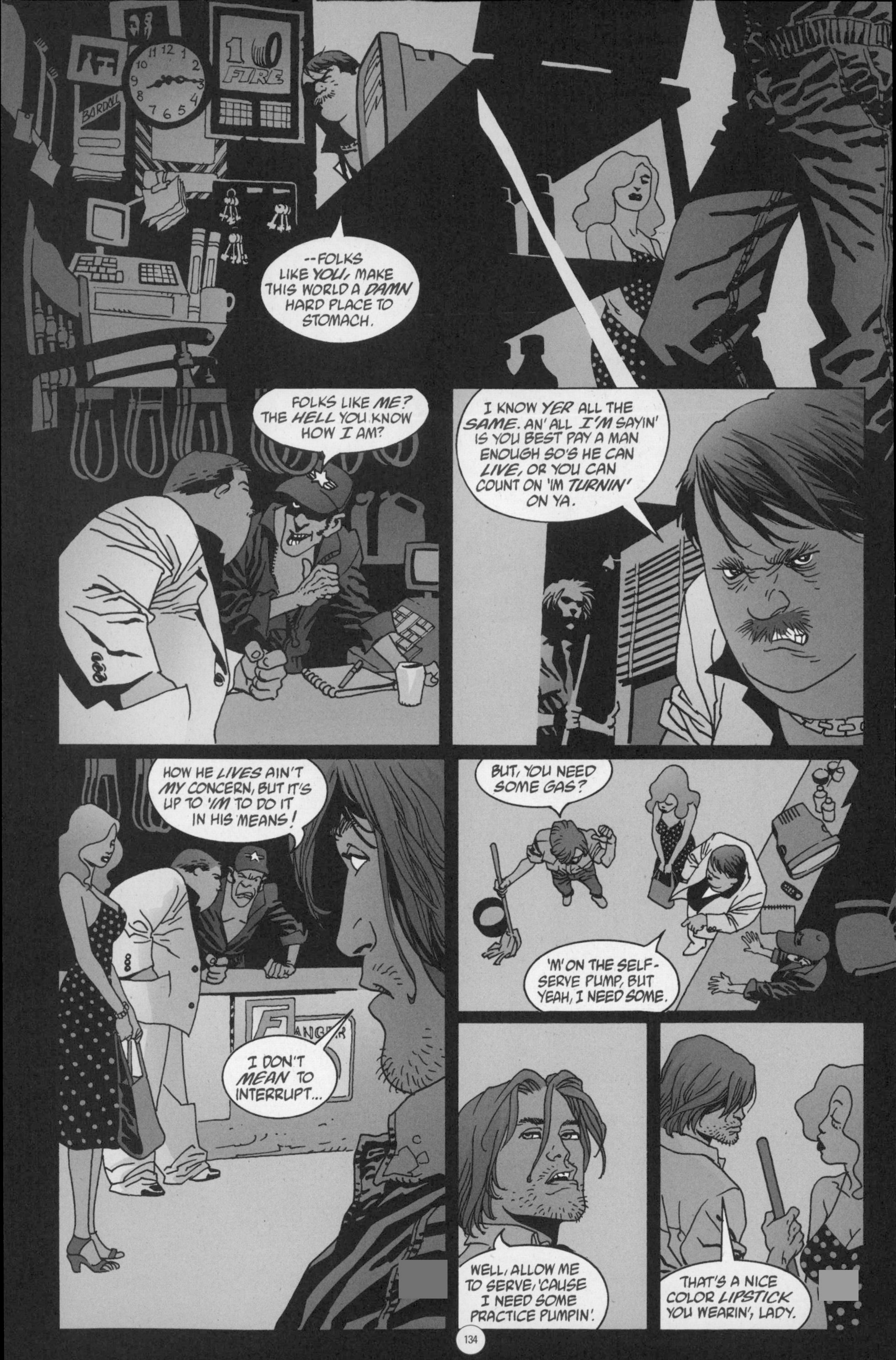

1 0
FIRE
BARDOLL
--FOLKS LIKE YOU, MAKE THIS WORLD A DAMN HARD PLACE TO STOMACH.
FOLKS LIKE ME? THE HELL YOU KNOW HOW I AM?
I KNOW YER ALL THE SAME. AN' ALL I'M SAYIN' IS YOU BEST PAY A MAN ENOUGH SO'S HE CAN LIVE, OR YOU CAN COUNT ON 'IM TURNIN' ON YA.
HOW HE LIVES AIN'T MY CONCERN, BUT IT'S UP TO 'IM TO DO IT IN HIS MEANS!
I DON'T MEAN TO INTERRUPT...
BUT, YOU NEED SOME GAS?
'M' ON THE SELF-SERVE PUMP, BUT YEAH, I NEED SOME.
WELL, ALLOW ME TO SERVE, 'CAUSE I NEED SOME PRACTICE PUMPIN'.
THAT'S A NICE COLOR LIPSTICK YOU WEARIN', LADY.

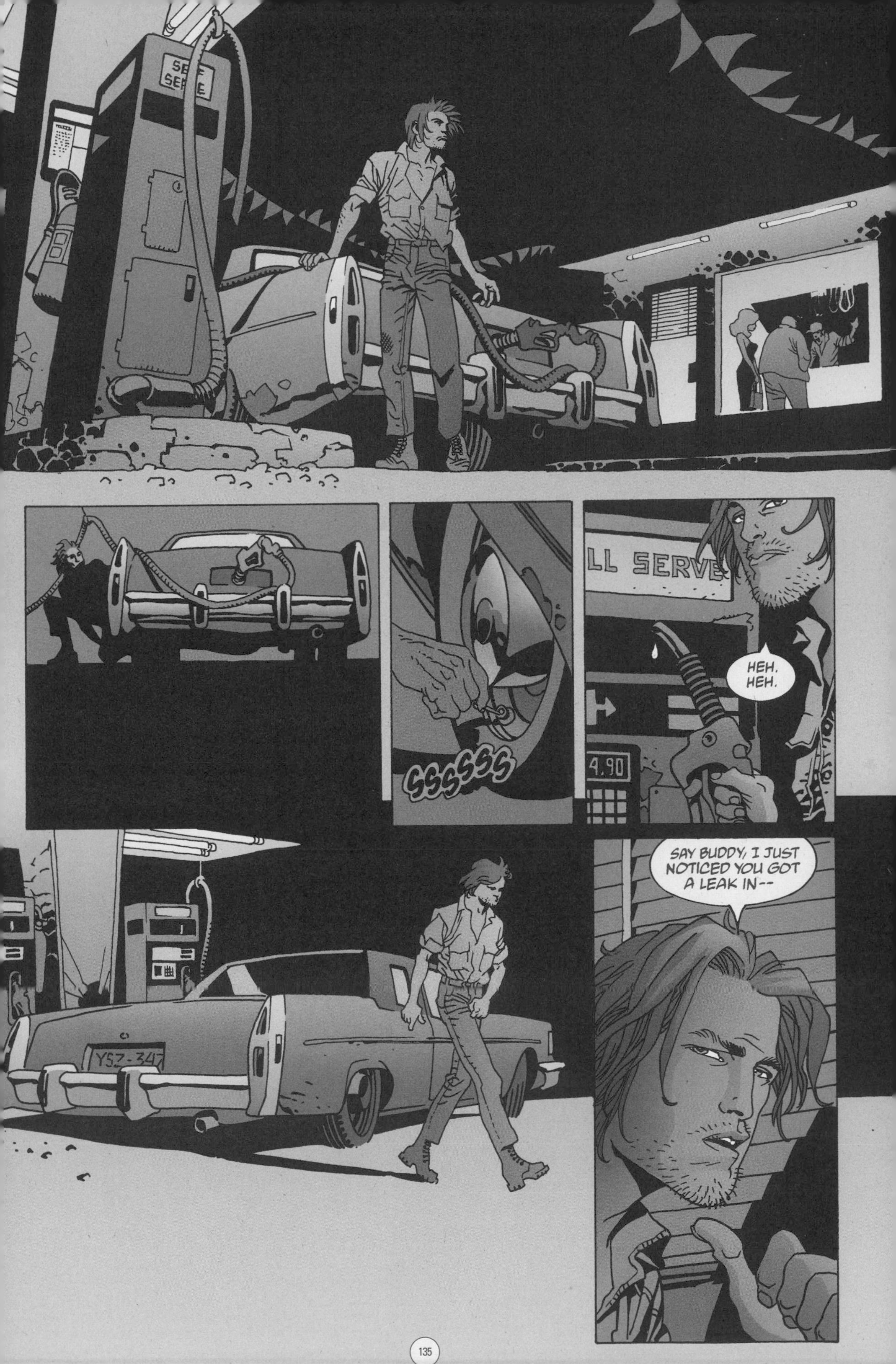
SELF SERVE
LL SERVE
4.90
SSSSSS
HEH. HEH.
YSZ-347
SAY BUDDY, I JUST NOTICED YOU GOT A LEAK IN--

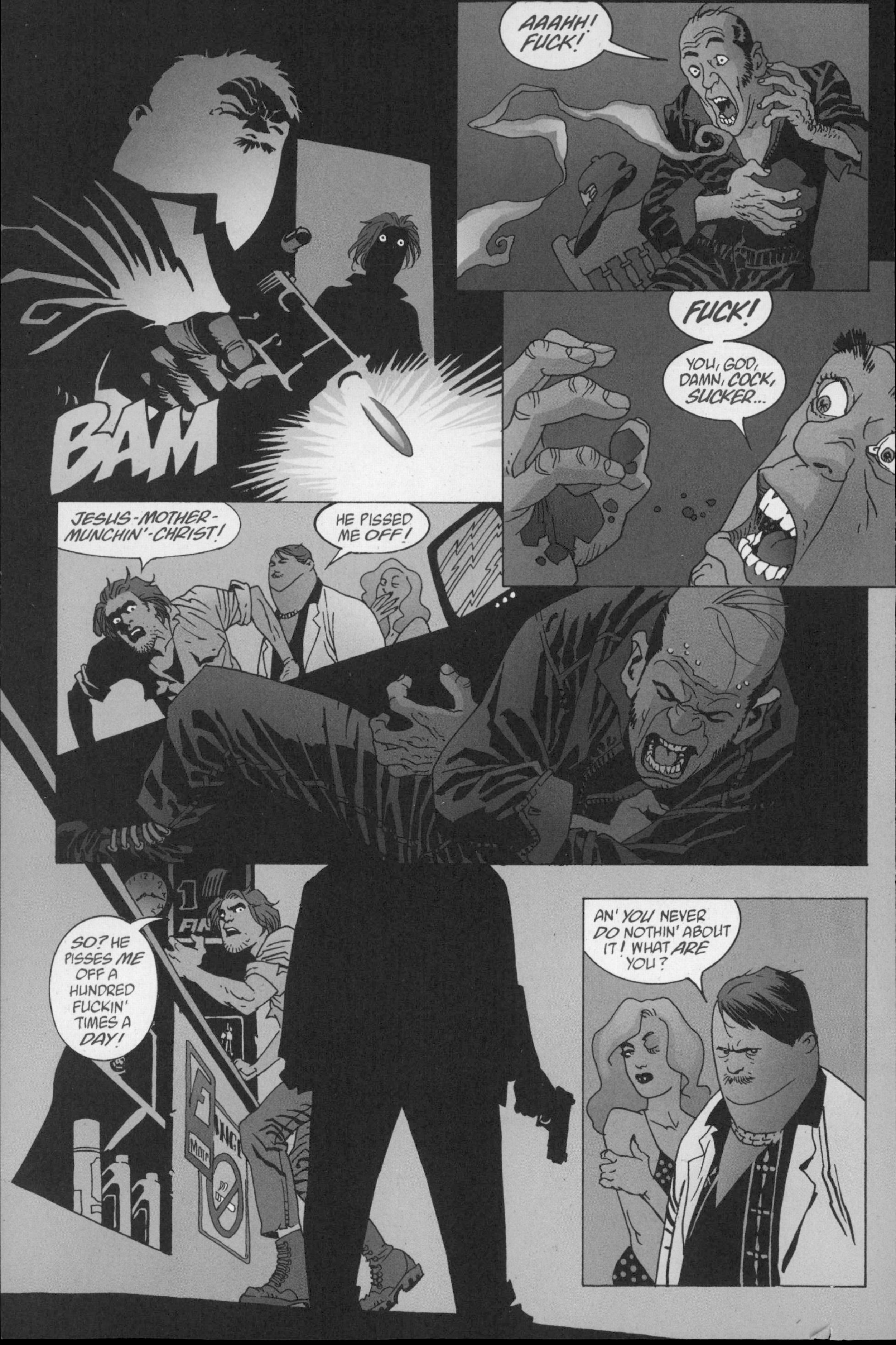
BAM
AAAHH! FUCK!
FUCK!
YOU, GOD, DAMN, COCK, SUCKER...
JESUS-MOTHER-MUNCHIN'-CHRIST!
HE PISSED ME OFF!
SO? HE PISSES ME OFF A HUNDRED FUCKIN' TIMES A DAY!
AN' YOU NEVER DO NOTHIN' ABOUT IT! WHAT ARE YOU?

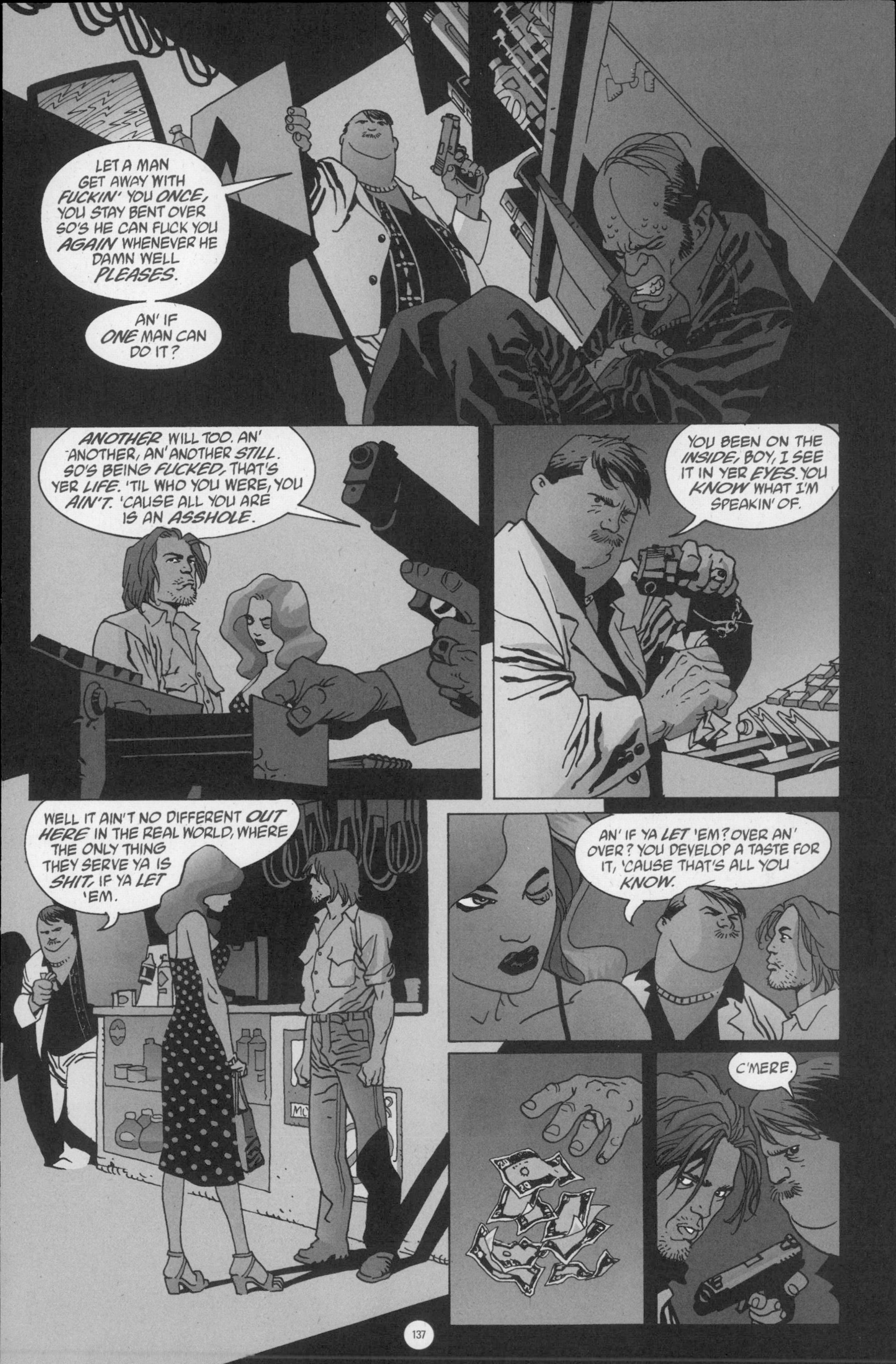
LET A MAN GET AWAY WITH FUCKIN' YOU ONCE, YOU STAY BENT OVER SO'S HE CAN FUCK YOU AGAIN WHENEVER HE DAMN WELL PLEASES.
AN' IF ONE MAN CAN DO IT?
ANOTHER WILL TOO. AN' ANOTHER, AN' ANOTHER STILL. SO'S BEING FUCKED, THAT'S YER LIFE. 'TIL WHO YOU WERE, YOU AIN'T. 'CAUSE ALL YOU ARE IS AN ASSHOLE.
YOU BEEN ON THE INSIDE, BOY, I SEE IT IN YER EYES. YOU KNOW WHAT I'M SPEAKIN' OF.
WELL IT AIN'T NO DIFFERENT OUT HERE IN THE REAL WORLD, WHERE THE ONLY THING THEY SERVE YA IS SHIT, IF YA LET 'EM.
AN' IF YA LET 'EM? OVER AN' OVER? YOU DEVELOP A TASTE FOR IT, 'CAUSE THAT'S ALL YOU KNOW.
C'MERE.

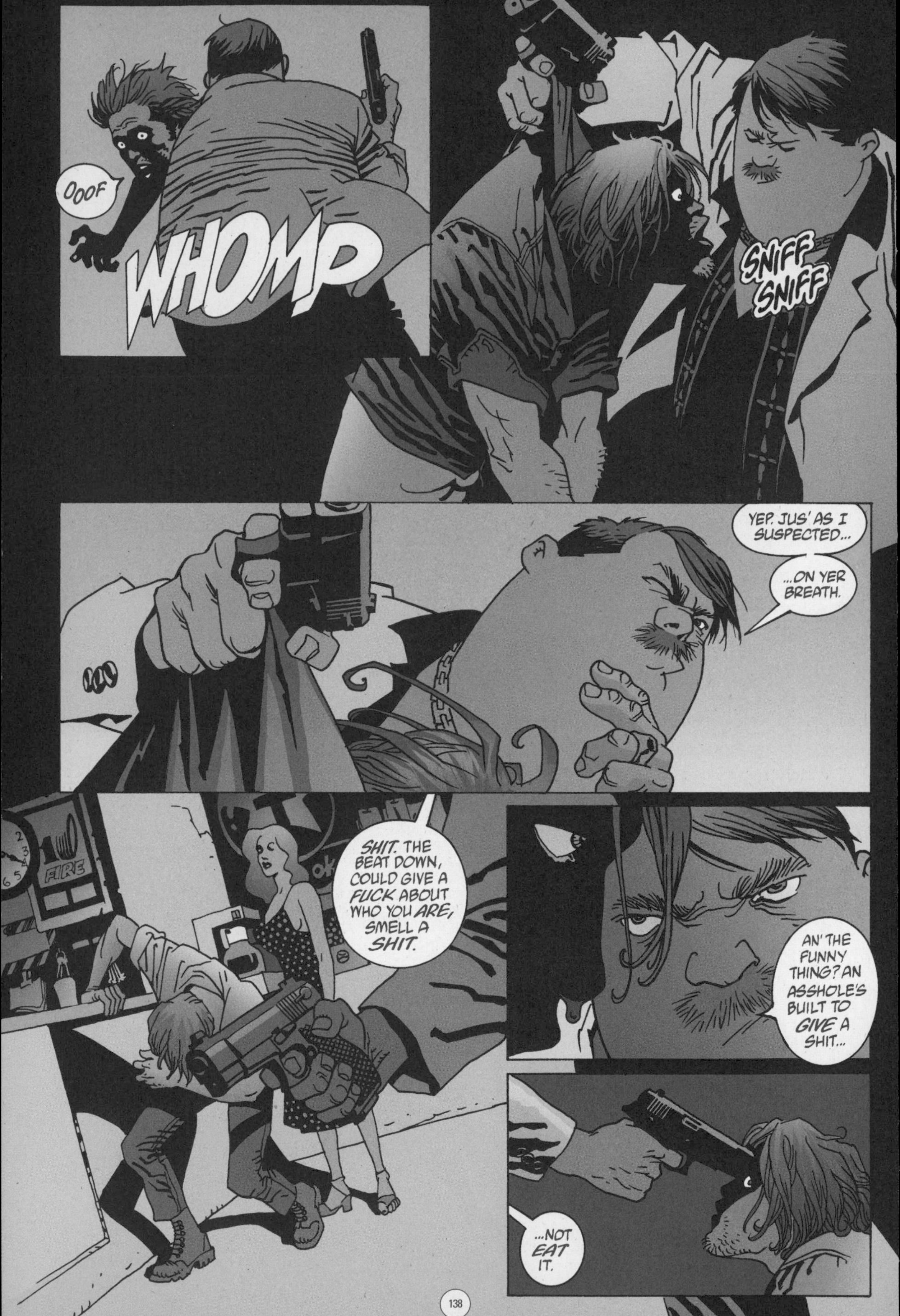
OOOF
WHOMP
SNIFF SNIFF
YEP. JUS' AS I SUSPECTED...
...ON YER BREATH.
SHIT. THE BEAT DOWN, COULD GIVE A FUCK ABOUT WHO YOU ARE, SMELL A SHIT.
AN' THE FUNNY THING? AN ASSHOLE'S BUILT TO GIVE A SHIT...
...NOT EAT IT.

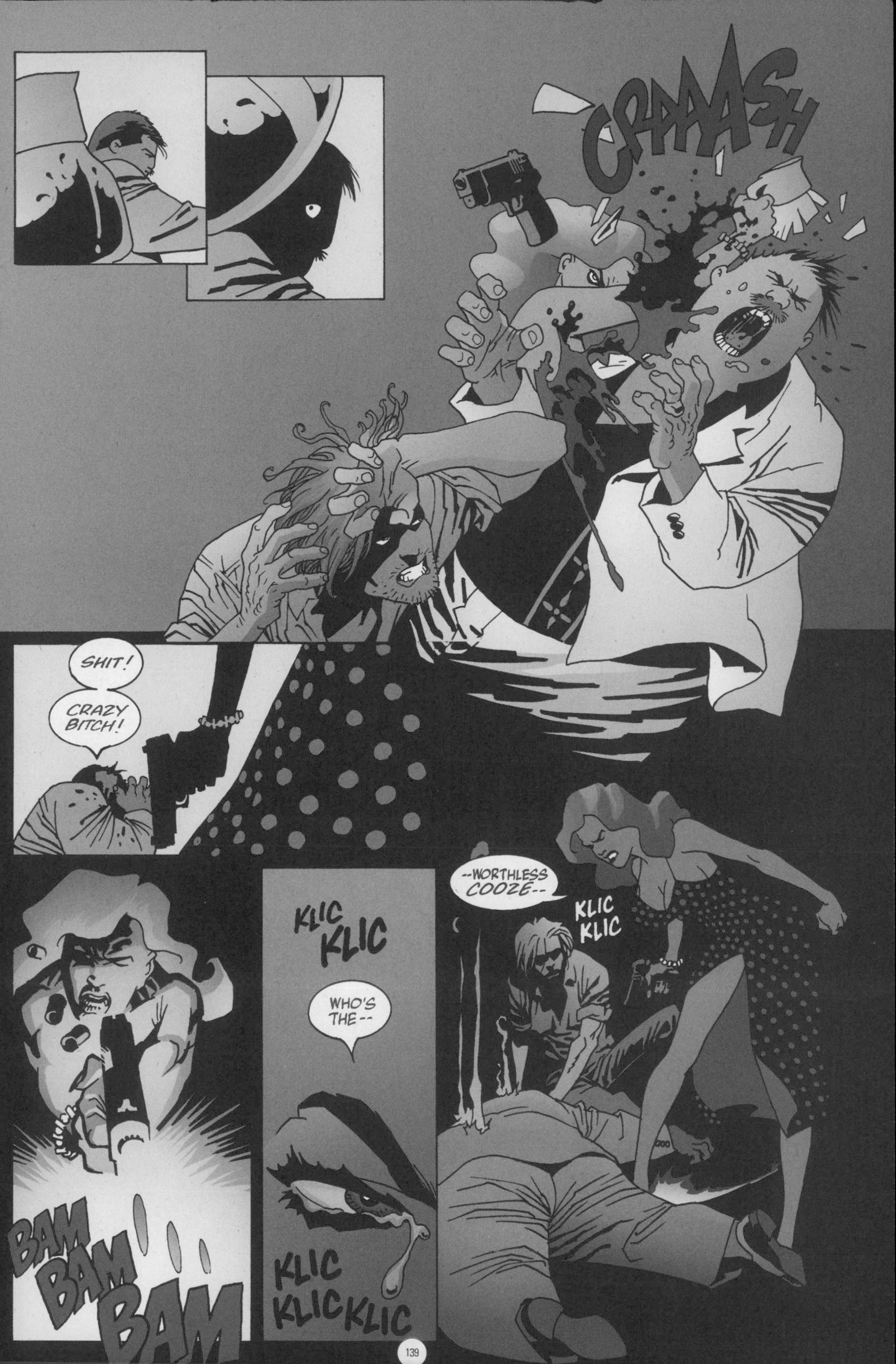
CRRAASH
SHIT!
CRAZY BITCH!
BAM BAM BAM
KLIC KLIC
WHO'S THE--
KLIC KLIC KLIC
--WORTHLESS COOZE--
KLIC KLIC

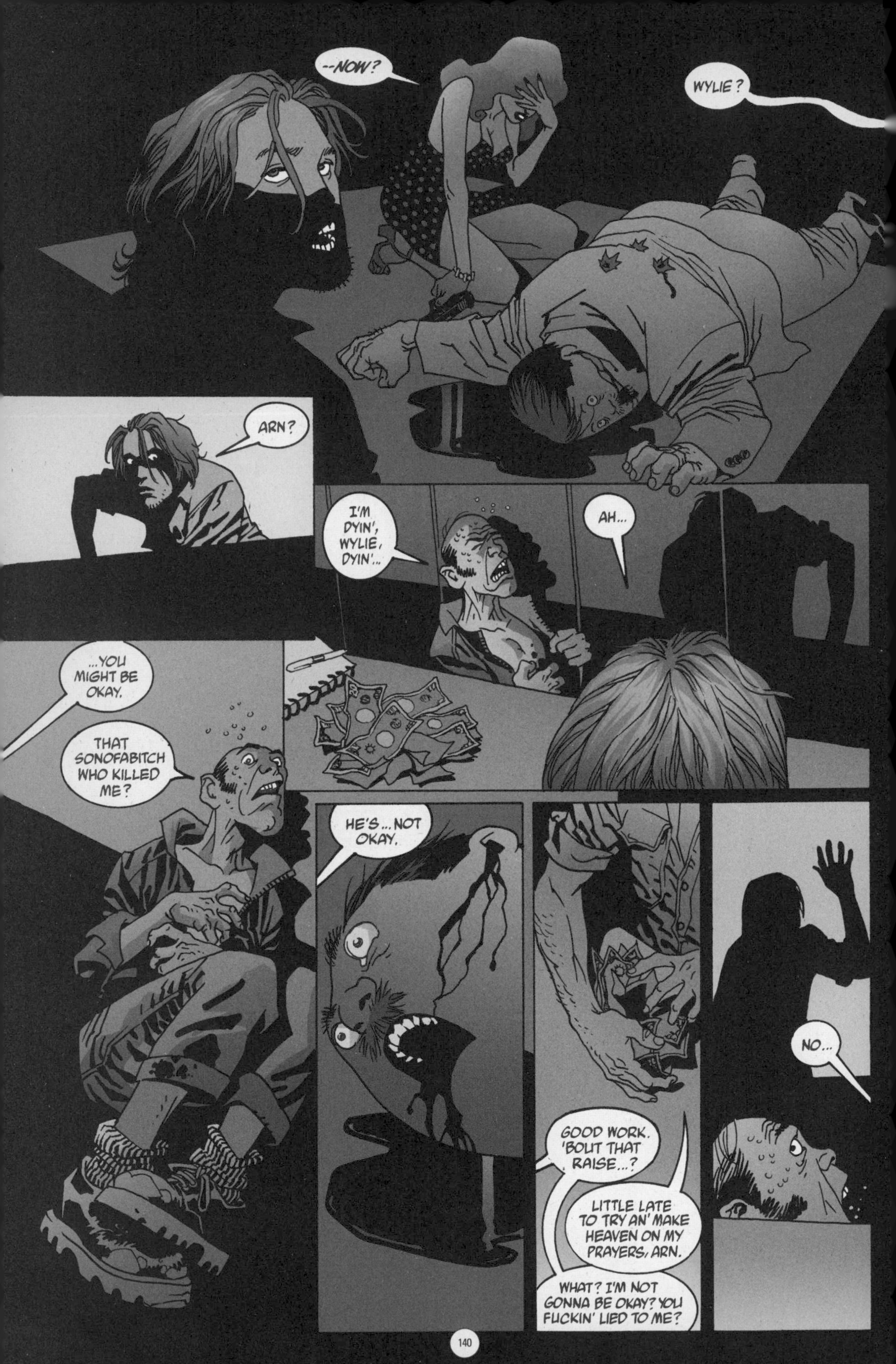
--NOW?
WYLIE?
ARN?
I'M DYIN', WYLIE, DYIN'...
AH...
...YOU MIGHT BE OKAY.
THAT SONOFABITCH WHO KILLED ME?
HE'S... NOT OKAY.
GOOD WORK. 'BOUT THAT RAISE...?
LITTLE LATE TO TRY AN' MAKE HEAVEN ON MY PRAYERS, ARN.
WHAT? I'M NOT GONNA BE OKAY? YOU FUCKIN' LIED TO ME?
NO...

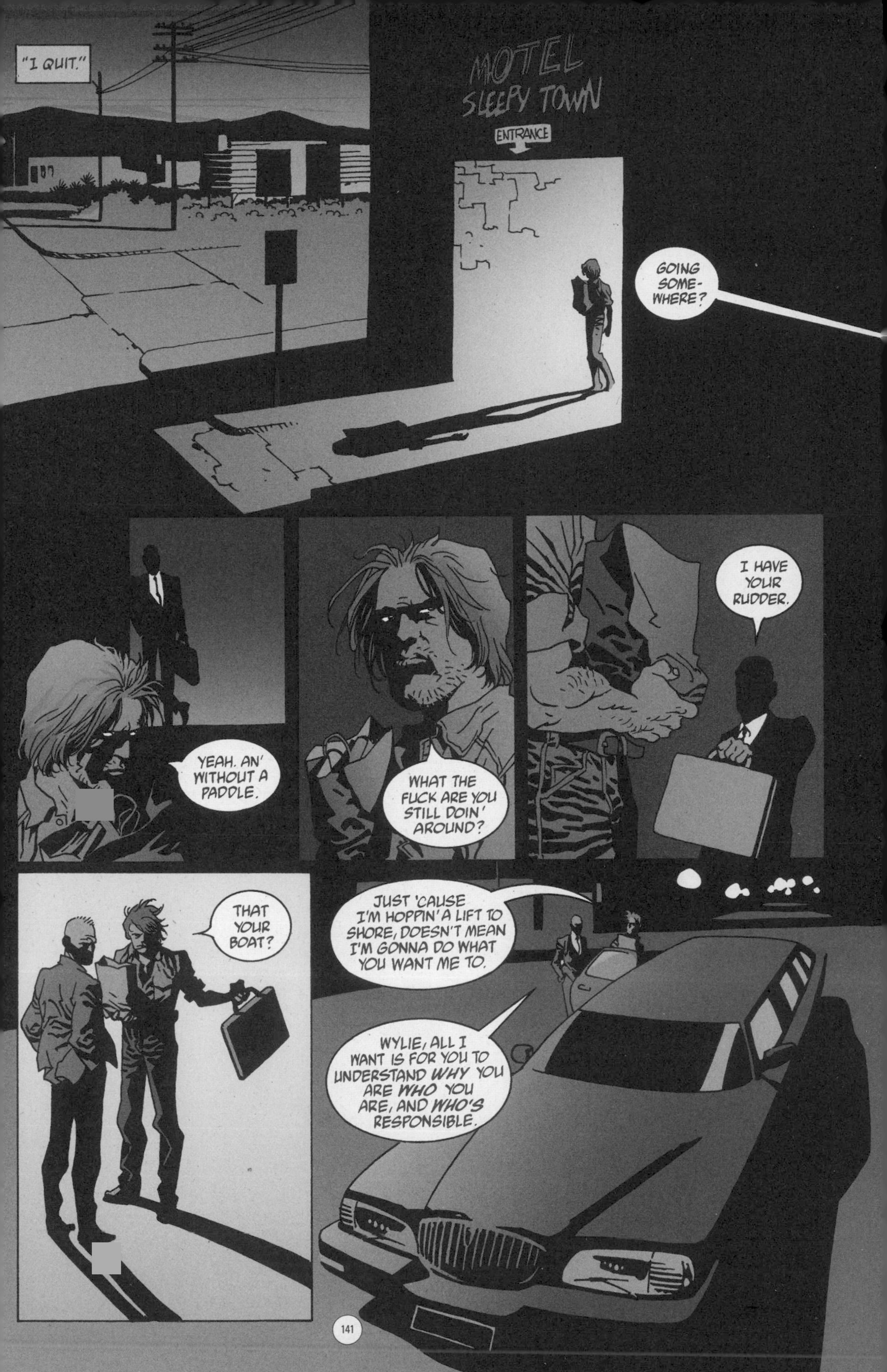
"I QUIT."
MOTEL SLEEPY TOWN
ENTRANCE
GOING SOME-WHERE?
YEAH. AN' WITHOUT A PADDLE.
WHAT THE FUCK ARE YOU STILL DOIN' AROUND?
I HAVE YOUR RUDDER.
THAT YOUR BOAT?
JUST 'CAUSE I'M HOPPIN' A LIFT TO SHORE, DOESN'T MEAN I'M GONNA DO WHAT YOU WANT ME TO.
WYLIE, ALL I WANT IS FOR YOU TO UNDERSTAND *WHY* YOU ARE *WHO* YOU ARE, AND *WHO'S* RESPONSIBLE.

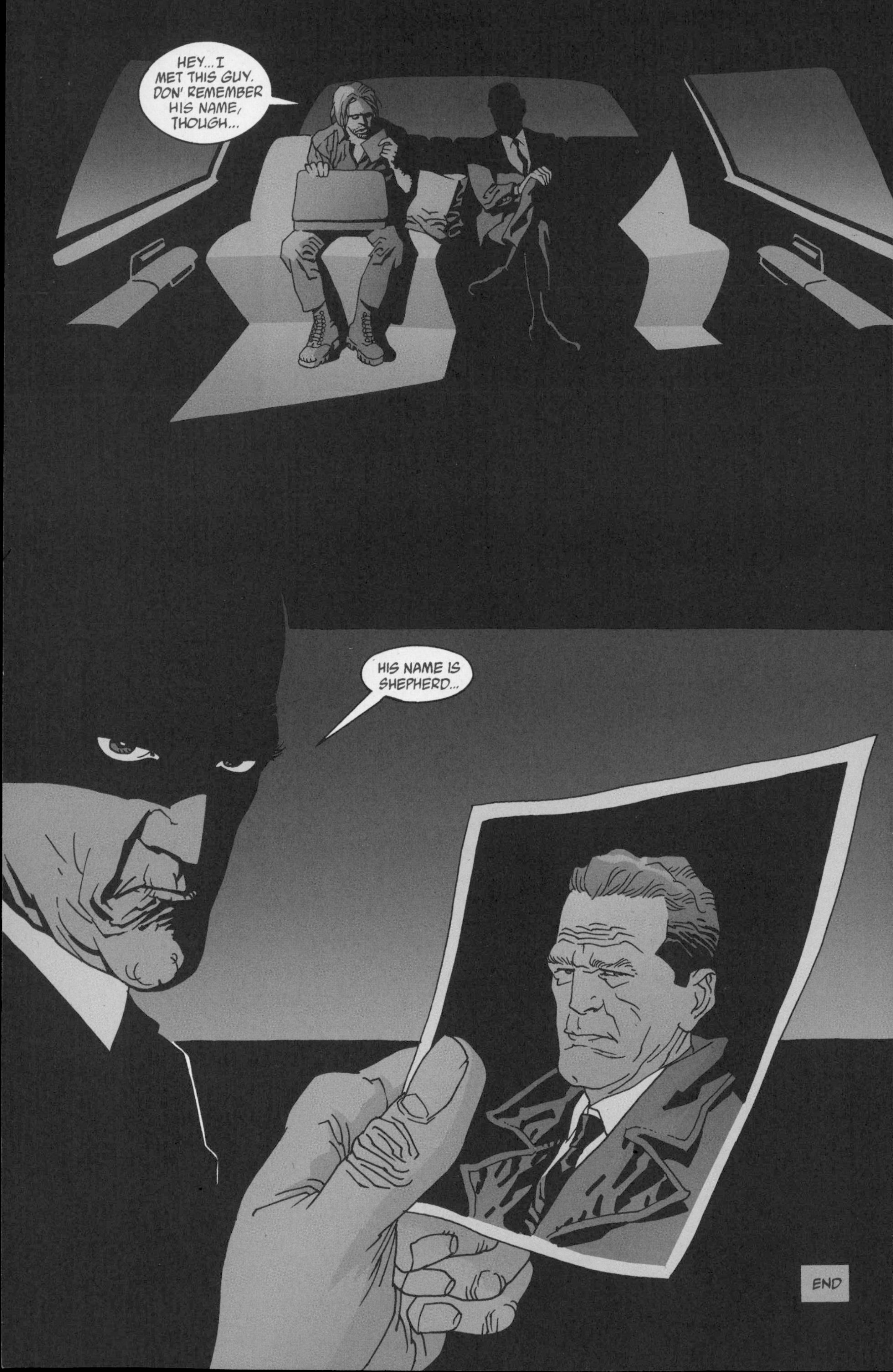
HEY... I MET THIS GUY. DON' REMEMBER HIS NAME, THOUGH...
HIS NAME IS SHEPHERD...
END

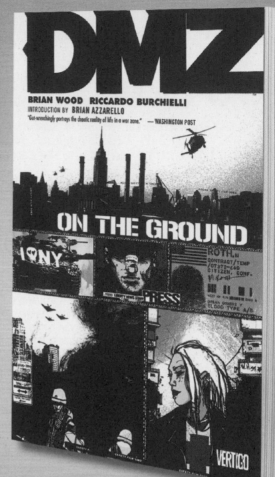

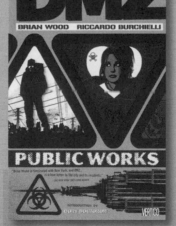
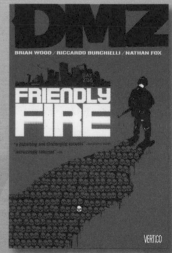